OTHER A TO Z GUIDES FROM
THE SCARECROW PRESS, INC.

1. *The A to Z of Buddhism* by Charles S. Prebish, 2001. *Out of Print. See No. 124.*
2. *The A to Z of Catholicism* by William J. Collinge, 2001.
3. *The A to Z of Hinduism* by Bruce M. Sullivan, 2001.
4. *The A to Z of Islam* by Ludwig W. Adamec, 2002. *Out of Print. See No. 123.*
5. *The A to Z of Slavery and Abolition* by Martin A. Klein, 2002.
6. *Terrorism: Assassins to Zealots* by Sean Kendall Anderson and Stephen Sloan, 2003.
7. *The A to Z of the Korean War* by Paul M. Edwards, 2005.
8. *The A to Z of the Cold War* by Joseph Smith and Simon Davis, 2005.
9. *The A to Z of the Vietnam War* by Edwin E. Moise, 2005.
10. *The A to Z of Science Fiction Literature* by Brian Stableford, 2005.
11. *The A to Z of the Holocaust* by Jack R. Fischel, 2005.
12. *The A to Z of Washington, D.C.* by Robert Benedetto, Jane Donovan, and Kathleen DuVall, 2005.
13. *The A to Z of Taoism* by Julian F. Pas, 2006.
14. *The A to Z of the Renaissance* by Charles G. Nauert, 2006.
15. *The A to Z of Shinto* by Stuart D. B. Picken, 2006.
16. *The A to Z of Byzantium* by John H. Rosser, 2006.
17. *The A to Z of the Civil War* by Terry L. Jones, 2006.
18. *The A to Z of the Friends (Quakers)* by Margery Post Abbott, Mary Ellen Chijioke, Pink Dandelion, and John William Oliver Jr., 2006.
19. *The A to Z of Feminism* by Janet K. Boles and Diane Long Hoeveler, 2006.
20. *The A to Z of New Religious Movements* by George D. Chryssides, 2006.
21. *The A to Z of Multinational Peacekeeping* by Terry M. Mays, 2006.
22. *The A to Z of Lutheranism* by Günther Gassmann with Duane H. Larson and Mark W. Oldenburg, 2007.
23. *The A to Z of the French Revolution* by Paul R. Hanson, 2007.
24. *The A to Z of the Persian Gulf War 1990–1991* by Clayton R. Newell, 2007.
25. *The A to Z of Revolutionary America* by Terry M. Mays, 2007.

26. *The A to Z of the Olympic Movement* by Bill Mallon with Ian Buchanan, 2007.
27. *The A to Z of the Discovery and Exploration of Australia* by Alan Day, 2009.
28. *The A to Z of the United Nations* by Jacques Fomerand, 2009.
29. *The A to Z of the "Dirty Wars"* by David Kohut, Olga Vilella, and Beatrice Julian, 2009.
30. *The A to Z of the Vikings* by Katherine Holman, 2009.
31. *The A to Z from the Great War to the Great Depression* by Neil A. Wynn, 2009.
32. *The A to Z of the Crusades* by Corliss K. Slack, 2009.
33. *The A to Z of New Age Movements* by Michael York, 2009.
34. *The A to Z of Unitarian Universalism* by Mark W. Harris, 2009.
35. *The A to Z of the Kurds* by Michael M. Gunter, 2009.
36. *The A to Z of Utopianism* by James M. Morris and Andrea L. Kross, 2009.
37. *The A to Z of the Civil War and Reconstruction* by William L. Richter, 2009.
38. *The A to Z of Jainism* by Kristi L. Wiley, 2009.
39. *The A to Z of the Inuit* by Pamela K. Stern, 2009.
40. *The A to Z of Early North America* by Cameron B. Wesson, 2009.
41. *The A to Z of the Enlightenment* by Harvey Chisick, 2009.
42. *The A to Z Methodism* by Charles Yrigoyen Jr. and Susan E. Warrick, 2009.
43. *The A to Z of the Seventh-day Adventists* by Gary Land, 2009.
44. *The A to Z of Sufism* by John Renard, 2009.
45. *The A to Z of Sikhism* by William Hewat McLeod, 2009.
46. *The A to Z Fantasy Literature* by Brian Stableford, 2009.
47. *The A to Z of the Discovery and Exploration of the Pacific Islands* by Max Quanchi and John Robson, 2009.
48. *The A to Z of Australian and New Zealand Cinema* by Albert Moran and Errol Vieth, 2009.
49. *The A to Z of African-American Television* by Kathleen Fearn-Banks, 2009.
50. *The A to Z of American Radio Soap Operas* by Jim Cox, 2009.
51. *The A to Z of the Old South* by William L. Richter, 2009.
52. *The A to Z of the Discovery and Exploration of the Northwest Passage* by Alan Day, 2009.

53. *The A to Z of the Druzes* by Samy S. Swayd, 2009.
54. *The A to Z of the Welfare State* by Bent Greve, 2009.
55. *The A to Z of the War of 1812* by Robert Malcomson, 2009.
56. *The A to Z of Feminist Philosophy* by Catherine Villanueva Gardner, 2009.
57. *The A to Z of the Early American Republic* by Richard Buel Jr., 2009.
58. *The A to Z of the Russo-Japanese War* by Rotem Kowner, 2009.
59. *The A to Z of Anglicanism* by Colin Buchanan, 2009.
60. *The A to Z of Scandinavian Literature and Theater* by Jan Sjåvik, 2009.
61. *The A to Z of the Peoples of the Southeast Asian Massif* by Jean Michaud, 2009.
62. *The A to Z of Judaism* by Norman Solomon, 2009.
63. *The A to Z of the Berbers (Imazighen)* by Hsain Ilahiane, 2009.
64. *The A to Z of British Radio* by Seán Street, 2009.
65. *The A to Z of The Salvation Army* by Major John G. Merritt, 2009.
66. *The A to Z of the Arab-Israeli Conflict* by P. R. Kumaraswamy, 2009.
67. *The A to Z of the Jacksonian Era and Manifest Destiny* by Terry Corps, 2009.
68. *The A to Z of Socialism* by Peter Lamb and James C. Docherty, 2009.
69. *The A to Z of Marxism* by David Walker and Daniel Gray, 2009.
70. *The A to Z of the Bahá'í Faith* by Hugh C. Adamson, 2009.
71. *The A to Z of Postmodernist Literature and Theater* by Fran Mason, 2009.
72. *The A to Z of Australian Radio and Television* by Albert Moran and Chris Keating, 2009.
73. *The A to Z of the Lesbian Liberation Movement: Still the Rage* by JoAnne Myers, 2009.
74. *The A to Z of the United States–Mexican War* by Edward R. Moseley and Paul C. Clark, 2009.
75. *The A to Z of World War I* by Ian V. Hogg, 2009.
76. *The A to Z of World War II: The War Against Japan* by Ann Sharp Wells, 2009.
77. *The A to Z of Witchcraft* by Michael D. Bailey, 2009.
78. *The A to Z of British Intelligence* by Nigel West, 2009.

79. *The A to Z of United States Intelligence* by Michael A. Turner, 2009.
80. *The A to Z of the League of Nations* by Anique H. M. van Ginneken, 2009.
81. *The A to Z of Israeli Intelligence* by Ephraim Kahana, 2009.
82. *The A to Z of the European Union* by Joaquín Roy and Aimee Kanner, 2009.
83. *The A to Z of the Chinese Cultural Revolution* by Guo Jian, Yongyi Song, and Yuan Zhou, 2009.
84. *The A to Z of African American Cinema* by S. Torriano Berry and Venise T. Berry, 2009.
85. *The A to Z of Japanese Business* by Stuart D. B. Picken, 2009.
86. *The A to Z of the Reagan–Bush Era* by Richard S. Conley, 2009.
87. *The A to Z of Human Rights and Humanitarian Organizations* by Robert F. Gorman and Edward S. Mihalkanin, 2009.
88. *The A to Z of French Cinema* by Dayna Oscherwitz and MaryEllen Higgins, 2009.
89. *The A to Z of the Puritans* by Charles Pastoor and Galen K. Johnson, 2009.
90. *The A to Z of Nuclear, Biological and Chemical Warfare* by Benjamin C. Garrett and John Hart, 2009.
91. *The A to Z of the Green Movement* by Miranda Schreurs and Elim Papadakis, 2009.
92. *The A to Z of the Kennedy–Johnson Era* by Richard Dean Burns and Joseph M. Siracusa, 2009.
93. *The A to Z of Renaissance Art* by Lilian H. Zirpolo, 2009.
94. *The A to Z of the Broadway Musical* by William A. Everett and Paul R. Laird, 2009.
95. *The A to Z of the Northern Ireland Conflict* by Gordon Gillespie, 2009.
96. *The A to Z of the Fashion Industry* by Francesca Sterlacci and Joanne Arbuckle, 2009.
97. *The A to Z of American Theater: Modernism* by James Fisher and Felicia Hardison Londré, 2009.
98. *The A to Z of Civil Wars in Africa* by Guy Arnold, 2009.
99. *The A to Z of the Nixon–Ford Era* by Mitchell K. Hall, 2009.
100. *The A to Z of Horror Cinema* by Peter Hutchings, 2009.
101. *The A to Z of Westerns in Cinema* by Paul Varner, 2009.

102. *The A to Z of Zionism* by Rafael Medoff and Chaim I. Waxman, 2009.
103. *The A to Z of the Roosevelt–Truman Era* by Neil A. Wynn, 2009.
104. *The A to Z of Jehovah's Witnesses* by George D. Chryssides, 2009.
105. *The A to Z of Native American Movements* by Todd Leahy and Raymond Wilson, 2009.
106. *The A to Z of the Shakers* by Stephen J. Paterwic, 2009.
107. *The A to Z of the Coptic Church* by Gawdat Gabra, 2009.
108. *The A to Z of Architecture* by Allison Lee Palmer, 2009.
109. *The A to Z of Italian Cinema* by Gino Moliterno, 2009.
110. *The A to Z of Mormonism* by Davis Bitton and Thomas G. Alexander, 2009.
111. *The A to Z of African American Theater* by Anthony D. Hill with Douglas Q. Barnett, 2009.
112. *The A to Z of NATO and Other International Security Organizations* by Marco Rimanelli, 2009.
113. *The A to Z of the Eisenhower Era* by Burton I. Kaufman and Diane Kaufman, 2009.
114. *The A to Z of Sexspionage* by Nigel West, 2009.
115. *The A to Z of Environmentalism* by Peter Dauvergne, 2009.
116. *The A to Z of the Petroleum Industry* by M. S. Vassiliou, 2009.
117. *The A to Z of Journalism* by Ross Eaman, 2009.
118. *The A to Z of the Gilded Age* by T. Adams Upchurch, 2009.
119. *The A to Z of the Progressive Era* by Catherine Cocks, Peter C. Holloran, and Alan Lessoff, 2009.
120. *The A to Z of Middle Eastern Intelligence* by Ephraim Kahana and Muhammad Suwaed, 2009.
121. *The A to Z of the Baptists* William H. Brackney, 2009.
122. *The A to Z of Homosexuality* by Brent L. Pickett, 2009.
123. *The A to Z of Islam, Second Edition* by Ludwig W. Adamec, 2009.
124. *The A to Z of Buddhism* by Carl Olson, 2009.
125. *The A to Z of United States–Russian/Soviet Relations* by Norman E. Saul, 2010.
126. *The A to Z of United States–Africa Relations* by Robert Anthony Waters Jr., 2010.
127. *The A to Z of United States–China Relations* by Robert Sutter, 2010.

128. *The A to Z of U.S. Diplomacy since the Cold War* by Tom Lansford, 2010.
129. *The A to Z of United States–Japan Relations* by John Van Sant, Peter Mauch, and Yoneyuki Sugita, 2010.
130. *The A to Z of United States–Latin American Relations* by Joseph Smith, 2010.
131. *The A to Z of United States–Middle East Relations* by Peter L. Hahn, 2010.
132. *The A to Z of United States–Southeast Asia Relations* by Donald E. Weatherbee, 2010.
133. *The A to Z of U.S. Diplomacy from the Civil War to World War I* by Kenneth J. Blume, 2010.
134. *The A to Z of International Law* by Boleslaw A. Boczek, 2010.
135. *The A to Z of the Gypsies (Romanies)* by Donald Kenrick, 2010.
136. *The A to Z of the Tamils* by Vijaya Ramaswamy, 2010.
137. *The A to Z of Women in Sub-Saharan Africa* by Kathleen Sheldon, 2010.
138. *The A to Z of Ancient and Medieval Nubia* by Richard A. Lobban Jr., 2010.
139. *The A to Z of Ancient Israel* by Niels Peter Lemche, 2010.
140. *The A to Z of Ancient Mesoamerica* by Joel W. Palka, 2010.
141. *The A to Z of Ancient Southeast Asia* by John N. Miksic, 2010.
142. *The A to Z of the Hittites* by Charles Burney, 2010.
143. *The A to Z of Medieval Russia* by Lawrence N. Langer, 2010.
144. *The A to Z of the Napoleonic Era* by George F. Nafziger, 2010.
145. *The A to Z of Ancient Egypt* by Morris L. Bierbrier, 2010.
146. *The A to Z of Ancient India* by Kumkum Roy, 2010.
147. *The A to Z of Ancient South America* by Martin Giesso, 2010.
148. *The A to Z of Medieval China* by Victor Cunrui Xiong, 2010.
149. *The A to Z of Medieval India* by Iqtidar Alam Khan, 2010.
150. *The A to Z of Mesopotamia* by Gwendolyn Leick, 2010.
151. *The A to Z of the Mongol World Empire* by Paul D. Buell, 2010.
152. *The A to Z of the Ottoman Empire* by Selcuk Aksin Somel, 2010.
153. *The A to Z of Pre-Colonial Africa* by Robert O. Collins, 2010.
154. *The A to Z of Aesthetics* by Dabney Townsend, 2010.
155. *The A to Z of Descartes and Cartesian Philosophy* by Roger Ariew, Dennis Des Chene, Douglas M. Jesseph, Tad M. Schmaltz, and Theo Verbeek, 2010.

156. *The A to Z of Heidegger's Philosophy* by Alfred Denker, 2010.
157. *The A to Z of Kierkegaard's Philosophy* by Julia Watkin, 2010.
158. *The A to Z of Ancient Greek Philosophy* by Anthony Preus, 2010.
159. *The A to Z of Bertrand Russell's Philosophy* by Rosalind Carey and John Ongley, 2010.
160. *The A to Z of Epistemology* by Ralph Baergen, 2010.
161. *The A to Z of Ethics* by Harry J. Gensler and Earl W. Spurgin, 2010.
162. *The A to Z of Existentialism* by Stephen Michelman, 2010.
163. *The A to Z of Hegelian Philosophy* by John W. Burbidge, 2010.
164. *The A to Z of the Holiness Movement* by William Kostlevy, 2010.
165. *The A to Z of Hume's Philosophy* by Kenneth R. Merrill, 2010.
166. *The A to Z of Husserl's Philosophy* by John J. Drummond, 2010.
167. *The A to Z of Kant and Kantianism* by Helmut Holzhey and Vilem Mudroch, 2010.
168. *The A to Z of Leibniz's Philosophy* by Stuart Brown and N. J. Fox, 2010.
169. *The A to Z of Logic* by Harry J. Gensler, 2010.
170. *The A to Z of Medieval Philosophy and Theology* by Stephen F. Brown and Juan Carlos Flores, 2010.
171. *The A to Z of Nietzscheanism* by Carol Diethe, 2010.
172. *The A to Z of the Non-Aligned Movement and Third World* by Guy Arnold, 2010.
173. *The A to Z of Shamanism* by Graham Harvey and Robert J. Wallis, 2010.
174. *The A to Z of Organized Labor* by James C. Docherty, 2010.
175. *The A to Z of the Orthodox Church* by Michael Prokurat, Michael D. Peterson, and Alexander Golitzin, 2010.
176. *The A to Z of Prophets in Islam and Judaism* by Scott B. Noegel and Brannon M. Wheeler, 2010.
177. *The A to Z of Schopenhauer's Philosophy* by David E. Cartwright, 2010.
178. *The A to Z of Wittgenstein's Philosophy* by Duncan Richter, 2010.
179. *The A to Z of Hong Kong Cinema* by Lisa Odham Stokes, 2010.
180. *The A to Z of Japanese Traditional Theatre* by Samuel L. Leiter, 2010.
181. *The A to Z of Lesbian Literature* by Meredith Miller, 2010.
182. *The A to Z of Chinese Theater* by Tan Ye, 2010.

183. *The A to Z of German Cinema* by Robert C. Reimer and Carol J. Reimer, 2010.
184. *The A to Z of German Theater* by William Grange, 2010.
185. *The A to Z of Irish Cinema* by Roderick Flynn and Patrick Brereton, 2010.
186. *The A to Z of Modern Chinese Literature* by Li-hua Ying, 2010.
187. *The A to Z of Modern Japanese Literature and Theater* by J. Scott Miller, 2010.
188. *The A to Z of Old-Time Radio* by Robert C. Reinehr and Jon D. Swartz, 2010.
189. *The A to Z of Polish Cinema* by Marek Haltof, 2010.
190. *The A to Z of Postwar German Literature* by William Grange, 2010.
191. *The A to Z of Russian and Soviet Cinema* by Peter Rollberg, 2010.
192. *The A to Z of Russian Theater* by Laurence Senelick, 2010.
193. *The A to Z of Sacred Music* by Joseph P. Swain, 2010.
194. *The A to Z of Animation and Cartoons* by Nichola Dobson, 2010.
195. *The A to Z of Afghan Wars, Revolutions, and Insurgencies* by Ludwig W. Adamec, 2010.
196. *The A to Z of Ancient Egyptian Warfare* by Robert G. Morkot, 2010.
197. *The A to Z of the British and Irish Civil Wars 1637–1660* by Martyn Bennett, 2010.
198. *The A to Z of the Chinese Civil War* by Edwin Pak-wah Leung, 2010.
199. *The A to Z of Ancient Greek Warfare* by Iain Spence, 2010.
200. *The A to Z of the Anglo–Boer War* by Fransjohan Pretorius, 2010.
201. *The A to Z of the Crimean War* by Guy Arnold, 2010.
202. *The A to Z of the Zulu Wars* by John Laband, 2010.
203. *The A to Z of the Wars of the French Revolution* by Steven T. Ross, 2010.
204. *The A to Z of the Hong Kong SAR and the Macao SAR* by Ming K. Chan and Shiu-hing Lo, 2010.
205. *The A to Z of Australia* by James C. Docherty, 2010.
206. *The A to Z of Burma (Myanmar)* by Donald M. Seekins, 2010.
207. *The A to Z of the Gulf Arab States* by Malcolm C. Peck, 2010.
208. *The A to Z of India* by Surjit Mansingh, 2010.
209. *The A to Z of Iran* by John H. Lorentz, 2010.

210. *The A to Z of Israel* by Bernard Reich and David H. Goldberg, 2010.
211. *The A to Z of Laos* by Martin Stuart-Fox, 2010.
212. *The A to Z of Malaysia* by Ooi Keat Gin, 2010.
213. *The A to Z of Modern China (1800–1949)* by James Z. Gao, 2010.
214. *The A to Z of the Philippines* by Artemio R. Guillermo and May Kyi Win, 2010.
215. *The A to Z of Taiwan (Republic of China)* by John F. Copper, 2010.
216. *The A to Z of the People's Republic of China* by Lawrence R. Sullivan, 2010.
217. *The A to Z of Vietnam* by Bruce M. Lockhart and William J. Duiker, 2010.
218. *The A to Z of Bosnia and Herzegovina* by Ante Cuvalo, 2010.
219. *The A to Z of Modern Greece* by Dimitris Keridis, 2010.
220. *The A to Z of Austria* by Paula Sutter Fichtner, 2010.
221. *The A to Z of Belarus* by Vitali Silitski and Jan Zaprudnik, 2010.
222. *The A to Z of Belgium* by Robert Stallaerts, 2010.
223. *The A to Z of Bulgaria* by Raymond Detrez, 2010.
224. *The A to Z of Contemporary Germany* by Derek Lewis with Ulrike Zitzlsperger, 2010.
225. *The A to Z of the Contemporary United Kingdom* by Kenneth J. Panton and Keith A. Cowlard, 2010.
226. *The A to Z of Denmark* by Alastair H. Thomas, 2010.
227. *The A to Z of France* by Gino Raymond, 2010.
228. *The A to Z of Georgia* by Alexander Mikaberidze, 2010.
229. *The A to Z of Iceland* by Gudmundur Halfdanarson, 2010.
230. *The A to Z of Latvia* by Andrejs Plakans, 2010.
231. *The A to Z of Modern Italy* by Mark F. Gilbert and K. Robert Nilsson, 2010.
232. *The A to Z of Moldova* by Andrei Brezianu and Vlad Spânu, 2010.
233. *The A to Z of the Netherlands* by Joop W. Koopmans and Arend H. Huussen Jr., 2010.
234. *The A to Z of Norway* by Jan Sjåvik, 2010.
235. *The A to Z of the Republic of Macedonia* by Dimitar Bechev, 2010.
236. *The A to Z of Slovakia* by Stanislav J. Kirschbaum, 2010.
237. *The A to Z of Slovenia* by Leopoldina Plut-Pregelj and Carole Rogel, 2010.

238. *The A to Z of Spain* by Angel Smith, 2010.
239. *The A to Z of Sweden* by Irene Scobbie, 2010.
240. *The A to Z of Turkey* by Metin Heper and Nur Bilge Criss, 2010.
241. *The A to Z of Ukraine* by Zenon E. Kohut, Bohdan Y. Nebesio, and Myroslav Yurkevich, 2010.
242. *The A to Z of Mexico* by Marvin Alisky, 2010.
243. *The A to Z of U.S. Diplomacy from World War I through World War II* by Martin Folly and Niall Palmer, 2010.
244. *The A to Z of Spanish Cinema* by Alberto Mira, 2010.
245. *The A to Z of the Reformation and Counter-Reformation* by Michael Mullett, 2010.

The A to Z of Ancient South America

Martin Giesso

The A to Z Guide Series, No. 147

The Scarecrow Press, Inc.
Lanham • Toronto • Plymouth, UK
2010

Published by Scarecrow Press, Inc.
A wholly owned subsidiary of
The Rowman & Littlefield Publishing Group, Inc.
4501 Forbes Boulevard, Suite 200, Lanham, Maryland 20706
http://www.scarecrowpress.com

Estover Road, Plymouth PL6 7PY, United Kingdom

British Library Cataloguing in Publication Information Available

Library of Congress Cataloging-in-Publication Data

The hardback version of this book was cataloged by the Library of Congress as follows:

Giesso, Martin.
Historical dictionary of ancient South America / Martin Giesso.
p. cm. — (Historical dictionaries of ancient civilizations and historical eras ; 21)
Includes bibliographical references.
1. Indians of South America—Antiquities—Dictionaries. 2. South America—Antiquities—Dictionaries. I. Title.
F2229.G54 2008
980'.01203—dc22 2008006716

ISBN 978-0-8108-7574-6 (pbk. : alk. paper)

™ The paper used in this publication meets the minimum requirements of American National Standard for Information Sciences—Permanence of Paper for Printed Library Materials, ANSI/NISO Z39.48-1992.
Printed in the United States of America

To all who have contributed and continue to contribute
to our knowledge of ancient South America

Contents

Editor's Foreword

South America encompasses a vast and varied geography, so it is not surprising that in ancient times it gave rise to many different cultures, ranging from small and simple chiefdoms to larger, more sophisticated kingdoms and empires. Many have been long since forgotten by all but archaeologists, but others still impress us today with the grandeur of their surviving monuments, among them the Moche and the Inka. Yet they all contributed to a continent-spanning civilization that commenced several millennia ago and flourished until it was severed in its prime by Spain and its conquistadors. This book provides insight into ancient South America, describing the more significant groups as well as their settlements and architecture, agriculture and other means of subsistence, social structure and organization, art and religion. It also describes archaeological sites, tools and ceramics, mounds and monoliths, deities, and funeral practices.

The A to Z of Ancient South America was written by Martin Giesso, who hails from the region, being born in Argentina and having studied at the Universidad Nacional de La Plata. He received a doctorate in anthropology from the University of Chicago. Dr. Giesso is currently a lecturer of anthropology and archaeology at Northeastern Illinois University in Chicago. He has completed research and fieldwork from Argentina to Bolivia, and his primary area of interest is the Andean region. He is also interested in state formation and long-distance trade and knows main languages of the area. In this historical dictionary, he has tackled an amazing range of topics to give us a feel for the early period of a vast continent.

Jon Woronoff
Series Editor

Acknowledgments

This dictionary could not have been possible without the support and advice of several colleagues and friends: Victor Duran, Jorge Eremites de Oliveira, Nora Flegenheimer, Adolfo Gil, Santiago Giraldo, Andrés Laguens, Gustavo Neme, Joel Palka, Franz Scaramelli, and Edward Swenson. Ed carefully reviewed the entire manuscript and gave numerous suggestions on style and content, so to him goes my deepest gratitude.

Chronology

Prior to 13,000 BC First humans enter South America.

12,890 BC Earliest occupation of southern Patagonia (Piedra Museo site).

9800 BC First inhabitants of the end of the world (Tres Arroyos rock shelter in Tierra del Fuego).

9000 BC People have settled in all of the major environmental regions of South America.

9000 BC Beginning of plant and animal domestication.

7000 BC First shell mound in southern Brazil.

5000 BC First ceramics, Taperinha, Brazil.

5000 BC First artificial mummies, Chinchorro, northern Chile.

3200 BC Real Alto, Ecuador, first site with public architecture.

2700 BC Caral, in the Supe Valley of Peru, first urban settlement of the Americas.

400–200 BC Chavín cult expands through Central Andes.

AD 100–700 The florescence of Nasca and Moche culture.

AD 600–800 Circular villages become a common feature in the Amazon basin.

AD 700 Tiwanaku state and Wari empire begin expansion.

AD 1000–1400 The Chimú create the largest coastal state in the Andes.

AD 1400 Inka state begins expansion.

AD 1493 Columbus sails by northern Venezuelan coast.

AD 1500 Portuguese arrive in northeastern Brazil.

AD 1532–1571 Last independent Inka kingdom in eastern Andean valleys.

Introduction

THE SOUTH AMERICAN LANDSCAPE

South America is a vast landmass that includes twelve independent countries and one region (Guyane Française) with diverse ethnic groups speaking hundreds of different languages and dialects. Indigenous people have occupied its different habitats while transforming the landscape and themselves with extraordinary dedication and success. South America's geographic regions are as varied as those of other continents: from Patagonia and Tierra del Fuego—at "the end of the world"—to the vast grasslands of central Argentina; to the large river basins of the Amazon, La Plata, and Orinoco; to the plateaus of eastern Brazil; to the high Andean mountains. All climates are present in South America, from the arid Atacama desert to the very humid areas of the southern Andean forest of Patagonia and the Amazonian basin. Vast river systems, such as the aforementioned Amazon, La Plata, and Orinoco, served as routes of contact between peoples, facilitating the exchange of goods, ideas, and cultural practices.

South America can be divided into three large geographic regions: two elevated areas, one on the east (older hills and mountains) and one on the west (the Andes), and a central lower region in between. The eastern highlands are found mostly in Brazil and the central lowlands are the sedimentary plains formed by materials brought by rivers of both the eastern and western elevations. They include the three larger basins (the Amazon, the Orinoco, and the Paraná lowlands), the Pampas, Chaco, and eastern Patagonia. The Andes is one of the largest mountain chains in the world, extending from 10 degrees north to 56 degrees south and covering a distance of 8,000 kilometers. Geographically, the Andes are divided into four regions, closely related to the cultural traditions that once inhabited them. The northern Andes extend from the island of Trinidad to the Pasto Knot (Nudo de Pasto) in southernmost Colombia (between one and two degrees north), crossing the present-day countries of Venezuela and Colombia. The northern Andes witnessed the development of the large señoríos of the intermediate area. The central Andes extend from the Pasto Knot to southern Peru (where the Altiplano begins), around 14 degrees south. The central Andes is the backbone of the present-day countries of Ecuador and north and central Peru. The Altiplano region comprises the area from 14 degrees to 27 degrees south, including parts of southern Peru, western Bolivia, northern Chile, and northwestern Argentina. The southern Andes begin around 27 degrees south, where the Altiplano ends, and extend to the southernmost tip of South America at 56 degrees south. Smaller-scale societies adopted hunting and gathering ways of life, particularly with the resources that guanacos or maritime mammals provide, successfully adapting to life in this southernmost region of the Andes.

THE PEOPLE

The people who inhabited South America were organized in very different social arrangements, from the Tehuelche bands of guanaco hunters and the Tupí and Guaraní agricultural villages to the politically complex Andean states and empires that incorporated millions of inhabitants living in rural settlements, towns, and cities. The Inka formed a vast empire during the fifteenth and early sixteenth centuries AD, and its social, technological, and economic achievements have interested generations of archaeologists, anthropologists, historians, other social scientists, and the public in general. The Inka based their power on accumulating the experiences of many preexisting societies, including the Chimú, Moche, Wari, and Tiwanaku. The legacy of these extraordinary societies include Tiwanaku's massive stone architecture and religious tradition; Wari's agricultural terracing, roads, and political organization; Moche's elaborate crafts and architecture, including irrigation systems; and Chimu's organization and kingship system.

Despite obvious cultural and social differences distinguishing prehistoric South American societies, it is commonly believed that the social, transcendent, and natural realms that characterized many of the cultures of the continent were interconnected. For example, an underlying emphasis on animism and the reverence of unusual features of the natural landscape constituted an important dimension of ancient South American worldviews. Moreover, archaeologists have consistently documented creative adaptation to and transformation of diverse landscapes in the continent. Among the enduring contributions of South American peoples is a vast knowledge of the environment and its biological and mineralogical resources, as well as agricultural products, including maize, potato, manioc, quinoa, and peanuts. Indigenous societies of South America excelled in technical and artistic achievements, such as architecture, crafts, and art in different media.

The principal archaeological areas of the continent include the central Andes, northern Andes, southern Andes, Pampa-Patagonia, Chaco, the Amazonian basin, and the Orinoco area. Each can be described based on common cultural themes. These large areas with common cultural traditions were not self-contained or closed units; on the contrary, they were permeable and dynamic. Thus, one of the underlying themes is the contact and interaction between different societies throughout South America and with peoples living in the Caribbean and in Central America. Some societies, even those located several hundred kilometers apart from each other, exchanged valuable goods such as obsidian, green and blue stones, *Spondylus* and other shells, metals, textiles, ceramics, and tropical-forest feathers. While exchanging these material items, groups of people shared ideas that promoted change in their communities.

The Europeans came into contact with indigenous South American societies at different times. Originally, they established towns mostly on the coasts of tropical and subtropical South America and slowly reached the interior of the large tropical river basins (Amazon and Orinoco) in the seventeenth and eighteenth centuries and most of Patagonia in the nineteenth century. For this reason, written documents describe these societies at different historical moments.

Interest in pre-Columbian cultures began early in the Colonial period, but archaeological research intensified after the consolidation of the new independent states following the end of European colonial rule. It was in the first half of the nineteenth century, after the first museums of natural sciences were established, that scientific archaeology first began to be practiced. These museums include the Museo Argentino de Ciencias Naturales, established in Buenos Aires in 1823; the Museo de Ciencias

Naturales in Santiago de Chile in 1830; the Museu de Historia Natural of Rio de Janeiro; and the Museo de La Plata, 1877, among others. Expeditions from different local and foreign (mainly European) museums and academic societies set the basis for fieldwork and research in many areas at the time. Scholars have been publishing and meeting on a regular basis since 1875, when the first International Congress of Americanists met in Paris, after which they met at four-year intervals. Large collections of archaeological materials from South America can be found in South American, European, and U.S. museums (see appendix 1).

Research on South American archaeology has intensified in the last decades and will continue to expand in the future. The number of institutions, including departments of anthropology, museums, and research centers, as well as individuals with university degrees focusing on the study of South American prehistory, continue to grow. New publications in several languages (Spanish, Portuguese, French, English, and Dutch) appear every year in the region. Archaeological meetings convene on a regular basis now in most, if not all, countries of South and North America and in Europe. Archaeology is increasingly taught in many elementary and high-school curricula in several countries as a means to better illuminate the history of native peoples before the European conquest. More books on archaeology can be found in bookstores.

In the last decades, there has been a growing interest on the part of the public toward ancient South American societies and different aspects of the cultures and lifestyles, including indigenous religions. A growing consciousness of the relevance of the pre-Columbian past and of the preservation of sites and material items is evidenced in the increased support of local museums. Communities have come together to protect and display their heritage, and have more active participation in decisions that pertains to archaeological sites and materials, traditionally in the hands of national or regional governments. In many instances, this change has contributed to the promotion of local tourism.

At the same time that archaeology is growing in popularity, it is necessary to be aware that archaeological sites are more threatened than in the past: population growth, expansion of agriculture and cattle herding, exploitation of natural resources, pollution, looting, and the construction of roads have contributed to the increased destruction of archaeological sites throughout the continent.

The Dictionary

– A –

ABISEO. Late Intermediate Period site (AD 1000–1450) in the Chachapoyas region of the eastern Andes, northern Peru. The site is a **World Heritage site of UNESCO** located in Abiseo National Park. It is characterized by elaborate stone **architecture** and is in relatively close proximity to the related Chachapoyas settlements of Gran **Pajatén** and **Los Pinchudos**. *See also* CHULLPA.

ACHIRA (*CANNA EDULIS*). A cane plant tolerant of cold and warm weather that is cultivated in most of South America for its edible rhizomes or underground roots. It also functions as a living fence and as a break to protect houses from the wind. The earliest findings of achira date to 2000 BC in coastal Peru. *See also* HUACA PRIETA.

ACONCAGUA. 1. Highest mountain peak in the Americas (6,962 meters above sea level). A **high-altitude Inka** ceremonial site is located near its summit. Offerings associated with the shrine included gold and silver human **figurines**, fine textiles, **turquoise** beads, and the southernmost finding of ***Spondylus*** shell in the Andes. These valuable goods suggest that this region was firmly incorporated into the Inka empire. 2. Late Period culture in central Chile (AD 950–1450) that practiced **agriculture** and manufactured distinct **ceramics**. **Hunting** was the main source of animal protein, because the Aconcagua groups did not have **domesticated animals**. Aconcagua sites are located in intermontane valleys and upper sections of the Andean mountains, where they moved to hunt in summer. *See also* CAPACOCHA.

ACONCAHUA. **Obsidian** quarry in southern Peru located on the Aconcahua mountain (4,732 meters above sea level) in the department of Puno. Obsidian from Aconcahua was procured from at least 400 BC and is found in the nearby site of Quelcatani.

ADOBE. Spanish term for sun-dried bricks used by many indigenous groups of the Americas. Some of the largest **pyramids** in South America, including **Huaca del Sol** in the Moche Valley of Peru, were constructed entirely of adobe. Prehistoric adobes come in many different forms and shapes, were occasionally manufactured in molds, and are frequently impressed with makers' marks. The use of makers' marks in **Moche** platform **mounds** suggests segmentary labor practices and the participation of groups of people in pyramid construction. Adobe constructions are still common in many regions of South America. *See also* ARCHITECTURE; CHULLPA; QUINCHA; TAPIA.

AGRICULTURE. Agriculture was the main source of food procurement for most indigenous people of South America. Plant cultivation extended throughout most of South America, except in very high altitude and in the southernmost region, where it extended up to 42 degrees south along the Andes and 32 degrees south in the eastern plains. In high altitudes and latitudes, people depended on **hunting**, fishing, and gathering of wild plants and animals. There were several centers of early agriculture in South America, both in the lowlands and in the highlands, including the Amazon and Orinoco basins, the Ecuadorian and Peruvian coast, and the Andean range. Early evidences of agriculture can be traced to at least to 6000 BC. Agricultural subsistence practices expanded from these core zones to other regions. A wide variety of technologies, from tools such as foot plows or **chaki taklla** and clod breakers to construction features such as sophisticated terracing and **raised fields** (**sukakollos**), were developed by South American peoples in order to improve the natural conditions for agricultural production. They also controlled the excess or lack of water through **irrigation**, improved soil conditions, prevented soil erosion, mitigated the damaging effects of frost, and so on. *See also* ACHIRA; CAÑIWA; CHUÑO; COCA; COCOA; COTTON; MAIZE; MANIOC; MANO AND METATE; MASHWA; OCA; POTATO; QUINOA; TARWI; ULLUKU.

AGUA DE LA CUEVA. Late Pleistocene–Early Holocene cave site located at 2,900 meters above sea level in Mendoza, Argentina. The earliest occupation dates to 8900–7200 BC, as indicated by six radiocarbon dates. Stone tools were made of a variety of raw materials, mostly local, with some regional materials and a very small number of lithics originating from foreign locations. Most of the **hunted** animal remains recovered from the site were **guanaco**, but there were other **camelid** species present as well. **Ñandú** eggs constituted part of the diet and **algarroba** plants deriving from lower altitudes were further associated with this site.

AGUA DE LA TINAJA I. Rock shelter located at 2,050 meters above sea level in Uspallata, Mendoza, Argentina. This site is of particular importance given that a large quantity of both wild and domesticated botanical remains were recovered here. Evidence of early **agricultural** practices was identified at Agua de la Tinaja I: **quinoa** and squash were cultivated around 2500 BC in its earliest occupation, and these crops are also found in the three later occupations: 400 BC, AD 600, and post–AD 600. The two most recent occupations are very similar in terms of associated artifacts and subsistence practices. **Maize** is present in level II (400 BC),while in the lowest level there are fragments of **ñandú** eggs and **camelid** bones.

AGUADA. Cultural tradition of the central valleys of northwest Argentina, forming a discontinuous eight hundred–kilometer arch that includes part of the provinces of Catamarca, Tucumán, La Rioja, and San Juan. Aguada is characterized by elaborate **ceramics** (**polychrome** and **incised**), textiles, **metallurgy**, **rock art**, and ceremonial **architecture**. Aguada **religious** iconography includes **trophy heads**, the figure of the **sacrificer**, and felines. Some of the main ceremonial centers are located in the **Ambato** Valley (Catamarca). Originally it was believed that Aguada development took place during the Middle Period (AD 600–900), but recent research indicates that Aguada emerged during the first century AD and continued in some areas until around AD 1000. Aguada society increased in complexity around AD 500, and for the first time in the region a religious elite emerged, associated with **pyramidal mounds** and ceremonial centers. **Bronze metallurgy** was very advanced in Aguada, and included the use of the **lost-wax technique**. Aguada subsistence was based on **agriculture** and **camelid** husbandry. Resources from the **algarroba** and **chañar** trees were also important in their diet. *See also* SPINDLE WHORLS.

AGUAZUQUE 1. Open-air, mostly preceramic site in the department of Cundinamarca, in the central highlands of Colombia. This settlement is characterized by six occupations (3000 BC to 700 BC), with only the last associated with **ceramics**. The main faunal resource was deer (constituting approximately 70–80 percent of all faunal bones recovered from the site) throughout the preceramic sequence. There is some evidence of cannibalism in several occupations. The first settlers lived in circular huts made of perishable materials and the stone tools are unifacial. Several hearths and primary burials were found in Aguazuque. The second occupation, dating to 1850 BC, is of particular note for its large burials: one had twenty-one individuals with offerings forming a circle.

ALAKA PHASE. Group of **shell-mound** sites with early **ceramics** of Suriname and northern Guyana. This phase is estimated to date around 4000 to 2500 BC. The mounds contain dense refuse of shells and fish and animal bones. Human burials were placed in different parts of the mounds. *See also* CONCHERO; SAMBAQUÍ.

ALAMITO. Early Period culture of the central valleys of northwestern Argentina. It was dated to between AD 300 and 500. Alamito sites occupy less than one hectare and are characterized by a small group of dwellings of **tapia**, **adobe**, and stone columns with an entrance corridor, all configured around a central space with two **mounds**. *See also* SUPLICANTE.

ALCA. Obsidian source located in the upper Cotahuasi valley, southern Peru. It was transported to the **Cuzco** valley and northern Titicaca basin. Alca obsidian predominates over other types in the Cuzco area. Alca obsidian was used continuously from 11,000 BC, at the site of **Quebrada Jaguay**, to the Late Horizon. During **Wari** times (Middle Horizon), it was transported as far north as **Marca Huamachuco** in the northern Peruvian highlands, some 1,000 kilometers away.

ALCARRAZA. Spanish term used in Colombia for a single- or **double-spout vessel**.

ALGARROBA/O (*PROSOPIS* SP.). Large tree that grows in dry and warm areas of South America, and which was very important for the inhabitants of those regions. Its seeds, rich in vitamins and protein, are ground to make flour or are fermented to make an alcoholic drink. In large parts of northwestern Argentina, algarroba was a main staple in the pre-Columbian diet, and it is still consumed nowadays. Algarroba was consumed by some of the earliest inhabitants of the central Andes including **Paiján** populations of northern Peru and **Las Vegas** of Ecuador. Algarroba was a staple in the diet of humans and **domesticated animals** for millennia; it was found among archaic populations of **La Paloma** (central coast of Peru) and in other sites of the Peruvian coast, including **Pampa Grande**, where it was used as fodder for **llamas**. In Colombia, the algarroba *Prosopis juliflora* grows from sea level to 1,000 meters above sea level, while in Venezuela, algarroba grows in the Orinoco basin. Apart from its fruits, algarroba was also an important source of wood for both construction and fuel, as in the site of **Caserones**. *See also* CAÑONCILLO; GUATACONDO-1; LA MINA; LAS MERCEDES; LOS MORRILLOS; SAN PEDRO DE ATACAMA; VILUCO.

ALICE BOER. Late Pleistocene open-air site in the state of São Paulo, Brazil. Finely flaked stone tools were found at Alice Boer, including bifacial projectile points. The dates assigned are around 12,000 BC, but are questionable.

ALPACA (*LAMA PACOS*). One of the two **domesticated** South American **camelids**. Alpacas were domesticated in the central highlands of Peru around 4000 BC. The distribution of alpacas in the Andes is more limited than that of **llamas**. Alpacas were raised mostly in higher altitudes, while llamas were also raised in coastal areas. Alpacas are shorter than llamas and have thinner wool. Alpaca bones have been found in many archaeological sites of the Peruvian, Bolivian, Chilean, and Argentine highlands. *See also* CHOROQOLLO; NASCA CULTURE.

ALTIPLANO. Spanish term that designates the central section of the Andes, from Venezuela (*tierra fría* or *altoandina*, 2,000–3,000 meters above sea level); Colombia (2,500–2,800 meters above sea level); and Ecuador, Peru, and Bolivia (3,500–4,000 meters above sea level) to northern Chile and Argentina (3500–4000 meters above sea level). In Peru, Bolivia, Chile, and Argentina, the local term for altiplano is ***puna***. It was the highest continuously inhabited region during pre-Columbian times, and in Peru and Bolivia **camelids** and Andean tubers (**potato**, **oca**, and **ulluku**) were domesticated here. The highest mountain peaks are found above the altiplano, where population densities were much lower. Here groups **hunted**, quarried rocks, partook in other extractive activities, and/or practiced certain rituals in **high-altitude sanctuaries**.

ALTO RAMIREZ. Culture that developed in Arica, northern Chile between 1000 BC and AD 500, after the end of the **Chinchorro** cultural tradition. The early phase (1000–500 BC) is characterized by **agricultural** villages with intensive **irrigation**, ceremonial and funerary **mounds**, **copper metallurgy**, textiles, and **trophy-head iconography**. **Hallucinogenic** paraphernalia is also present at Alto Ramirez. Many elements have an **altiplano** origin, particularly from the Titicaca basin, which relates Alto Ramirez with the site and culture of **Pukara**.

ALTO SALAVERRY. Preceramic site in the **Moche** Valley, Peruvian north coast. It dates to the **cotton** preceramic. Cotton, gourd, squash, chili, lúcuma (fruit), guava, avocado, pacae (fruit), *ciruela de fraile*, common bean, and lima bean were all recovered from this early site.

AMAZONIAN POLYCHROME TRADITION. Ceramic style dated to the first and second millennium AD associated with the emergence of complex societies in the Amazon basin. Some authors use the term *Polychrome Horizon* due to the vast geographic extent of the distribution of this complex of ceramics in Amazonia. One of the earliest peoples to manufacture polychrome wares is the **Marajoara** culture, after AD 400. The main features of Amazonian cultures associated with **polychrome** ceramics are large settlements and earthworks, large cemeteries with **funerary urns**, and the development of specialized crafts. The territories of these societies covered tens of thousands of square kilometers and were possibly unified under the leadership of a paramount, warlike chief. Ancestor worship among chiefs was an important vehicle of ideological production and political legitimacy. **Trade**, especially in shells and green stones, was another uniting element among these societies. **Maize** was the main crop cultivated in the Amazon and Orinoco basins at this time.

AMBATO. A small valley in northwestern Argentina, near the city of San Fernando del Valle de Catamarca, that served as one of the centers of **Aguada** culture. The ceremonial centers of **La Rinconada** and **Iglesia de los Indios** are among the two most important Aguada sites in Ambato. These ceremonial centers were built around AD 500 and are formed by **mounds**, plazas, and residential areas. Residential **architecture** is of **adobe**. **Ceramics** are mostly gray and black **incised** with felines and human figures ("the sacrificer") with trophy heads. The Ambato Valley is in the western fringes of the area of distribution of cebil or **vilca** trees, one of the **hallucinogenic substances** used in pre-Columbian times.

AMBER. Amber was a precious raw material for some South American societies and was transported over long distances. Amber beads were found in elite **tombs** from the Huaca Loro platform at the **Sican** site of **Batán Grande** (La Leche River valley, north coast of Peru), which date to the Middle Sican Period (AD 1000). They probably originated in northeastern Colombia. Amber is also present at the site of Camay in northwestern Venezuela, a site characterized by large cemeteries with **funerary urns** for children and adults and the manufacture of shell ornaments. Amber artifacts were also documented at the cemetery of Las Locas, Quíbor valley, northwestern Venezuela (200 BC–AD 200). *See also* SERPENTINITE.

AMBROSETTI, JUAN BAUTISTA (1865–1917). Known as the father of Argentine archaeology, Ambrosetti was also a pioneer in the study of folklore. He founded the Ethnographic Museum of Buenos Aires in 1906, the first museum in Argentina dedicated exclusively to anthropology, which later took his name. Even though Ambrosetti conducted his first expeditions in the northeastern section of the country, most of his research was done in the Andean area of northwestern Argentina. Among his main publications are *La antigua ciudad de Quilmes (Valle Calchaquí)* (1897), *Los monumentos megalíticos del valle de Tafí* (1897), *Antigüedades calchaquíes: Datos arqueológicos sobre la provincia de Jujuy* (1902), *El bronce en la región Calchaquí* (1904), *Exploraciones arqueológicas en la Pampa Grande* (1906), and *Exploraciones arqueológicas en la ciudad prehistórica de La Paya* (1907).

AMEGHINO, FLORENTINO (1854–1911). Argentinean paleontologist and archaeologist. He presented a theory that the first human beings originated in what is now the Argentine **Pampas**. Among his many important publications are *L' homme préhistorique dans La Plata* (1879) and *La antigüedad del hombre en el Plata*, published in Buenos Aires and Paris in 1880–1881. Ameghino traveled to Europe to visit early sites and to present several papers. His theory was not only popular in academia but also in Argentine society of the time. His written work was published together in 1935 in *Obras completas y correspondencia científica*.

AMPAJANGO. Quarry site in Catamarca, northwest Argentina. Like **Chivateros** in Peru, it was originally thought to be a very early site, due to its lack of projectile points.

AMPATO. One of the northernmost **high-altitude sites**, located in Arequipa, Peru. Three children were **sacrificed** and buried close to the summit of Mount Ampato during the **Inka** Period. The offerings that accompanied the bodies were of typical Inka style: silver tupu, ***Spondylus*** shell figurines, and textiles. Two camps with **pirca** structures were built at 4,890 and 5,760 meters above sea level to serve as resting areas for people and animals (corrals for **camelids**) on their way to the summit. *See also* ACONCAGUA; CAPACOCHA; CERRO EL PLOMO; LLULLAILLACO.

ANANATUBA PHASE. Sites of this **ceramic** stylistic phase are located in the Marajó Island in the mouth of the Amazon, Brazil. These sites date to between 1400 and 1000 BC. The ceramics are characterized by zoned incisions. For this reason, the Ananatuba is a phase of the **Zoned Hatchured Horizon**. The earliest phase of this horizon is the Early **Tutishcainyo** in the Peruvian Amazon, which likely dates to around 2000 BC.

ANCON. Hunter and gatherer/fisher sites located along the central coast of Peru, from around 6000 to 4000 BC. Members of this cultural tradition used leaf-shaped (**Lauricocha**) projectile points for **hunting** in the ***lomas*** (coastal hills).

ANGUALASTO. Late Period (AD 1200–1450) culture of San Juan, central Argentina, characterized by **agriculture**, **llama** husbandry, and well-developed textile industries. Angualasto communities built and maintained large systems of **irrigation** canals that cover some 15,000 hectares in the northern valleys of San Juan. Large **ceramic** vessels used to store grains are also associated with this culture and foreign artifacts have been recovered from Angualasto sites. These include snuffing tablets from northern Chile as well as **Diaguita** ceramics and other ceramics from north-central Chile. Other material elements that relate to neighboring groups are some garments, which are similar to those used by contemporaneous people in northwestern Argentina and northern Chile. **Metallurgy** was also important in Angualasto society. Angualasto settlements were villages with houses made of **quincha** and **adobe** (some houses are semisubterranean) and are situated close to agricultural fields. Some have corrals made of adobe. **Geoglyphs** and petroglyphs are some of the artistic manifestations of Angualasto. The geoglyphs are associated with the road system, and petroglyphs have figures that appear in Angualasto ceramics, textiles, and other media. Some elements are related to **camelids**. *See also* TURQUOISE.

ANSILTA. Late preceramic/early **ceramic** culture in San Juan, central Argentina, dated to 1800 BC–AD 50. Ansilta groups settled at altitudes of 2,500–3,000 meters above sea level and in encampments that were isolated from **hunter** and gatherer groups to the east. Many material elements were preserved due to the extremely dry climate in the region, including burials with hair and skin. Ansilta groups were the first **agriculturalists** in the region; they cultivated **quinoa**, squash, beans, and **maize**. Basketry and weaving with **camelid** wool, vegetable fibers, and human hair were common practices among Ansilta communities. They also used **tembetá** and nasal plugs. Wool was used for **clothing**. Ansilta **rock art** includes painted figures in caves. The first ceramic vessels were made around 500 BC, but were not used as burial offerings by Ansilta groups (only much later is this practice evident in the **Angualasto** culture). *See also* GRUTA DEL INDIO.

ARATÚ TRADITION. A **ceramic** cultural tradition of eastern Brazil related to but predating the **Uru Tradition**. The first circular villages emerged in the Aratú region around AD 600 and became the most common type of settlement in eastern Brazil by AD 800. The origin of these circular villages is unclear, but they have had a long history continuing into the Colonial Period and into the present day in some areas. These villages occupied areas of up to five hundred meters in diameter, and usually consisted of several rows of houses arranged around an open space or plaza. Village inhabitants cultivated **maize** among other cultigens. After AD 850, the Aratú groups coexisted with **Tupiguaraní** settlements in the area.

ARAUQUINOID. Dating to between AD 600 and 1530, Arauquinoid is one of the latest pre-Hispanic **ceramic** series in the Middle Orinoco and forms part of the **Incised and Punctate Horizon** of the tropical lowlands of northern South America. Contrary to the earliest cultures, often associated with **Arawak**-speaking peoples, Arauquinoid and **Valloid** are believed to represent the arrival of Carib-speaking populations in the area. Whether or not the relationship is valid, there was a significant change in the occupational history of the area between AD 350 and 600. Archaeological remains pertaining to this period are characterized by the presence of Arauquinoid ceramic and larger sites often associated with a large number of **manos and metates**. **Pottery** during this period tends to be made of an orange-brown paste tempered with sponge spicules (***cauixí***). Although **polychrome** decoration characterizes the early part of the series, later or classic Arauquinoid bowls are commonly decorated on the rims with fine-line incise zigzags and punctation. This series has often been associated with an expanding population, apparently related to the production of **maize**. In the middle Orinoco, the Arauquinoid series represents a long-term tradition with considerable spatiotemporal variation and stylistic diversity. This series is represented by two subtraditions, **Corozal** and **Camoruco**, each of them subsequently subdivided in three temporal periods or subphases. Because the geographical distribution of sponge-tempered Arauquinoid pottery coincides with the distribution of Carib-speaking populations, the relationship between the two has been proposed. This movement would be the result of a second migratory movement coming north from the Amazon, associated with the southeast-to-northwest movement of Carib-speaking populations. *See also*

CUEVA DEL CERRO GAVILÁN; CUEVA DEL SANTO; CUEVA SUSUDE INAVA; THÉMIRE.

ARAWAK. Language family widely dispersed throughout South America and the Caribbean. At the time of the European conquest, Arawak-speaking people lived in several large regions of lowland areas. These included the upper Paraguay and Tapajós basins (southwestern Brazil and parts of Paraguay), the upper Madeira basin or part of the Llanos de Mojos (northeastern Bolivia), the upper Purus and Ucayali basins (southwestern Brazil and southeastern Peru), the Río Negro basin and the upper Amazon (western Brazil), the upper Orinoco and western Venezuela, and the northern coast of Guyana, Suriname, and Guyane and the coast of Brazil to the north of the mouth of the Amazon. Terms such as canoe, cacique, hammock, **maize**, and tobacco are of Arawak origin. *See also* SAN; SALADOID.

ARCHITECTURE. Architectural features are found throughout many different regions and geographic environments of South America, from the lowlands to the highest mountain peaks (**Llullaillaco**). People have modified large portions of the South American landscape throughout the millennia to create new spaces of interaction using earth, stone, wood, hides, and other materials. Constructions were organized in hamlets, small towns, large towns, and cities. Massive **adobe pyramids** such as the **Huaca del Sol** and the monumental walls of **Sacsaywaman** represent some of the most impressive constructions built by indigenous people of South America. Houses, temples, terraces, and other built environments were represented in **ceramics** (**Chorrera**, **Moche**, **Recuay**), stone (**Tiwanaku**), wood (**Chimú**), **metallurgy** (several Colombian cultures), and **rock art**. *See also* ADOBE; ASANA; ASPERO; ATERROS; BAHÍA; CALIMA COMPLEX; CERRITO; CHUCUITO; CHULLPA; CIUDAD PERDIDA; FORTIFICATIONS; KALLANKA; LOMAS; MALOCA; MISTOL; MOUND; PIRCA; PUKARA; PYRAMID; QUINCHA; SUNKEN COURT; TAPIA; TOLA; USHNU; WATTLE AND DAUB.

ARISTÉ. Cultural complex of Guyane and neighboring areas of Brazil dated to between AD 350 and 1750. There are different types of Aristé sites: open-air sites of up to four hectares are found along the rivers, and small rock-shelter sites are situated in higher places. The open-air sites there could have supported several large multifamily houses with hundreds of individuals in each. Rock shelters were occupied for short periods of time, probably for ritual activities such as rites of passage and initiation. There are also funerary sites, some in open air, other sites in rock shelters. In early Aristé sites, burials were placed in **funerary urns**. In late Aristé sites, cremation was common. Some open-air sites on the tops of hills have large vertical granite stones forming ceremonial enclosures. Aristé has three phases: early, middle, and late. **Ceramics** are characterized by incision and punctation in the early and middle phases. The late period ceramics are **polychrome**.

ARROYO MALO-3. Preceramic rock-shelter site in southern Mendoza, Argentina, one of the earliest evidence of human occupation of northern Patagonia. Arroyo Malo-3 is located at an altitude of 2,000 meters above sea level. The site seems to have been occupied sporadically from 6900 BC to 200 BC. Tools were made of local **basalts**; **obsidian** from Andean sources was also present. The most abundant animal remains recovered from the site are **guanaco**.

ARROYO SECO-2. Late Pleistocene site in the province of Buenos Aires, Argentina. There is evidence that hunters congregated at this site to **hunt** horse, giant **ground sloth**, and armadillo, three species that are now extinct. The dates obtained for this site range between 9000 and 7000 BC. Only unifacial tools were found here and twenty human skeletons were encountered during the course of excavation.

ASANA. Preceramic open-air site located in the high mountains of southern Peru. Asana was occupied for several millennia, and its earliest occupation dates to 7400 BC. It has one of the earliest known public **architectures** in the south-central Andes, which dates to 3360 BC and consists of a circular ceremonial structure surrounded by dwellings. Asana's latest occupation dates to 1600 BC. The inhabitants of Asana were **hunters** and **pastoralists** who exploited the surrounding high plateau or **puna**.

ASIA. Large preceramic site in the central coast of Peru. Several **tombs** were found in or close to residential areas. Some of them contained

trophy heads. Among the objects that accompany the body are textiles. The presence of a tomb with more offerings than the rest evidences early forms of social stratification. The site of Asia is also known for one of the earliest evidences of **coca** consumption.

ASPERO. Large preceramic site with **mounds** located on the north side of the Supe Valley, north-central coast of Peru. There are seven monumental mounds as well as plazas, terraces, and extensive **middens** or refuse deposits. The site covers approximately twelve hectares and was first occupied around 2700 BC. The ceremonial **architecture** of Aspero constitutes one of the oldest public constructions in the Americas. The structures were made with bundles of entwined stone (quarried and cobbles) and rubble called shicra bags, a common feature of other coastal ceremonial architecture of the preceramic period. Two of the largest ceremonial mounds at Aspero are Huaca de los Idolos and Huaca de los Sacrificios. The name of the first comes from a group of unbaked clay human **figurines** recovered from near the summit of the structure. These could have been used in rituals of curing. ***Spondylus*** was found in an Aspero midden, suggesting its ritual use in the foundations of central Andean civilization.

ASTRONOMY. South American cultures observed and recorded astronomical events. One of the examples of these astronomical studies is the orientation of main monuments in ceremonial and urban sites such as **Tiwanaku** and **Cuzco**. The **Inka** and other Andean people studied the movement of the Milky Way, which is called *Mayu* or "celestial river" in **Quechua**. They divided the Mayu in four parts or *suyu*, which have a parallel to the division into four parts of the Inka empire. Lunar phases were used to determine planting time, and the movement of the Pleiades and other constellations and planets were also integral to plotting for the **agricultural** cycle. One of the elements used in Inka astronomy was the **intihuatana**.

ATAWALLPA (ATAHUALPA). Last **Inka** ruler, captured and put to death by the Spaniards under the direction of Francisco Pizarro in AD 1532. He was apprehended in the Inka city of **Cajamarca**, where he was encamped on his return to **Cuzco** from the northern province of Quito. *See also* METALLURGY.

ATERROS. Portuguese term that designates partial or complete artificial **mounds** located in southern Brazil and Uruguay (the Spanish term is ***cerritos de indios*** or ***lomas*** in **Moxos**, Bolivia). They are usually found in groups and in areas subject to flooding and were constructed by either **hunter**/gatherers or **agriculturalists**.

ATURES TRADITION. This tradition is defined by Archaic sites in the Orinoco basin, Venezuela, and the Colombian lowlands. In the middle Orinoco, Atures designates the earliest human occupations yet found. The first phase, Atures I, dates to 7200–5000 BC. There are no projectile points associated with this cultural tradition. It is probable that Atures I derives from earlier, post-Pleistocene cultures of the Colombian highlands that have similar tools and lowland faunal remains. The second phase, Atures II, dates approximately to 5000–2000 BC. This phase has projectile points, similar to those of the **Canaima** Complex (Venezuela) and other areas in Panama, northern South America, and central and southern Brazil (**Vinitú**). The rest of the lithic instruments are similar to those of Atures I.

AUKAPATA. Name of the main square in the city of **Cuzco**. The term in **Quechua** means *auka* (soldier) *pata* (square or terrace), suggesting that one of its main uses was for military training or parades.

AUSTRAL, ANTONIO G. (1927–). Argentine archaeologist who has conducted research in the pampa region, particularly in the province of Buenos Aires, as well as in Uruguay. Among his published articles are "Investigaciones prehistóricas en el curso inferior del río Sauce Grande (Partido de Cnel. de Marina Leonardo Rosales, Pcia. de Buenos Aires, República Argentina)" (1965), "Prehistoria del sur de la region pampeana" (1968), "El yacimiento de los Flamencos II: La coexistencia del Hombre con fauna extinguida en la Región Pampeana" (1972), "Arqueología en el Sudoeste de Buenos Aires" (1994), and "Variabilidad de la ergología indígena en el sur de Córdoba" with Ana María Rocchietti (1995).

AXE MONEY. Axe money is small **bronze** artifacts of regular sizes associated primarily with the **Lambayeque** culture. Apparently, they were manufactured in northern Peru in the Late Intermediate Period.

Axe money is found in Ecuador, where it was probably exchanged for ***Spondylus***. *See also* MANTEÑO CULTURE.

AYAMPITÍN. Leaf-shaped type of projectile point found in sites throughout northern and central Argentina. This site type is in northern Cordoba, Argentina. Similar points have other names in other South American countries such as **Lauricocha** in Peru and **El Jobo** in Venezuela. The first radiocarbon samples obtained for contexts associated with Ayampitín points date to around 6000 BC, from the **Intihuasi** Cave. These points were found in preceramic and **ceramic** sites, although they are less abundant in the latter. *See also* HUACHICHOCANA; LOS MORRILLOS; PURIPICA-1; TILIVICHE; VISCACHANI.

AYLLU. An ayllu is the traditional socioeconomic and ritual unit of the Andes. An ayllu is a descent group that recognizes a common ancestor, shares usufruct rights to lands, **irrigation** systems, and **camelid** herds in common, and performs **religious** ceremonies related to ancestor worship (local **wacas**). **Kinship** bonds, real or fictive, underscored affiliation in particular ayllus. Ayllus were an important basis of Andean life. *See also* CEQUE SYSTEM; PANAQA.

AYMARA. Large social group that inhabited the Peruvian-Bolivian **altiplano** or **puna** at the time of the Spanish conquest. The Aymara were organized in ***señoríos*** based on **camelid pastoralism**. Señoríos were divided into halves or moieties following a northwest-southeast axis along the Desaguadero River and Lake Titicaca. Today, several million Aymara speakers live in highland areas of southern Peru, Bolivia, and northern Chile. With **Quechua**, the Aymara language is one of the most widely spoken indigenous languages in South America. *See also* AYMARA KINGDOMS; CHULLPA.

AYMARA KINGDOMS. Term commonly used for the polities of Aymara speakers that existed at the time of the **Inka** conquest, around AD 1450–1480. These kingdoms had their political centers along the axis formed by the Titicaca and Poopó lakes and the Desaguadero River. Each Aymara kingdom was divided in two parts: the *urku* or *orqo*, the upper part, and the *uma*, the lower part. The Aymara kingdoms include the Lupaka, Pacajes, Carangas, and Quillacas, among others. *See also* AYMARA.

AZÁNGARO (INKARAQAY). Planned **Wari** site in the Huanta valley, southern Peru. Azángaro was built from around AD 650 to 800, some fifty kilometers north of the capital city of Wari. Azángaro is a rectangular enclosure with three sectors. The north and central sectors are rigidly planned. The southern sector has buildings irregularly distributed. Large numbers of local **ceramics** suggest that the site was a center for recruitment of labor.

AZAPA PHASE. Early part of the **Formative Period** in the north coast of Chile (1400–500 BC). The type sites are **Faldas del Morro**, El Laucho, and Azapa 71. Subsistence was based on **hunting** and gathering and cultivation of **achira** and peppers using digging sticks. The Azapa settlements were small, and houses were made of wood and totora reeds. The cemeteries were close to the dwellings; bundles were made with totora reeds. Some undecorated **ceramics**, **copper** elements, and **incised** gourds are elements that characterize Azapa sites. Several members of these communities had **cranial deformation**. The Azapa Phase is followed by the **Alto Ramirez** groups.

– B –

BAHÍA. This culture was centered in the area of coastal Ecuador in the vicinity of the city of Manta and dates from approximately 200 BC to AD 600, during the **Regional Development Period**. Bahía is closely related to **Jama-Coaque**. Bahía sites have **pyramidal** earthen **mounds** or **tolas**, which anchored urban or quasi-urban centers. Bahía society was hierarchical, and a group of religious figures were among its leaders. Religious iconography is complex, including feline figures. Moldmade hollow **ceramic** figures depict a variety of human activities (**hunters**, warriors, **musicians**, dancers, and so on) and individuals, including figures with elaborate costumes and headdresses. Other ceramic forms include **compoteras**, **architectural** models, and whistling bottles. Bahía people had a very diverse diet based on **agriculture** (**maize**, beans, squash, and **manioc**), fish, related maritime resources, and land animals, both wild and **domesticated**. The latter included dog, **guinea pig**, and **Muscovy duck**. *See also* LOS ESTEROS.

BARABINA HILL. A **shell mound** dated to 5000–4000 BC, Barabina Hill is one of the oldest sites in Guyana. Snail (brackish-water nerite) and crabs were the main sources of protein for the groups that occupied this site. Other sources of protein were provided by **hunting** and fishing.

BARBAKOEBA. Cultural complex of coastal Guyane and Suriname (AD 1000–1400) related to the **Arauquinoid** groups of northern South America. Sites are formed by layers of **terra preta** and are associated with drained fields. Barbakoeba is closely related with the **Thémire Complex**. Most **ceramics** are undecorated; those that have decoration are mostly with incisions and finger marks. Many polished lithic tools were made by specialized groups of the **Brownsberg Complex** of Suriname.

BARRANCOID. A widely distributed **ceramic** style from northern South America. The type site is Barrancas in the lower Orinoco River drainage, Venezuela. The origin of this series is unknown. Its relationships with other stylistic traditions in the area, such as the **Saladoid**, are also unknown. Barrancoid ceramic exhibits polished surfaces and is tempered with fine sand. The series includes large vessels beautifully decorated with wide **incised** curvilinear motives and designs depicting animal and human figures. Some scholars consider Barrancoid to predate the appearance of Saladoid in the Orinoco basin. According to these authors, Barrancoid represents a long-term tradition (1000 BC–AD 1500) subdivided into three distinguishable style periods, the earliest of which is believed to be associated with a western **Formative** development such as **Valdivia** in Ecuador or **Puerto Hormiga** in Colombia. **Maize agriculture** among Barrancoid people is suggested by the presence of **manos and metates** in their sites. *See also* CUEVA DEL SANTO; MABARUMA.

BASALT. Many indigenous people of South America used this type of volcanic rock for tools, ornaments, and as construction material. There are different types of basalt according to its chemical composition, grain size, color, and so on. Fine-grained basalt, such as that from the **Querimita** quarry in Bolivia, was used for cutting tools and hoes. Coarser grain basalt was used to make grinding tools (**manos**

and metates) and for ornamental and ritual objects, such as the **chachapuma** of **Tiwanaku**. **Culebras**, in the central coast of Peru, provides one example of an archaeological site where basalt was used as a construction material. *See also* CUEVA EPULLAN.

BATÁN GRANDE. Large **Lambayeque** and **Sican** ceremonial center located in the La Leche valley in the region of Lambayeque, northern Peru. Batán Grande was inhabited from around 1500 BC to AD 1100. The majority of its standing **architecture** dates to the Middle Sican Period: seventeen monumental **adobe mounds**, multi-room enclosures, roofed terraces with colonnades, and adobe-limestone flagstone floors. Batán Grande was an important center of **bronze metallurgy** in the ninth century AD. Wealthy lords were accompanied in their **tombs** by retainers and valuables, such as gold or **tumbaga** funerary masks encrusted with semiprecious stones, shells, metal spangles, and feathers. One of the major tombs, which was **looted** several decades ago, contained more than one hundred and fifty gold and silver **keros**, a thousand gold beads, twenty necklaces, and a **tumi** or ceremonial knife, as well as **emeralds**, pearls, and **ceramics**. *See also* TÚCUME.

BATUNGASTA. *See* WATUNGASTA.

BELÉN. Ceramic style of the southern valleys of northwestern Argentina, particularly in the Catamarca province, that can be dated to the **Regional Development Period**, which extends from AD 1000 to 1400. Most of the early findings were large cemeteries with **funerary urns** for infants. Belén ceramics have black paint over a red slip.

BENNETT MONOLITH. The largest **monolith** found in **Tiwanaku** and one of the largest in South America. It was originally located in the semisubterranean temple, and consists of one block of sandstone, carved to represent a human figure with a headdress holding a **kero**. Other smaller monoliths were found in the same temple. Shortly after its discovery in the 1930s, the Bennett Monolith was taken to the city of La Paz and has recently been returned to Tiwanaku, where it was placed at a new museum for stone sculpture. The monolith takes the name of American archaeologist Wendell Bennett. *See also* STAFF GOD.

BENNETT, WENDELL (1905–1953). American archaeologist who conducted archaeological research in Bolivia (*Excavations in Tiwanaku*, AMNH, 1934; *Excavations in Bolivia* 1936), Peru, Ecuador, and Venezuela (*Excavations at La Mata, Maracay, Venezuela*, 1937). His *North Western Argentine Archaeology* with E. Bleiler and F. Sommer (1948) was an important synthesis. His work on **Tiwanaku** settled the first relative chronology for the Titicaca basin. He published *Andean Culture History* with **Junius Bird** in 1948 and then in 1960. Other important publications are *Excavations at Wari, Ayacucho, Peru* (1953); *Excavations in the Cuenca Region, Ecuador* (1946); *The North Highlands of Peru: Excavations in the Callejón de Huaylas and at Chavín de Huántar* (1944); and *Ancient Arts of the Andes* (1954).

BINGHAM III, HIRAM (1875–1956). American scholar who reported of the existence of **Machu Picchu** in 1911. He traveled through Venezuela, Colombia, Argentina, Bolivia, and Peru. He published several articles and books, including *Inca Land: Explorations in the Highlands of Peru* (1922), *Machu Picchu, a Citadel of the Incas* (1930), and *Lost City of the Incas: The Story of Machu Picchu* (1948).

BIRD, JUNIUS B. (1907–1982). American archaeologist who conducted key archaeological research in Peruvian coastal preceramic (**Huaca Prieta**) and in Late Pleistocene–Early Holocene cave sites in southern Chile (**Fell** and **Palli Aike** caves). His main publications are *Antiquity and Migrations of the Early Inhabitants of Patagonia* (1938), *Excavations in Northern Chile* (1943), *The Archaeology of Patagonia* (1946), and *South American Radiocarbon Dates* (1951). Some of his writings were published after his death as *The Preceramic Excavations at Huaca Prieta, Chicama Valley, Peru* (J. Hyslop, ed., 1985), and *Travels and Archaeology in South Chile* (Hyslop, ed., 1988). This last book contains reports on the sites of Cañadón Leona, Palli Aike, Fell Cave, Cerro Sota Cave, and Mylodon Cave.

BOLA (BOLEADORA). Ground stone artifact used for **hunting** by many South American groups since Late Pleistocene times and into the Colonial and Republican periods. Some of the Late Pleistocene sites that contain bolas are **Monte Verde** (southern Chile, 10,500

BC), **Fell Cave** (9000 BC), **Marazzi** (7500 BC), and sites in eastern Brazil (9500–9000 BC). More recent sites associated with bolas are those of the **Casapedrense** (5000–3000 BC). Bolas became a more effective hunting device with the introduction of the horse after the 16th century AD. One possible iconographic representations of bolas in southern South America can be found at the **Cueva de las Manos Pintadas** (Santa Cruz, Argentina). *See also* CHACO; ITAPARICA TRADITION; OSOIDE TRADITION; UMBÚ TRADITION; VILUCO.

BOMAN, ERIC (1867–1924). Swedish-born archaeologist who in 1887 traveled to South America and explored northwest Argentina, north Chile, and southern Bolivia with the Swedish and French expeditions. He lived most of his life in Argentina. Among his main works are *Antiquités de la region andine de la République Argentine et du Desert d'Atacama* (two volumes, 1908), *Una momia de Salinas Grandes (Puna de Jujuy)* (1918), *Los ensayos de establecer cronología prehispánica en la región Diaguita* (1923), and *Estudios arqueológicos riojanos* (1927–1932). The Archaeological Museum of Santa Maria (Catamarca, Argentina) takes his name.

BORDO DE LOS INDIOS. Aguada ceremonial center in the **Ambato** Valley, Catamarca, northwest Argentina. Bordo de los Indios consists primarily of an elevated **mound** made of earth and stones and residential dwellings. The site was dated to AD 500–1000.

BRAY, WARWICK. British archaeologist who conducted research in Colombia. He wrote *Investigaciones arqueológicas en el valle del río Calima* (1962), *An Archaeological Sequence from the Vicinity of Buga, Colombia* (1971), *The Gold of Eldorado* (1979), *Across the Darien Gap: A Colombian View of Isthmian Archaeology* (1984), *Calima: diez mil años de historia en el suroccidente de Colombia* (coedited with M. Cardale, T. Gahwiler, and L. Herrera, 1992), and edited *The Meeting of Two Worlds: Europe and the Americas, 1492–1650* (1993).

BRONZE METALLURGY. The most sophisticated bronze **metallurgy** in the Americas developed in the central and southern Andean regions. Bronze metallurgy was lacking in the northern Andes (Colombia and Venezuela). The primary evidence of large-scale production of arsenic bronze in the central Andes comes from the site of **Batán Grande**. The extraordinary discoveries at **Sipán** also indicate that the **Moche** were experts in **copper** and bronze smelting as well as in gilding techniques. During the Middle Horizon (**Tiwanaku-Wari** expansions), bronze metallurgy became a technological marker throughout the Andes and was practiced from northwest Argentina to Ecuador. In the Titicaca basin, bronze alloys included those of tin and copper and copper and arsenic, as well as ternary alloys of copper, arsenic, and nickel. Bronze was used for the manufacture of decorative items and tools such as knives and nails (Tiwanaku). In northwest Argentina, the most common form of bronze is a copper-arsenic-zinc alloy. In northern Chile (**San Pedro de Atacama**), axes were made of a ternary alloy of copper, arsenic, and nickel, and there is one case of a Quaternary alloy: copper, arsenic, nickel, and tin. In **Inka** times, bronze items became disseminated throughout **Tawantinsuyu**. *See also* LAMBAYEQUE; RUMIQOLCA; SAN JOSÉ DE MORO; SANTA MARÍA; VILUCO.

BROWNSBERG CULTURE. A mining culture that processed metabasalt to make axes, which they **traded** with coastal groups. Brownsberg culture developed in the interior of Suriname and can be dated to AD 1000–1500. *See also* BARBAKOEBA.

BUDARES. A type of clay griddle which is an indirect index of **manioc** cultivation in many parts of northern South America. Small stone chips were used to make grater boards in the soft clay. In **La Gruta** (Middle Orinoco), there are some early budares. They are present in **Arauquinoid** and **Valloid** sites as well. *See also* HOKOMO STYLE; HOSSORORO CREEK; MOMIL; MONT GRAND MATOURY; RANCHO PELUDO; SALADOID; TUMACO.

BUENA VISTA. Large site in the northern bank of the Chillón River, slightly north of Lima, Peru. The site of Buena Vista was occupied since 1500 BC and has ceremonial constructions in which there are the oldest well-dated niches and windows in the New World.

BURITICÁ. A paramount-headed **chiefdom** in the northern Cauca River valley (Colombia). The main Buriticá settlement was an important center of **trade** that linked macro-**Chibchan**, macro-Caribbean, and

Arawakan-speaking groups in Central America and northern South America.

– C –

CABALLO MUERTO. Large **Cupisnique** site in the **Moche** Valley, north coast of Peru. The site occupies 200 hectares and contains eight **mounds**. The best preserved is **Huaca de los Reyes**, a **U-shaped structure** with a central platform six meters high and lateral wings surrounding a large central courtyard. As with other U-shaped structures, the opening of the U faces east, up-valley. Near the main façade of the platform, there were four **adobe** heads two meters high representing feline creatures with large canine teeth. Some apparently domestic **architecture** was found in the vicinity of Caballo Muerto.

CACHIMBO. Portuguese term for **pipe**.

CAHUACHI. Important ceremonial center of the **Nasca Culture** in the Nazca Valley of the south coast of Peru. There are a multitude of **adobe mounds** and plazas and the site occupies an area of over 150 hectares. Cahuachi served primarily as a **pilgrimage** center. There is domestic **architecture**; however, it seems to be temporary. Cahuachi is close to the San José pampa, where the famous **geoglyphs** or **Nazca lines** are located. The site was abandoned around AD 500. *See also* VENTILLA.

CAJAMARCA. 1. **Inka** administrative center in the northern Peruvian highlands where the Spanish *conquistador* Francisco Pizarro met and captured Inka **Atawallpa**. 2. Culture and **ceramic** style in the Cajamarca basin, which consists of several temporal-stylistic divisions that date from 500 BC to the Inka conquest. Cajamarca ceramics, renowned for their floral cursive designs and **polychrome** paint, are common in much of Peru, both in the coast and in the highlands, especially during the first centuries of the Middle Horizon (AD 550–800). Cajamarca society appears to have been stratified, with a complex settlement hierarchy and a chiefly elite. The sites of Collor, Santa Delia, and Tantarica were large ceremonial and administrative settlements characterized by elaborate stone precincts, **tombs**, and dense domestic areas. *See also* HUACALOMA; LAYZÓN.

CAJAMARQUIILLA. Large urban site extending over six square kilometers in the Rimac valley, central coast of Peru, associated with the **Lima Culture** (Nivería). Cajamarquilla represents one of the largest prehistoric cities of the Andes with a population of 20,000 people or more at the height of its occupation during the Middle Horizon (AD 600–1000). Seven occupation levels have been identified here, dating from 200 BC (Early Intermediate Period) to the Middle Horizon 2 (AD 700–800). The city appears to have been organized into neighborhoods centered on a platform **mound** and a large open plaza.

CALIMA COMPLEX. Long-lasting cultural tradition in the Cauca Valley, western Colombia. The Calima Complex is divided into three phases: Ilama (1000 BC–AD 100), **Yotoco** (AD 200–1300), and Sonso (AD 1200–Spanish conquest). **Ceramic** production included modeled representations of humans, animals, and houses, among other elements of their daily life. Many of these figures are single- or **double-spout** vessels (***alcarraza***). The Calima made **funerary urns**, usually with little or no decoration. Calima people manufactured ornaments in gold, including pectorals, masks, bracelets, and necklaces.

CALZADAS. Spanish term for elevated earth structures that were built in lowland sites of the Amazon and Orinoco basins as roads to unite other structures, such as **mounds**. They were particularly useful during the rainy season, when the waters cover the lowland areas between sites. The site of **Gaván** in the Orinoco and several sites in the Mojos area of northern Bolivia are examples of sites with calzadas.

CAMELIDS (*CAMELIDAE*). Four species of camelids were **hunted** or herded in South America: **guanaco**, **llama**, **alpaca**, and **vicuña**. They constituted one of the main sources of protein, wool, leather, tendons, fuel/fertilizer (dung), and/or **transport** in South America. Guanaco and vicuña are wild camelids, while llamas and alpacas were **domesticated** and herded for more than four millennia. A fifth species, *Paleolama*, lived during the Late Pleistocene and is now extinct. By **Formative** times, domesticated camelids were common throughout the central and south-central Andes as well as in Ecuador. The **Inka** introduced domesticated camelids to central Argentina, central Chile, and other frontier areas of their empire. *See also* AGUA DE LA CUEVA; AGUA DE LA TINAJA I; ALTIPLANO; AMPATO; ANGUALASTO; ANSILTA; AYLLU; AYMARA; CATARPE; CERRO BLANCO; CERRO COLORADO; CERRO SOMBRERO; CIÉNAGA; CLOTHING; CUMBE CAVE; EL INDÍGENO; HIGH-ALTITUDE SANCTUARIES; LA BARCA; LAS ANIMAS CULTURE; SAN FRANCISCO CULTURE; TELARMACHAY; TIWANAKU; YURAJ MOLINO.

CAMELLONES. Spanish term for **raised fields**.

CAMORUCO PHASE. The Camoruco Phase constitutes the latest component of the **Arauquinoid** sequence (AD 600–1500). This phase is often considered as emblematic Arauquinoid. Previous painted motifs are absent during this period, while at the same time there is a strong emphasis on fine-line incisions, zigzag, rectilinear geometric designs, and punctation. During this period there is a tremendous intensification in the use of spicule temper across the middle Orinoco, where Camoruco seems to represent the local expression of a much wider horizon style. Sites corresponding to this period are larger and occur along the middle Orinoco and most of its tributaries, including vast portions of the northwestern llanos. There is little agreement about the origin or the widespread expansion of the Camoruco Phase in the middle Orinoco. To some scholars, the rapid spread of this **ceramic** along the middle Orinoco is the product of a local process of cultural change. Nevertheless, these authors also consider the possibility that the Camoruco Phase may the product of a much wider Amazonian Horizon (the fine-line and **incise punctate** zone) that spread north into the middle Orinoco and even further. On the other hand, this process could represent the intensification of an ongoing migratory pattern fueled by increasing demographic pressures along the main rivers of the tropical lowlands. *See also* COROZAL.

CAÑADÓN SALAMANCA. Obsidian source in northern Patagonia, Argentina.

CANAIMA. Campsite in Venezuela associated with stemmed points of the Late **El Jobo** Tradition.

CANDELARIA. Ceramic style from the eastern valleys of northwestern Argentina. It dates to approximately AD 300–900. Large ceramic vessels, some of which functioned as **funerary urns**, with **incised** and modeled ornaments (human faces) are one of the more characteristic elements of this cultural tradition.

CAÑIWA (KAÑIWA OR KAÑAWA) (*Chenopodium pallidicaule*). Pronounced kan-*yi*-wa, cañiwa is a very nutritious grain first domesticated in the south-central Andes. Similar to its relative, **quinoa**, it is extremely resistant to frost and can be cultivated up to 4,500 meters above sea level. Thus it was and continues to be an important staple for the communities that live at the highest altitudes. Today it is grown in the Andean highlands from central Peru to southern Bolivia.

CAÑONCILLO (JATANCA/TECAPA). Cañoncillo emerged as one of the most significant Late **Moche** sites on the south bank of the Jequetepeque River. However, the majority of its standing **architecture** was built in the Transitional and **Chimú** periods. Some authors argue that it served as a provincial elite center for the south valley in the Late Moche Period and Early Transitional Era. Typical Late Moche face-neck jars were found in the **algarroba** forest of the site (Tecapa) and smaller percentages in the vicinity of the acropolis on the sandy plain (Jatanca). However, Tecapa appears to represent the late Chimú portion of the site (characterized by large compounds with **adobe** bricks), while the **tapia** constructions of the Jatanca suggest an earlier occupation on the desert pampa. Constructions built of rectangular adobe bricks and rows of square column bases may have been associated with a Late Moche presence at Cañoncillo. Huaca Santa María and a large network of plazas adjacent to expanded **agricultural** fields are thought to date to the Late Intermediate Period.

CAPACOCHA. Ritual **sacrifice** of children in the **Inka** empire. The children were left as offerings to sacred **wacas** and revered mountain peaks. Famous examples include the well-preserved remains of child victims found near the summits of **Llullaillaco**, **Cerro El Plomo**, and **Aconcagua**, among others.

CARAJUANA. This is a site located between Yunguyu and Copacabana (Bolivia). It consists of the largest major **pukara** in the Titicaca basin in terms of area enclosed by **fortification** walls. Similar to other pukara in the region, it dates to the Late Intermediate Period (AD 1000–1400).

CARAL. Recent finds indicate that Caral in the Supe Valley is the earliest ceremonial center and perhaps urban conglomeration in the Americas. The construction of this site dates to 3200 BC in the early preceramic period. The center of the site is dominated by large **mounds** and circular plazas. Residential areas are also present in different sectors of the site. The inhabitants of Caral were **agriculturalists** and fishers, but did not use **ceramics**.

CARDAL. An Early Period **U-shaped ceremonial complex** in the Lurín valley, central coast of Peru. The site was occupied from 1300 to 900 BC and consists of a large plaza surrounded by low platforms and a high **pyramid** forming the basal portion of the ceremonial complex. In the summit of this central **mound**, rooms were found containing remains of an **adobe** frieze with a fanged feline.

CARDICH, AUGUSTO (1923–). A Peruvian-born archaeologist, Cardich lived most of his life in La Plata, Argentina, where he taught and conducted research at the Museo de La Plata. His research focused on Late Pleistocene and Early Holocene settlers in Peru and Argentina and ancient **agriculture** in the Peruvian highlands. His work includes *Los yacimientos de Lauricocha. Nuevas interpretaciones de la prehistoria peruana* (1958), *Lauricocha. Fundamentos para una Prehistoria de los Andes Centrales* (1964), *Secuencia arqueológica y cronología radiocarbónica de la cueva 3 de Los Toldos (Santa Cruz, Argentina)* (1973), *El fenómeno de las fluctuaciones de los límites superiores del cultivo en los Andes: su importancia* (1980), and *Civi-*

lización Andina: su formación (1988). His most recent book compiles his early work: *Hacia una Prehistoria de Sudamérica: Culturas Tempranas de los Andes Centrales y de Patagonia* (2003).

CARIAPÉ. Tempering substance (particles that are added to the clay before firing it) made with ash. Cariapé characterizes the **ceramics** made by many Amazonian groups, such as the **Uru**, **Aratú**, and **Mossamèdes**. *See also* MABARUMA.

CARIBBEAN AREA. Cultural area that defines the prehistoric people living in the Caribbean and part of the northernmost coast of the South American mainland. In South America, it includes central and northern Venezuela and the northern half of the Guianas. Some of the groups that lived in the mainland migrated to the Caribbean islands and thus share elements of the general cultural tradition.

CARONÍ TRADITION. This tradition refers to the early settlers of the Lower Orinoco. Caroní sites are camps or lithic workshops. Little is known about their subsistence. It is suggested that the Caroní were **hunters** of small animals (small rodents, birds, turtles), fishers, and collected riverine mollusks and vegetables. This lithic tradition is characterized by rustic quartzite choppers and flakes and was developed in the Early Holocene of the Lower Orinoco, eastern Venezuela. These stone tools are similar to those found in sites dating to 10,000–8000 BC in other parts of South America, for example, in the **Itaparica** Tradition of the Matto Grosso. **Ño Carlos** and Remigio are two Caroní sites dating to 3300–2500 BC.

CASAPEDRENSE. One of the few stone-tool industries of South America with a high proportion of blades (long and narrow flakes with the shape of a knife blade). Casapedrense sites are located in the central **altiplano** of the Santa Cruz province, southern Argentina; **Los Toldos**, Cueva Grande del Arroyo Feo (Río Pinturas valley), La Martita, and **Cerro Tres Tetas** are among the more important sites of this tradition. This lithic industry dates to the Middle Holocene, ranging between 5000 and 3000 BC. There are no projectile points in this industry, suggesting that **guanacos** were hunted mainly by encirclement. The end-scrapers are thought to be for preparing guanaco hides. There is an abundance of **rock art** associated with the Casapedrense culture.

CASAS SUBTERRÂNEAS. Groups of sites located in the highlands and coast of the Rio Grande do Sul and Santa Catarina states, southern Brazil. Some were also found further north, in the state of São Paulo. These sites were dated to AD 800–1700, with some scholars arguing that the first sites originated 2,000 years ago. The Portuguese term refers to partially subterranean houses that characterize these sites. Villages are formed by several subterranean houses, up to eighty, in open areas with pine (*Araucaria*) forests of the highlands, usually above 400 meters. Houses contain hearths and postholes and have diameters of between five and twenty meters. Not all sites of this culture are in open-air villages; some are in rock shelters. Subsistence was probably based on pine nuts. **Ceramics** found in these sites are of the Taquara or **Itararé** Tradition; they are small and usually have limited decoration.

CASERONES. (Large houses in Spanish.) Large village or town 1.5 hectares in size located in the Tarapacá valley of northern Chile and dating to 500 BC. Caserones is larger than contemporaneous sites in the region and was surrounded by a double wall. There is evidence of **agriculture** involving **maize**, **quinoa**, squash, peppers, and gathering of **algarroba** seeds. Maize and algarroba seeds and flour were stored in communal warehouses and algarroba posts were used for building houses. Part of the food came from the sea, mainly fish and shellfish. Caserones inhabitants had contacts with people from the eastern Andean valley from whom they obtained feathers of tropical birds. **Ceramics**, metals, and basketry items were common in Caserones houses.

CATARPE. Inka tampu and administrative center located a few kilometers north of the town of **San Pedro de Atacama** in northern Chile. It was probably also a manufacturing and storage center of **camelid** products.

CATEQUIL (SITE OF NAMANCHUGO). Important provincial **huaca** in the Huamachuco region of the northern highlands of Peru described in the Early Colonial Period. At Catequil, there were two construction moments; the earliest, associated with a rectangular building, dates to AD 670–800. The building is similar to the contemporaneous Classic niched halls at **Marca Huamachuco**. The later building is believed to have been the sanctuary of Catequil. It had an oracular canal and a subterranean libation canal. Among the offerings were ***Spondylus*** shells, stone cobbles, and **ceramics**.

CAUIXÍ. Sponge spicules that were added to clay in the manufacture of **ceramics** by some groups in the greater Amazonia. *See also* ARAUQUINOID.

CEBIL. *See* VILCA.

CEDEÑOID. Cedeñoid is a long-term **ceramic** tradition of the middle Orinoco, Venezuela. Tempered with rounded clay pellets, ash, sand, and vegetable fibers, this ceramic is often decorated with **incised** bands and zigzags. Some authors believe that Cedeñoid series represent western **Arawak**-speaking people who came into the middle Orinoco area about AD 700–800 and subsequently spread westward across the western Llanos. The beginning of this series is considered to be contemporary with the **La Gruta** Phase of **Saladoid**, dating at least between 2000 and 1000 BC or even earlier. According to some scholars, populations associated with this ceramic tradition may have experienced a demographic increase related to improved adaptation strategies and heightened interaction with other Guyana populations.

CEQUE SYSTEM. Complex system of 342 **wacas** and interconnecting, though invisible, site lines located in and around the city of **Cuzco**. This system was described in detail by the Jesuit priest Bernabé Cobo in the sixteenth century. Different social groups (**ayllus** or **panaqas**) were in charge of maintaining these series of shrines, which were related to their ancestors, the a**gricultural** cycle, and **Inka** narratives of royal history, legitimacy, and political privilege. *See also* KORICANCHA.

CERAMIC MOLD. Fired clay potters' molds first appear shortly before AD 1 in Ecuador and northern Peru. This technique allowed the mass production of numerous identical vessels and came to florescence in northern Peru. The earliest examples have been uncovered in coastal Ecuador: **Chorrera** potters used a single-piece mold to form the front half of hollow **figurines**. Molds were commonly used by coastal **Chavín** cultures (**Cupisnique**) and later underwrote the famous **Moche** ceramic tradition. The Moche employed two-piece and multiple molds. *See also* CERAMICS; LA MINA; LOMA NEGRA.

CERAMICS (POTTERY). Fired clay artifacts (vessels, **figurines**, and so on) were manufactured and used in most of South America, from northern Patagonia in the south to the Caribbean coast in the north. Archaeologists use ceramics as one of the main indicators of cultural affiliation and relative chronology. The earliest ceramics in South America come from the northern areas (Ecuador, Colombia, and Venezuela) and the Amazon and were dated to between 6000 and 5000 BC. In the central Andes, people began manufacturing ceramics several centuries after the first villages and ceremonial centers appeared. Ceramics were exchanged among different groups; in some cases, foreign wares can be identified by their style or by trace element analysis of the clay. One of the most common manufacturing techniques is using coils. Once manufactured, the vessel can be decorated through incision, burnishing, smoothing, corrugation, modeling, pressing fingers, corncobs, cords or basketry, slipping, and painting. Several groups in Peru, including the **Moche**, used **ceramic molds** to produce large quantities of vessels of standardized shapes. *See also* ALCARRAZA; CARIAPÉ; CAUIXÍ; CIÉNAGA; COMPOTERA; CONDORHUASI; DOUBLE-SPOUT BOTTLE; FIGURINES; FUNERARY URN; KERO; MARAJOARA; PEDRA PINTADA CAVE; PORTRAIT VESSELS; STIRRUP BOTTLE; TAPERINHA; TECOMATE.

CERRITOS DE INDIOS. Spanish term for artificial **mounds** found in Uruguay (see **aterros** for their Brazilian counterpart).

CERRO ARENA. Cerro Arena is the largest and most prominent **Salinar** Period site in the Moche Valley, north coast of Peru. Cerro Arena dates to 350–100 BC and occupied two square kilometers. It is distinguished by ceremonial structures, administrative **architecture**, and densely clustered, agglutinated domestic residences, around two thousand of them, exhibiting differences in quality and construction. The constructions were made of quarried granite and range from one-room dwellings to dwellings formed by twenty-four rooms. The prominence and diversity of purported administrative architecture (as opposed to the more subdued religious monuments) is seen as evidence for the development of a "secular" and specialized administration during the Salinar Period. The Salinar centers of **Puémape** and Cerro Arena were abandoned sometime around AD 1, an event which appears to have coincided with the emergence of **Gallinazo** and **Moche** cultures on the north coast.

CERRO AZUL. Inka site in the lower Cañete valley, southern coast of Peru. It is unique for its elaborate stone masonry (on the coast, Inka constructions are of **adobe**). Cerro Azul was also an important fishing center during the Late Intermediate Period prior to the Inka expansion. There are monumental complexes and storage areas for anchovies and sardines, which were dried and sent to other parts of the valley and probably even farther afield.

CERRO BAÚL. Wari site located at 2,300 meters above sea level on a high and steep hill overlooking the Moquegua valley, southern Peru. This **fortified** ceremonial center is close to the site of **Cerro Mejía**. Both sites were located in the southern frontier of the Wari empire and very close to **Tiwanaku** sites. **Obsidian** at Cerro Baúl comes from six different sources, including **Alca** (main source), **Quispisisa**, and **Chivay**.

CERRO BLANCO. 1. Early Horizon site in the Nepeña Valley, north coast of Peru. With **Moxeke-Pampa de las Llamas** and **Huaca de los Reyes**, it represents an important Initial Period pre-**Chavín** site with multicolor mural art. 2. The site of Cerro Blanco (also referred to as **Huaca del Sol** and **Huaca de la Luna**) is located six kilometers inland on the south bank of the **Moche** Valley at the base of the eponymous coastal hill. The site was first settled by communities producing **Gallinazo** material culture at the beginning of the millennium. The earliest foundations of Huaca del Sol were in fact built during this time, and after eight stages of further construction (most of which were undertaken in the Middle Period), the immense **pyramid** would emerge as one of the largest religious monuments ever built in the ancient Americas.

The expansive plain located between the towering pyramids of Cerro Blanco was once thought to have been largely destroyed by movement of dunes and El Niño–related rains. Recent research, however, has uncovered the foundations of large residential and craft production sectors in this central zone, revealing the urban character and dense settlement of the Moche capital. That is to say, Cerro Blanco was a true city and not simply a vacant ceremonial center.

A number of large residential areas have been excavated, consisting of a series of architectural compounds containing patios, corridors, habitation areas, workshops, and storage facilities. An intricate network of streets, plazas, and water canals interconnected these residential compounds and shops. The large multifunctional compounds and the labyrinthine road system indicate a high level of urban planning. Scholars who worked at the site argue that the compounds housed corporate groups organized according to occupational specialization, transcending low-level familial and kinship units. A compound associated with **ceramic** production has been analyzed, and comparable precincts dedicated to textile manufacture, **metallurgy**, **chicha** production, fishing, and **camelid** husbandry were identified. Restricted access within the precincts, such as sealed entries, are interpreted as signifying the presence of tightly integrated groups who carefully guarded stored wealth and group-specific identities and activities.

Significantly, **agricultural** tools common at smaller sites in the Moche and Chicama valleys are conspicuously absent at Cerro Blanco, indicating that the large urban population was largely removed from primary food production (similar to the later **Chimú** city of **Chan Chan**). Indeed, scholars inferred the presence of a "prosperous urban class" ("middle class") at Cerro Blanco, which was instrumental in financing the political economy of the priestly elite. In effect, architectural and funerary remains within the compounds suggest that potters, **metallurgists**, and other artisans who resided in the urban sector were a privileged community patronized by the state. On the basis of excavated architectural remains, it was argued that the lower classes resided outside the city, although they took part in public work projects such as the manufacture of **adobe** bricks and canal maintenance within Cerro Blanco. Other scholars, however, infer pronounced social distinctions and lower-class habitation from a patterned variation in architectural quality and configuration in the residential area near Huaca del Sol. This variation was reinterpreted as signaling gradations within the middle class itself. For example, thirty-six secondary elite compounds (of one hundred which might exist) have been identified, distinguished by larger storage rooms, elaborate burials, a high percentage of gold and nonutilitarian objects, and large public spaces for ceremonial feasting and related displays of power. Smaller and poorer quality structures (though superior in construction to rural **architecture**) served as housing for people of lower classes.

Regardless of varying interpretations on the nature of social hierarchy at Cerro Blanco, recent research emphatically demonstrates a complex and heterogeneous social structure at Moche during the Middle Moche Period, characterized by occupational specialization, a diversified ruling class (comprised possibly of noble families that headed sectors or compounds within the city), and sophisticated economic and administrative systems. The growing military and economic power of the urban elite at Cerro Blanco would enable the conquest and administrative incorporation of southern polities as well as the far-flung propagation of Moche religious and political ideology.

CERRO CHEPÉN (ALSO KNOWN AS KOLSACHEC). This site represents one of the largest and most complex archaeological sites in the Jequetepeque Valley dating to the Late **Moche** Period. Situated on a high coastal cerro (Cerro Chepén) overlooking the modern city of Chepén below, it is characterized by a wide variety of elaborate **architecture** and is dominated by a ring of massive **fortification** walls built of stone. It is apparent that defense was one of its main functions, and convoluted corridors and checkpoints indicate restricted movement and controlled access. However, Kolsachec also served as an important residential and ceremonial nucleus, and centrally placed terraced complexes with ramps (*tablados*) are almost identical to ritual architecture documented in the hinterland. A complex network of quadrilateral stone structures with high walls, recessed niches, and large door lintels probably served in an administrative or ceremonial function.

Interestingly, the only examples of two-storied buildings in the Jequetepeque Valley were found at Cerro Chepén. Indeed, the site exhibits among the finest examples of Middle Horizon masonry on the north coast, which betrays a highland influence. These structures could have been warehouses. Rooms constructed of **adobe** with niched walls were also built at Cerro Chepén, and a large number of stone terraces indicate that a sizeable residential population lived at this important site. Kolsachec was likely the seat of a powerful polity during the Late Moche Period and Transitional era. Evidence of orthogonal planning and large agglutinated domestic structures suggest the urban character of Cerro Chepén. It is possible that this inaccessible hilltop redoubt served as the most powerful city in the Jequetepeque Valley during the Late Moche Period.

CERRO COLORADO. 1. Large **rock art** site in the Sierra de Ambargasta, north of the province of Cordoba, central Argentina. Red, white, black, and gray paintings include human and numerous animal figures, including reptiles, insects, **guanaco**, **puma**, deer, fox, condor, **ñandú**, and **llama**, as well as geometric motifs. They were tentatively dated to AD 1000–1500, and also depict scenes of the Spanish conquest as indicated by representations of men on horseback. This site is one of Argentina's national historical monuments. 2. Area with a half-hectare of domestic residences and vast cemeteries on the **Paracas** peninsula, southern coast of Peru. This site dates to approximately 300 BC–AD 200 and the cemeteries correspond to the Paracas Cavernas and Paracas Necropolis phases. Several hundred **mummies** were placed wrapped with large, highly decorated **cotton** and **camelid** wool textiles in the pit **tombs** of these cemeteries; they are among the most outstanding textiles of pre-Columbian times. The textiles are very well preserved due to the extremely dry climate. 3. A large Late Intermediate Period site associated with the **Lambayeque** and **Chimú** cultures in the Zaña Valley of the north coast of Peru.

CERRO EL PLOMO. One of the southernmost **Inka high-altitude sanctuaries** in central Chile. Cerro El Plomo has several circular and rectangular stone enclosures located between 5,100 and 5,400 meters above sea level. A **mummy** of a boy was found close to its summit, a **sacrifice** to the mountain **deities** or *Apus*, together with gold and silver human and **llama** figurines and textiles. As with the site of **Aconcagua** and others of the region, Cerro El Plomo suggests that the **Inka** had incorporated this region in their empire. Cerro El Plomo is one of Chile's national monuments. *See also* CAPACOCHA.

CERRO EL SOMBRERO. Preceramic site in the Sierra de Tandilia, province of Buenos Aires, Argentina. Numerous **fishtail projectile points** and fragments were found on the top of this hill, suggesting a Late Pleistocene or Early Holocene date. El Sombrero is close to **Cerro La China**, and their lithic industries are similar.

CERRO GRANDE DE LA COMPAÑÍA. Southernmost **Inka** fortress in the Cachapoal Valley of central Chile. The site has Inka defensive **architecture**, storage units, and Inka **ceramics**. Cerro Grande has a pre-Inka (Late Period) occupation without defensive walls and was inhabited after the first Europeans settled in the region, becoming a focus of resistance to the conquest. Cerro Grande de la Compañía is one of Chile's national monuments.

CERRO HUENUL. An **obsidian** quarry located in Neuquén, northwest Patagonia, Argentina. Obsidian from this quarry was found 550 kilometers to the northeast in the late prehistoric levels of the cave site of **Intihuasi**, along with other Patagonian cultural elements. The quarry is some 1,000 meters west of the **Cueva del Huenul** Cave.

CERRO LA CHINA. Late Pleistocene-Early Holocene rock shelter in the Sierra de Tandilia, Buenos Aires, Argentina. Cerro La China is the first eastern South American site where **fishtail points** were found in a stratified, multicomponent site. These points date to roughly 8700 BC. Most of the stone tools were made of local quartzites. One plaque of giant armadillo (*Eutatus seguini*) suggests that the early settlers of Cerro La China coexisted with **megafauna**, as in the contemporaneous site of **Cueva Tixi**.

CERRO LOS BURROS. Open-air site in Uruguay with **fishtail points**. No dates are available yet for Cerro Los Burros, but it is highly probable that these points were made in the Late Pleistocene Period.

CERRO MEJÍA. Wari site located in the Moquegua valley, southern Peru, close to **Cerro Baúl** in the southern frontier of the Wari state. Some of the structures on the summit were built of fine-quality stone masonry. There are several monumental walls and a staircase that leads to the summit.

CERRO NARRÍO. Formative and post-Formative site and culture of the upper valleys of southern Ecuador, close to the city of Cuenca. The earliest occupation of the site of Cerro Narrío dates to 2850 BC, contemporaneous with the Middle **Valdivia** phases. Cerro Narrío is one of the earliest sites with ***Spondylus princeps***, suggesting that it was one of the **trade** centers for this precious Andean commodity into the highlands and eastern lowlands. The end of Cerro Narrío culture can be placed in the **Regional Development Period** (500 BC–AD 800).

CERRO OREJAS. The site of Cerro Orejas, located on the southern Moche Valley, extends for three kilometers on the slopes of the hill and is comprised of irregular agglutinated domestic dwellings, built of masonry, and two sizeable **adobe** platform **mounds**. It probably represented the premier seat of **Gallinazo** power in the Moche Valley from 250 BC to AD 50. However, the **Moche** built over a Gallinazo settlement at **Cerro Blanco**, and the first stages of construction at **Huaca del Sol** were initiated by **Vicú** inhabitants.

CERRO SAPO. Sodalite mine located in Cochabamba (Bolivia). Sodalite, a bluish mineral, was exploited for the manufacture of beads and other ornaments since the second millennium BC and was exchanged over long distances. Cerro Sapo is the only sodalite mine known in South America. *See also* TRADE.

CERRO SECHÍN. Early **ceramic** site in the Casma Valley, Peru, contemporaneous to **Las Haldas**, and dated to around 1200 BC. It is one of the few coastal sites in Peru with stone carvings. The perimeter wall of the main temple is covered with stone slabs that depict warriors and slain, dismembered victims (enemies captured in **warfare** or possibly **sacrificial** victims): limbs, heads, and other body parts, both external and internal, are graphically depicted in the sculptures.

There are earlier buildings inside the temple, the oldest one (phase I) dating to around 1800 BC, is made of **adobe** and has painted images of felines and humans.

CERRO SOMBRERO. A site in the Azapa Valley of northern Chile distinguished by the presence of **geoglyphs**. They represent two huge massive **camelids**. Cerro Sombrero is one of Chile's national monuments.

CERRO TRES TETAS. A group of caves and rock shelters in the central plateau of Santa Cruz, southern Argentina. Cave 1 was occupied by five different groups, from the earliest at around 9500–8200 BC to the Tehuelche, who occupied the cave at the time of the European conquest. Cerro Tres Tetas is fifty-five kilometers north of **El Ceibo** and seventy-five kilometers southwest of **Piedra Museo**. Material of the earliest occupation, which represents the phase of first human colonization of Patagonia, includes stone tools (sidescrapers, retouched flakes, knives, a chopper, and a hammer). Most tools were made of flint and petrified wood and projectile points were absent. Hearths were excavated and animal bones, mainly **guanaco**, were relatively rare. Cave 1 is known for its **rock art** preserved on the walls of the shelter. *See also* CASAPEDRENSE.

CHACHAPUMA. Monolith that represents a **jaguarlike** figure with a human mask in **Tiwanaku** art. The name derives from *chacha* or *yaya* (man) and **puma**. One was found in archaeological excavations at the base of the stairs of the Akapana **pyramid** at the site of Tiwanaku. Chachapumas are strong emblems of Tiwanaku **religion**. *See also* YAYA-MAMA.

CHACO (Quechua term). 1. Savanna region located in western Paraguay, northern Argentina, and parts of Bolivia and Brazil. The archaeology of this region is poorly understood. Around AD 1500, many Chaco groups cultivated **maize**, **manioc**, beans, tobacco, and **cotton** and manufactured **ceramics**, which were usually decorated with cord impressions. Many Chaco indigenous groups resisted the Spanish and Portuguese well into the Late Colonial Period. Among their **weapons** were bows and arrows as well as slings (**bolas**). 2. **Hunting** technique utilized by the **Inka**, which entailed driving animals such as **vicuña**, deer, and **ñandú** into large corrals made with ropes or plants.

CHAKI TAKLLA. Quechua term for the foot plow used in the Andean region. The chaki taklla was made of a wooden stick with a sharpened edge or with a stone hoe. These stone hoes were found in many Andean sites and are an indication of **agricultural** practices.

CHAN CHAN. Large urban site and capital of the **Chimú** state located in the **Moche** Valley on the north coast of Peru near the modern city of Trujillo. The constructions were made of **adobe** and the largest consist of massive compounds or *ciudadelas* (small cities), which were the residences of Chimú rulers. These compounds are located in the center of the ancient city and occupy approximately six square kilometers. The compounds are several hectares in surface, they are surrounded by high adobe walls often with decorated reliefs, and they have only one entrance. Inside the compounds are rooms for residential use and warehousing, burials, and sunken gardens and wells. Burials were placed in a burial platform. Around these compounds were residences of the lesser nobility and dwellings of retainers who specialized in weaving and in **metallurgy**. These dwellings were made of cane and surrounded central patios. Chan Chan is in the list of the **World Heritage Sites of UNESCO**. *See also* FARFÁN; MANCHAN; PAMPA GRANDE; TALAMBO.

CHANCAY. Cultural and political unit that occupied part of the central coast of Peru during the Late Intermediate Period (AD 1000–1400) in the area of the Chancay and Chillón valleys north of Lima. The main elements that identify Chancay culture are its black-on-white **ceramics**, elaborate ceramic "tomb guardians," and fine textiles used to wrap **mummies**. Ceramics usually are molded in the form of birds, **camelids**, and humans. Many Chancay cemeteries have been **looted**, and most of the information we have on Chancay comes from looted materials. Chancay **architecture** consisted mostly of **tapia** precincts and dwellings.

CHANKA. According to ethnohistoric documents, the Chanka were an ethnic group that lived in the **Cuzco** valley and fought against the **Inka**. The victory over the Chanka by Pachakuti, which took place in the mid thirteenth century AD, triggered the Inka expansion outside of the Cuzco valley.

CHANKILLO (ALSO SPELLED CHANQUILLO). Fortified hill in the Casma Valley, central coast of Peru. It is an oval-shaped fortified site consisting of three concentric stone walls surrounding two circular towers and a rectilinear compound of rooms and courts. Chankillo dates to 340–120 BC and is associated with the **Salinar** culture. It exemplifies the heightened militarism that characterized the north coast during the end of the Early Horizon and the beginning of the Early Intermediate Period.

CHAÑAR (*GEOFFROES DECORTICANS*). An important tree for many South American indigenous populations. The chañar grows in warm and dry regions. Like **algarroba/o**, it is of the family *Leguminosae* and has edible fruits that are rich in carbohydrates. Indigenous people ate these fruits in many ways: grounded (flour), toasted, boiled, fermented (**chicha**), and so on. *See also* LAS MERCEDES; LOS MORRILLOS; VILUCO.

CHAVÍN. Style associated with the **religious** center of **Chavín de Huantar**. The apogee of the Chavín cult dated to 400–200 BC and is associated with innovations in textiles (resist technique similar to batik and tie-dye; tapestry) and **metallurgy** (soldering, sweat-welding, repoussé decoration, and alloying of gold and silver) to make portable religious elements. Items with Chavín-style decoration were found in the highlands and coast of Peru. Chavín **architectural** and iconographic elements were found in **Pacopampa**, **Caballo Muerto**, and other coastal sites. Scholars argue that at Chavín de Huantar there were full-time craft specialists. Several coastal and valley sites with Chavín-style elements also contain **obsidian** from the **Quispisisa** source. This suggests that Chavín had direct or indirect control over the source. See also OCUCAJE; RAIMONDI STELA; SHILLACOTO; STAFF GODDESS; STIRRUP BOTTLE; TELLO, JULIO CESAR.

CHAVÍN DE HUANTAR. A ceremonial site, the center of the **Chavín** cult (800–200 BC), located in the confluence of the Mosna and Wacheqsa rivers in the central highlands of Peru 3,000 meters above sea level, equidistant to the coast and the tropical lowlands to the east. The earliest occupation of Chavín is called the Urabarriu Phase (1000–500 BC) and the original site occupied approximately six hectares. The U-shaped Old Temple is symmetrical and embraces a sunken circular courtyard with stone walls decorated with feline figures and San Pedro cactus. The New Temple was constructed in several stages and has a megalithic stairway framed on one side by a black stone and on the other by a white stone (perhaps expressing principles of dualistic opposition). In its interior there is a series of passages or galleries, which were related to Chavíns's role as an oracle center. Several **monoliths** were found in situ in Chavín de Huantar, including El Lanzón, which represents the **fanged deity**; the **Tello** Obelisk; and the **Raimondi Stela**. The Gallery of the Offerings includes the remains of eight hundred broken **ceramic** vessels and bones. Chavín de Huantar is on the list of **World Heritage Sites of UNESCO**.

Chavín was the base of a widespread religious and ideological "horizon," and emblems of Chavín art and ritual were disseminated throughout the central Andes during the Early Horizon. It probably functioned as a panregional oracular and **pilgrimage** center (similar to the later site of **Pachacamac**), attracting devotees from across the Andes. However, its immediate political influence was likely limited to the Mosna Valley area. *See also* SMILING GOD; *SPONDYLUS*.

CHECUA. Preceramic site located in the municipality of Nemocón in the savanna of Bogotá, Colombia. Checua has seven occupations, which date from 6500 to 1000 BC. The earliest occupation, dated to 6500 BC, is characterized by short-term occupation: there are a small number of stone tools and faunal remains. Hearths and posts were present, but clearly delineated dwellings were not identified. In the second-oldest occupation, which dates to 5800 BC, a bone flute was encountered, the oldest **musical** instrument found in Colombia to date.

CHENA (ALSO KNOWN AS PUCARÁ DE CHENA). One of the southernmost **Inka** sites in central Chile. The Pucará de Chena is located at 640 meters above sea level and dominates the Maipo Valley. It is a small site with two defensive walls and a series of rectangular rooms around a patio on top of the hill. The site has an Inka cemetery. The remains of an earth and stone **mound** eight meters in diameter were interpreted as an **ushnu**.

CHERT. One of the main raw materials used in manufacturing stone tools in many regions of South America. Chert has a fine grain and sharp natural edges. Chert can be found in the form of cobbles in streams and rivers or in veins (quarries). It was procured locally or imported from long distances.

CHIBCHA. An indigenous language, also known as **Muisca**, spoken in the valleys and highlands of Colombia at the time of the Spanish conquest. Chibcha was part of the Chibchan language family, which was widespread in Central America and northern South America. *See also* JEWELRY; ZAQUE; ZIPA.

CHICAMA-MOCHE (LA CUMBRE) INTERVALLEY CANAL SYSTEM. The coast of Peru is one of the most arid regions of the Americas. During pre-Columbian times, many canals were constructed to bring water from coastal rivers to the flat valley plains. The La Cumbre system is the largest **irrigation** system in the Americas. It was constructed by the **Chimú** state after AD 1000 in the north coast of Peru, and it diverted water from the Chicama drainage to the northern portion of the **Moche** Valley. Some scholars believe that the massive canal, extending over 113 kilometers, was never finished.

CHICHA. Quechua term for an alcoholic drink made from **maize** (corn) and other crops or vegetables. Chicha was consumed throughout most of South America, usually in rituals and in chief- and state-sponsored feasts. The elaboration of chicha was usually communally processed and the liquid was stored in large **ceramic** vessels. Certain Andean people, such as the **Inka** and **Tiwanaku**, used **keros** to drink chicha. *See also* CERRO BLANCO; CHAÑAR; CONCHOPATA; GUADALUPE PHASE; PACHACAMAC; SAN JOSÉ DE MORO.

CHIEFDOMS. *See* SEÑORÍO.

CHIMÚ (ALSO KNOWN AS CHIMOR). Late Intermediate Period state of the north coast of Peru dated to AD 900–1400. Chimú was the second-largest empire in pre-Columbian South America, after the **Inka**. It stretched along the north coast of Peru for approximately one thousand kilometers, from the Chillón River in the south to the Tumbes River in the north. The economic base of the Chimú state was **irrigation agriculture** and fishing. Provincial centers, following the model of the capital, were built in several strategic points on the coast, including **Farfán**, **Túcume**, and **Manchán**. The Chimú state was conquered by the Inka around AD 1470. Its capital was **Chan Chan**. According to the Spanish chroniclers, Nancenpinco was the Chimú cultural hero and founder of the group. *See also* CERRO COLORADO; LAMBAYEQUE; STIRRUP BOTTLE; TALAMBO; TÚCUME.

CHINCHA. Late Intermediate Period **señorío** (chiefdom) of the south coast of Peru. The valley of Chincha is broad and has a large area for cultivation. According to Spanish documents, Chincha society was divided into three notable groups: farmers, fishermen, and merchants. Some Chincha people were sea **traders** who traveled to the north coast in search of ***Spondylus*** and were actively patronized by the **Inka** state. The main Chincha sites are La Centinela (characterized by **adobe platform mounds**), probably the capital, and Tambo de Mora. At La Centinela there were three main roads, with each one possibly associated with one of the large three principal social groups based on occupation specialization.

CHINCHORRO. Cultural tradition from northern Chile and southern Peru characterized by its carefully prepared **mummies**, which are the oldest in the world, and an early evidence of ancestor worship, dating from 5000 to 1600 BC. Chinchorro populations were present along some seven hundred kilometers of the Pacific coast. The earliest Chinchorro settlements date to 7000 BC and consist of **shell middens** and cemeteries. Chinchorro people obtained most of their food resources from the sea. They were fishermen, they **hunted** marine mammals, and they gathered shellfish. The Chinchorro also lived in seasonal camps in valleys. Bioanthropological studies indicate that the Chinchorro were biologically linked to people of the Amazon basin. Chinchorro people invested significant amounts of time in preparing mummies. Mummies are of men and **women** of different ages, children, newborns, and even fetuses. They used vegetable products, such as totora reeds and sticks, clay, and pigments. Mummies were placed in extended position and in groups. Some individuals show more elaborate techniques of mummification than others. Most of the Chinchorro mummies are stored in the Azapa Museum. *See also* LA PALOMA.

CHIRIBAYA. Late Intermediate Period culture that emerged in the lower Moquegua valley of the southern coast of Peru shortly before the collapse of the **Tiwanaku** state. Chiribaya was dated to between AD 1000 and 1400. The site of Chiribaya Alta has several large cemeteries with very well-preserved **mummy** bundles.

CHIRIPA. Large **Formative** site and culture on the southern shores of Lake Titicaca, Bolivia. As the largest site of the region in its time, it was probably the capital of a regional polity. Chiripa is characterized by a semisubterranean temple or **sunken court** of the **Yaya-Mama** Tradition, surrounded by sixteen one-room buildings that formed a roughly circular configuration. The site was reoccupied in **Tiwanaku** times and its temple was rebuilt. Most of the **architectural** features from Chiripa constitute the source of Titicaca traditions.

CHISI. Yaya-Mama tradition site in the Copacabana peninsula, Lake Titicaca, Bolivia. Chisi was dated to 200 BC–AD 1. At the entrance of the semisubterranean temple, a Yaya-Mama carved stone was found.

CHIVATEROS. Lithic (quartzite) workshops close to the modern city of Ancón in the central coast of Peru. As no projectile points were found at the site, it was thought originally that Chivateros represented an older population. Further studies indicated that the artifacts in these workshops are the debris of the manufacture of **Paiján** projectile points.

CHIVAY (ALSO KNOWN AS COTALLAULLI). Obsidian quarry located in the Colca valley, Arequipa, Peru). Obsidian from the Chivay source was used since the Late Pleistocene. In the southern highlands site of **Asana**, Chivay obsidian was used at least since 7400 BC. During **Formative** and Tiwanaku (Middle Horizon) times, it was the main type of obsidian used by the inhabitants of the Titicaca basin, and its distribution was probably controlled by **Pukara** and **Tiwanaku** elites.

Most of the obsidian used from this source is transparent, in contrast with that of other sources, suggesting that its transparency made it symbolically important. *See also* CERRO BAÚL.

CHOBSHI CAVE. Preceramic cave site located in the southern highlands of Ecuador. The occupations were dated from 8000 to 5500 BC. **Obsidian** from Chobshi Cave was provenienced to **Yanaurco-Quiscatola**, **Mullumica**, some 300–350 kilometers to the north, and to other unknown sources.

CHOKEPUKIO. Site in the valley of **Cuzco**, Peru. Chokepukio has occupations dating from the Early Intermediate Period to the Late Horizon (AD 375–1500). There are large niched walls here dating between AD 860 and 1410. Two shrines were discovered at Chokepukio, each associated with a large stone **waca** and offerings. Both wacas were ritually buried.

CHONGOYAPE. Site in the upper section of the **Lambayeque** valley of north Peru. Elaborate, Early Horizon **tombs** were excavated here in the late 1920s. The undisturbed burials of three individuals were associated with sixty-six hollow gold beads, a gold headband, and two **pottery** beads encased in gold, as well as gold rings, pins, gorgets, and other ornaments. The other finds include greenstone disks, **stirrup-spouted bottles**, a red plate, and a polished **mirror**. The principal occupant of the tomb was a female interred with a gold crown embossed with the image of the supreme **deity** of the **Chavín** cult. The burials are thought to have been contemporaneous with the Janaburriu Phase of **Chavín de Huantar**. They belong to the **Northern Peruvian Coastal Metallurgical Tradition**, one of the most prominent of pre-Columbian America.

CHOQE K'IRAW. Inka site on the Apurimac River, located 150 kilometers west of **Cuzco**. Choqe K'iraw is situated at 3,100 meters above sea level and was built on the top and sides of a mountain, similarly to **Machu Picchu**, to which it is connected by a road. There are terraces, platforms, temples, **qolcas**, water fountains, canals, corrals, and an **ushnu** at Choqe K'iraw. The site has a **hanan** sector and a

hurin sector. A park was created to protect the site, part of which was reconstructed.

CHOROQOLLO. Early **Formative** site in the Santivañez valley (Cochabamba, Bolivia). It dates to between 1320 and 980 BC and is one of the earliest **agricultural** villages in the region. The site has several sectors with evidence of **ceramic** production (burning areas). **Camelids**, both **alpacas** and **guanacos**, and deer were two main elements in the diet. The relative absence of stone projectile points (or other **hunting** implements) could suggest that hunting implements were made of wood, as in lowland areas.

CHORRERA. Early culture that developed in the coast of Ecuador from around 1300 to 300 BC. The sites of this tradition consist of small and medium villages. Luxury goods in some of the burials suggest the existence of status differentiation. **Ceramics** are very elaborate, usually modeled, and depict many elements of Chorrera daily life and **religion**. The vessels have iridescent and organic resist painting. Modeled clay human **figurines**, some with elaborate body paint and other ornaments, are common. *See also* STIRRUP BOTTLE; TABUCHILA PHASE.

CHOTUNA. Large urban site with a series of platform **mounds** located in the lower portion of the Lambayeque River, north coast of Peru. It was founded in Early **Sican** times (after AD 750) and was occupied into the Late Horizon after the **Inka** conquest.

CHUCARIPUPATA. This is a large **Tiwanaku** site on the **Island of the Sun** located some one hundred meters southeast of the **Inka** ceremonial site of the Titikala rock in the northern part of the island, Lake Titicaca, Bolivia. This site was one of the first ceremonial sites in the island, suggesting that the Inka continued Tiwanaku **religious** traditions, which included making offerings of **ceramic**, stone, and metal objects to the lake. Such offerings were found in subaquatic archaeological expeditions.

CHUCUITO. The largest **Inka** site in the Collao **señorío** after **Hatunqolla**. The site, located on the western Titicaca basin, Peru, follows a grid pattern and occupied some fifty to eighty hectares. There is no evidence of pre-Inka occupation of the site. A masonry building locally known as Inka Uyu combines local **architecture** techniques with Inka stylistic canons.

CHULLPA. Aymara term for an aboveground burial construction found in the central and south-central Andes. Some chullpas were made of **adobe** (usually painted on the exterior) and others of stone, some of which were made with fine-cut masonry blocks in the region of Sillustani (southern Peru). They could be square or circular. Some chullpas were built in the eastern valleys of the Andes (**Abiseo** and **Los Pinchudos**). In northwestern Argentina, the term applies to small constructions built under rock shelters or caves for the same mortuary purpose.

CHUMBIVILCAS. Obsidian used in an area between the departments of **Cuzco** and Arequipa in the southern highlands of Peru since at least 4150 BC. Its source has not yet been identified.

CHUÑO. Potato that has been dehydrated by leaving it exposed to frost during three nights in the Andean highlands. By transforming the potatoes into chuño, Andean people preserve potatoes for several years. Chuño does not decompose and is a food source readily available. Nowadays it is mostly eaten in soups.

CHUQUITANTA. *See* EL PARAÍSO.

CIÉNAGA. Ceramic style from the early period of northwestern Argentina that dates to between 500 BC and AD 300. Ciénaga style is characterized by **incised** graywares with geometric and zoomorphic motifs (**camelids**) as well as painted ceramics (black on cream). Typical vessel forms are jars and bowls. *See also* CONDORHUASI; PIPE; SUPLICANTE.

CIGLIANO, EDUARDO M. (1926–1977). Argentine archaeologist who conducted research in the northwest of the country. Among his publications are *Arqueología de la zona de Famabalasto (Prov. Catamarca)* (1958); *Investigaciones Arqueológicas en el Valle de Santa María*, with collaborators (1960); *Contribución a los fechados radio-*

carbónicos argentinos (1966); *Investigaciones Antropológicas en el Yacimiento de Juella (Depto. Tilcara, Jujuy)* (1967); *Tastil, una ciudad preincaica Argentina*, with several collaborators (1973); and *La Aldea Formativa de Las Cuevas*, with R. Raffino and H. Calandra (1976).

CIUDAD PERDIDA. Large **Tairona** site in northern Colombia, located 1,300 meters above sea level. The site occupies several hectares and has numerous stone structures including hundreds of residential terraces, plazas, staircases, ditches, and other **architectural** features united by stone roads overviewing the valley of **Buriticá**. Ciudad Perdida, which means "Lost City" in Spanish, is close to the archaeological site of **Pueblito**. Both are in protected areas.

CLOTHING. The indigenous people of South America used a variety of clothes. The main materials were **cotton**, other vegetable fibers, **camelid** wool, and animal skins. Clothing deteriorates very rapidly and thus is not common in archaeological sites, except for very dry areas, such as the Pacific coast of northern Chile and Peru and other dry areas of the Andes, or in extremely cold areas, such as **high-altitude sanctuaries**. Some caves are sufficiently dry as to preserve organic remains. *See also* FIGURINES; LOS MORRILLOS.

COCA (*ERYTHROXYLON COCA, E. NOVAGRANATENSE*). Tree that grows in low-altitude tropical areas of the Andes. Its leaves are and were used throughout the north, central, and southern Andes and in lowland areas in domestic and ritual contexts as well as to alleviate discomfort related to working in high altitudes. Its use can be traced to the preceramic period. According to studies of hair and teeth derived from archaeological samples, coca was consumed by both men and **women** and by different social groups. There is both direct and indirect evidence of coca consumption in the archaeological record. Direct evidence comes from coca leaves in **tombs**, sometimes in textile bags (Niño Korín in Bolivia and so on). Indirect evidence of coca consumption comes from coastal Ecuador. The recovery of lime containers or pots in the **Las Vegas** and Late **Valdivia** contexts suggests that coca leaves were consumed. In Peru, the earliest evidence of coca leaves comes from the site of **Culebras**, which dates to approximately 2000 BC. At the site of **Asia**, in the central coast, coca leaves and burned lime were dated to 1800 BC. Some **Tiwanaku waco retratos** show individuals (men) with coca tucked in their cheeks. *See also* HIGH-ALTITUDE SANCTUARIES; PANZALEO; QUECHUA; QUIMBAYA.

COCOA (*THEOBROMA* SP.). A plant, the source of chocolate, cultivated in pre-Columbian times in the upper Orinoco and Amazon. There are several possible areas of origin of cocoa: the upper Amazon region, the upper Orinoco region, the Andean foothills, or more likely the northern part of Central America. It is still uncertain where the cocoa plant was domesticated.

COMPOTERA (OR COPA). Spanish term used by Ecuadorian and Colombian archaeologists for **ceramic** bowls or plates with a high annular base. See MANTEÑO CULTURE.

CONCHERO. Spanish term applied to coastal or riverine **mounds** composed of massive accumulations of shellfish and other faunal remains. These concheros are found on both the Atlantic and Pacific coasts and at all latitudes, from Tierra del Fuego in the south to Venezuela and Colombia in the north. In Brazil, the term used is **sambaquí**. *See also* CHINCHORRO; HUENTELAUQUEN; LAMINA; MANICUAROID; MIDDEN; ÑO CARLOS; PUERTO HORMIGA; QUIANI.

CONCHOPATA. An important **Wari** site in the Ayacucho valley, Peru, near the Wari state capital. Elaborate **polychrome** vessels were found there, including two groups of finely decorated large vessels used for storing **chicha**, which highlight the importance of communal ritual drinking in the Wari state.

CONCHU PATA. Large **Formative mound** in the valley of Mizque, Cochabamba, Bolivia. The site was occupied from around 1200 to 600 BC and was surrounded by a peripheral stone wall. There are numerous burials with offerings that include exotic materials such as **sodalite** beads, coral, Pacific seashells, and **ceramics** from other regions of Cochabamba. All of these items indicate connections exclusively with regions to the west. Ceramic and stone **keros** formed part of burial offerings and could be among the earliest in the Andes. The slightly earlier site of **Yuraj Molino** is located fifty kilometers north of Conchu Pata.

CONDORHUASI. Polychrome ceramic style from northwest Argentina. Condorhuasi ceramics are found mostly in **tombs**, together with vessels of other ceramic styles, such as **Ciénaga**. Plastic representations of individuals with headdress and corporal paint and zoomorphic creatures such as felines are among the typical Condorhuasi ceramic forms. Ceramic and stone **pipes** are also part of Condorhuasi material culture.

CONSENS, MARIO (1936–). Uruguayan archaeologist interested in archaeological theory, **rock art**, and the interaction of archaeology and the general public. He published numerous articles including "First Rock Paintings in the Amazon Basin" (1988). Consens edited *Arqueología en el Uruguay: 120 años después* with J. M. Lopez and M. C. Curbelo (1995) and is the author of *El pasado extraviado: Prehistoria y arqueología del Uruguay* (2003).

COPA. *See* COMPOTERA.

COPPER METALLURGY. Copper **metallurgy** began in the Bolivian **altiplano** between 1200 and 800 BC, marking the beginning of a southern Andean metallurgical tradition. Copper metallurgy was also very important among the **Moche**. *See also* DOS CABEZAS; GUANGALA; HUACA DE LA LUNA; LAMBAYEQUE; LAS ANIMAS CULTURE; LOMA NEGRA; MANTEÑO CULTURE; MILAGRO-QUEVEDO; NORTHERN PERUVIAN COASTAL METALLURGICAL TRADITION; PAMPA GRANDE; SAN JOSÉ DE MORO; SAN PEDRO DE ATACAMA; TILOCALAR PHASE; VILUCO; VIÑA DEL CERRO; WANKARANI.

COROZAL. Corozal (AD 350–600) represents a transition between Late **Saladoid** and the later **Camoruco Phase** and coincides roughly with **Ronquín** Period 2, which represents the introduction of **Arauquinoid** in the middle Orinoco. During this transitional period, there is gradual decrease of Ronquín attributes (white-on-red paintings and sand-tempered pastes) and there is an increasing utilization of spicule temper for **ceramics**. Decorative motifs during this transition are characterized by bichrome and **polychrome** painting and fine-line incision. This transition period represents a local development rather than the product of external influences. For some scholars, the Corozal Phase constitutes instead an abrupt transition and therefore external influences are perhaps more relevant to explaining its emergence.

CORTADERAS COMPLEX. Group of **Inka** sites located in the Calchaquí Valley, Salta, northwestern Argentina. The sites include Cortaderas Alto, Cortaderas Bajo, Cortaderas Izquierdo, and El Director or Cortaderas Derecho and cover some fifty hectares. Some buildings, design patterns, and masonry techniques are typical of Inka **architecture** and are very different from local **Santa María** architecture. The important site of Cortaderas Bajo is located along the Inka road.

COTALLAULLI. Important **obsidian** source located in southern Peru. *See also* CHIVAY.

COTOCOLLAO. Site in the Quito basin of the Ecuadorian Andes situated at 2,810 meters above sea level. The earliest obtained radiometric dates are from 1545 BC (Middle **Formative**), and around 500 BC—Late Formative—the site was destroyed by a volcanic eruption (the Pululahua eruption took place circa 467 BC). The earliest occupations have **maize**. There could be a pre-Cotocollao Phase occupation (Early Formative) below a first unidentified eruption associated with the first **agricultural** settlers of the Ecuadorian highlands. *See also* YANAURCO-QUISCATOLA.

COTTON (*GOSSYPIUM BARBADENSE*). One of the main fibers that South American people used in **clothing**. Cotton was cultivated in the Peruvian coast, where it was important for making nets for fishing, since at least 3000 BC. Cotton later became practically universal in warm areas of South America. *See also* CERRO COLORADO; KARWA; LAS HALDAS; MANTEÑO CULTURE.

CRANIAL DEFORMATION. Important cultural marker among many indigenous groups of South America since the Early Holocene Period, for example in **Lauricocha**, until the Iberian conquest. The heads of infants were wrapped tightly with cloths and wooden planks in order to slowly modify the growth and shape of the frontal and occipital bones. Cranial deformation was a permanent indicator of ethnic group, social status, and/or other types of community memberships. There are several types of deformations, such as tabular erect and annular, and usually there is more than one type present in any given site, making it difficult to establish a relation with other cultural elements. For instance, among the **Tiwanaku** there were two main types of cranial deformation: annular and fronto-occipital. Individuals in three different regions (Tiwanaku heartland, Katari, and Moquegua) presented distinct styles, suggesting different ethnic or group affiliations: individuals in the Tiwanaku valley had both annular and front-occipital cranial deformation, individuals living in the adjacent area of Katari valley had nearly all annular deformation, and individuals living in the Tiwanaku settlements of the Moquegua valley of southern Peru only were characterized by fronto-occipital cranial deformation. *See also* AZAPA PHASE; FIGURINES; KINSHIP; LLOLLEO; VILUCO.

CRUXENT, JOSÉ MARÍA (1911–2005). Spanish-born archaeologist who conducted archaeological research in Venezuela and the Caribbean islands in Late Pleistocene to Colonial Period sites. Among his publications are *Pinturas Rupestres de El Carmen, en el Río Parguaza, Estado Bolívar, Venezuela* (1946–1947) and *An Archaeological Chronology of Venezuela* (1959), *Arqueología Cronológica de Venezuela* (1961), and *Venezuelan Archaeology* (1963), the last three with Irving Rouse as coauthor. In 1987, he received the National Science Prize of the Consejo Nacional de Investigaciones Científicas y Tecnológicas (CONICIT), Venezuela's national research institution.

CUBILÁN. Late Pleistocene open-air campsite in the southern highlands of Ecuador, situated at 3,100 meters above sea level. Cubilán was dated to between 8300 and 7100 BC. The flake tools and bifacial points of Cubilán are finely worked in local jasper and chalcedony.

CUEVA CUYÍN MANZANO. A site located near a small tributary of the Traful River, Neuquén, southern Argentina. The earliest occupations were dated to 7300 BC. **Guanaco** and rodent bones dominate the faunal assemblage. The most abundant stone tools are different types of sidescrapers and endscrapers, knives, and other unifacial tools. No projectile points were found in the earliest occupations.

CUEVA DE LAS MANOS PINTADAS. Important **rock art** site in Alto Rio Pinturas, Santa Cruz, southern Argentina. The earliest paintings date to 7400 BC. The paintings on the cave walls were grouped in three sectors, known as A, B, and C. There are several hundred depictions of hands, **guanaco**, and other animals as well as geometric figures (circles, crosses, dots, and lines of dots) painted in red, yellow, and black. Cueva de las Manos Pintadas is one of Argentina's national historical monuments and a **World Heritage Site of UNESCO**.

CUEVA DEL CERRO GAVILÁN. In the middle Orinoco, Venezuela, this cave has one of the highest concentrations of **rock art** in the region. Red, white, and black were used to paint animals (reptiles, mammals, and fish). There are also geometric figures and some anthropomorphic representations. As for other caves of the area (**Cueva del Santo**, **Cueva Susude Inava**), there are several occupations including **Saladoid**, **Arauquinoid**, and **Valloid**, implying that the cave was occupied from around 1000 BC to AD 1500. In recent decades, the cave was used as a burial ground by the local Piaroa or Mapoyo indigenous groups.

CUEVA DEL HUENUL. Cave with **rock art** located in northern Neuquén, northwest Patagonia, Argentina. The cave has a Late Pleistocene occupation dated to 10,000 BC. Close by is the **obsidian** quarry **Cerro Huenul**.

CUEVA DEL MEDIO. A site near Seno Ultima Esperanza on the Pacific coast of southern Chile and located one kilometer from the **Cueva del Milodon**. There is a clear association between human activity and extinct fauna (**ground sloth** and horse) at this site. Stone artifacts include **fishtail projectile points**, endscrapers and sidescrapers, and knives.

CUEVA DEL MILODON. Close to Seno Ultima Esperanza on the Pacific coast, southern Chile. Located one kilometer from the **Cueva**

del Medio. Dung, hide, and bones of extinct **ground sloth** (milodon) date to between 11,500 and 8500 BC, but the earliest human occupation date to only 6000 BC. This occupation is associated with contemporary fauna such as **guanaco**.

CUEVA DEL SANTO (CUEVA BOULTON). Cave site located in the middle Orinoco, Venezuela. This rock shelter was occupied by **Barrancoid**, **Saladoid**, **Arauquinoid**, and **Valloid** populations, from 1000 BC to AD 1500. **Ceramic** styles from all four periods are represented here, along with **manos and metates**. Numerous rock paintings, mostly geometric figures in red and white, decorate the roof and a wall of the cave. Until recently, the cave was also used as a burial ground and ritual site. Other caves and rock shelters of the region also have **rock art** and were used as burial grounds.

CUEVA EPULLAN. Located on the left bank of the Limay River, Neuquén, southern Argentina. The earliest occupations date to between 7900 and 5500 BC and include **obsidian** and **basalt** stone tools, along with **guanaco**, rodents, and other modern fauna.

CUEVA PINTADA. Cave located in the middle Orinoco, Venezuela. The cave, as with others of the region, has rock paintings, hence the name *painted cave*. Here there are animals, humans, and geometric figures. *See also* ROCK ART.

CUEVA SUSUDE INAVA. Cave located in the middle Orinoco region, Venezuela. Its name means rock house (*Casa de piedra*). Cueva Susude Inava has an impressive collection of **rock art** consisting of drawings in red and white. Animal representations predominate, but there are also geometric and anthropomorphic designs. The cave is associated with **Saladoid** and **Arauquinoid ceramics**.

CUEVA TIXI. One of the earliest sites in the Pampa region, province of Buenos Aires, Argentina. Two radiocarbon dates range from 8300 to 8000 BC. Stone tools were made of local (quartz and quartzite) and exotic raw materials (**chert** and **basalt**). No projectile points were found and tools were associated with **megafauna**. Among them are the bones of the extinct giant armadillo (*Eutatus seguini*), as in the contemporaneous site of **Cerro La China**, and of a large rodent (*Myocastor coypus*). There is a great variety of faunal remains at Cueva Tixi, including **guanaco**, deer—these two are the most abundant—vizcacha, and many other smaller mammals; reptiles; birds, including **ñandú**; and fish. Cueva Tixi is five kilometers from the **Los Pinos** rock shelter, which dates to the same period.

CUEVA TRAFUL 1. Cave located on the right bank of the Traful River near the confluence of the Limay River, Neuquén, southern Argentina. This cave has three meters of cultural deposits. The first inhabitants occupied the site around 7500 BC. A hearth and a few flakes are the only remains from this first occupation. From the second level, dating to 7200 BC, there are triangular projectile points and modern fauna.

CULEBRAS. Site (and group of sites under the term Culebras Complex) in the valley of the same name, department of Ancash, north-central coast of Peru. This complex was dated to the later preceramic, from around 2500 to 1800 BC, and includes the site of **Las Haldas**. Culebras can be characterized as a large village or a small town, and constructions were made with **basalt** blocks and mortar; the Culebras Complex as a whole suggests a high population density in the area for that time period. The main food resources associated with the site were fish, shellfish, marine mammals, and **guinea pig**. **Maize** appears in the latest occupation levels of Culebras. Most of the dead were buried underneath house floors, but there is also evidence of a cemetery. Culebras has the earliest evidence of **coca** use in Peru, circa 2000 BC.

CUMBE CAVE. Rock shelter in the department of **Cajamarca**, northern highlands of Peru. The oldest occupation dates to approximately 8500 BC. The lithic industry is simple, consisting of a few retouched instruments and no projectile points. The complex shows similarities with **El Abra**, Talara Complex, and **Tibitó** (Colombia). Cumbe inhabitants **hunted** deer and rodents (as well as **guinea pig** and others) and the first **camelids** appear in levels with the earliest **ceramics** (**Huacaloma**, **Layzón**, and **Cajamarca** styles) around 1300 BC.

CUMBEMAYO CANAL. This elaborate canal runs for nine kilometers along the slopes west of the city of **Cajamarca** in the northern highlands of Peru. The first 850-meter stretch was carved into the bedrock, often in an elaborate, ceremonial zigzag path. The canal diverts runoff from the Pacific drainage into the Atlantic drainage and is associated with elaborate stone sculpture adorned with elaborate Initial Period iconography (1000 BC).

CUPISNIQUE. Early Horizon culture, art style, and **religion** that characterizes the northern Peruvian coast from the Virú to the **Lambayeque** valleys. Some of the most important sites are **Garagay**, **Sechín Alto**, and **Caballo Muerto**. The **architectural** tradition includes monumental platform **mounds** with rectangular forecourts and inset stairways. Colonnades and painted **adobe** sculptures or friezes often adorn the summit temples of these ceremonial platforms. The religious ideology of Cupisnique was based on **trophy heads**; **hallucinogenic substances**; and cult of felines, birds, and reptiles, as well as ***Strombus*** and ***Spondylus*** shells probably associated with fertility and water cults. *See also* CERAMIC MOLD; KUNTUR WASI; LIMONCARRO; PUÉMAPE; SALINAR; STIRRUP BOTTLE.

CUY (*CAVIA PORCELLUS*). *See* GUINEA PIG.

CUZCO (ALSO SPELLED CUSCO). Political, administrative, and **religious** center of the **Inka** empire, in the valley of the same name, in southern Peru. Cuzco is one of the most well-known and most-visited archaeological sites in South America. Cuzco is one of the oldest continuously inhabited cities in South America, having been first inhabited around AD 1200–1300 or earlier. Inka constructions in Cuzco, mainly palaces, temples, and elite residences, are characterized by elaborate masonry, consisting of carefully fitted cyclopean stone work. Important sections of streets and buildings, such as the Loreto street and the curved wall of the **Koricancha** (the Inka Temple of the Sun, converted into a Dominican church), are still extant, while many other constructions were destroyed by the Spaniards. The Spaniards dismantled many buildings and used the carved stone blocks to construct private residences, public buildings, and churches. On a hill to the north of Cuzco are the massive zigzag stone wall constructions of the **fortification** and ritual complex of **Sacsaywaman**. Similar to other Andean settlements, Cuzco was divided in two halves: **Hanan** Cuzco and **Hurin** Cuzco. Most of the constructions were built as compounds for members of the royal **ayllu** or **panaqas**. Several roads originated in Cuzco's main plaza, the **Aukapata**, and connected the city with the rest of the empire. Cuzco is a **World Heritage Site of UNESCO**. *See also* CHANKA; CHOKEPUKIO; TOMEBAMBA.

– D –

DABAJUROID (DABAJURO). Northwestern Venezuelan sites that date to the first centuries AD. The earliest phases are found in the coastal region of Maracaibo-Cobo **(Rancho Peludo)**; later it expanded into the Andean region and the Caribbean. It represents one of the examples of the **First Painted Horizon** of northern South America. **Ceramics** were decorated with red paint, and fabric impressions and corrugation were also common. The presence of clay griddles indicates that **agriculture** of **manioc** was important, while **hunting** and fishing also represented a significant part of the diet. Later Dabajuro sites are characterized by **manos and metates**, suggesting that **maize** was grown. Some Dabajuro buried their dead in **shell middens**, while others made use of **funerary urns**.

DEITIES. As every indigenous group believed in several deities or supernatural forces or entities, there are large groups of gods or pantheons in South American cultures. In many cases, deities are associated with natural elements or phenomena, such as the sun, moon, lightning, stars, rain, mountains, plants, and animals. Deities are represented in several media, including textiles, stone, **ceramics**, metal, and bone, as well as in **rock art**. *See also* FANGED DEITY; ILLAPA; INTI; KORICANCHA; LAMBAYEQUE; LORD OF THE SEA; MAIZE GOD; OCULATE BEING; RELIGION; SMILING GOD; STAFF GOD; STAFF GODDESS; VIRACOCHA.

DIAGUITA. 1. Late Period culture in north-central Chile or Norte Chico, from the Copiapó River valley in the north to the Aconcagua River in the south. The Diaguita emerged after AD 1200 as a continuation of the **Las Animas** Complex. The term Diaguita was used by the Spaniards to identify all local people living in this area. Archaeologists began using the term *Diaguita chilena* to differentiate the culture from the Diaguita of Argentina. In coastal sites, food sources were mostly of marine origin. In upper valley sites, there is evidence of **agriculture** and **pastoralism**. The Diaguita are characterized by elaborate **ceramics** painted on the outside with black and/or red over a white or red base with geometric or anthropomorphic motifs. The Diaguita resisted the **Inka** conquest, and after annexation to the Inka empire some groups were deported to other areas. These groups had to perform different tasks such as agricultural production, crafts, and road building in their new placement and were known as *mitmakuna*. The Inka established a **metallurgic** production center at **Viña del Cerro**. Ceramics from this period have a combination of Inka and Diaguita forms and decorative styles. 2. Term applied in northwest Argentina archaeology until the 1950s to refer to all sixteenth-century inhabitants and their ancestors. *See also* EL INDÍGENO.

DOMESTICATED ANIMALS. The **llama**, **alpaca**, dog, and **guinea pig** were some of the most important domesticated animals (mammals) in South America. The dog was domesticated outside of South America, but some varieties were native to the continent. The llama, alpaca, and guinea pig were domesticated and raised in western South America; the dog was common also in other regions. The **Muscovy duck** (*Cairina moschata*) was a domesticated bird of many indigenous groups of South America.

DOS CABEZAS. Dos Cabezas, a major **Moche** site in the Jequetepeque Valley, is by far the largest site on the north coast of Peru associated with characteristic Moche I **ceramics**. Dos Cabezas is dominated by a massive pyramid 31.5 meters high built of solid **adobe** brick. A monumental trench bisects the summit of the **huaca**, artificially forming two peaks, hence the pyramid's name. This massive excavation was conducted in the Early Colonial Period by Spanish **looters**. The pyramid, however, towers over an extensive site consisting of a number of subsidiary temples, domestic zones, and **shell middens** that date to the **Formative** and Moche periods.

Excavations on the lower seaward side of the main edifice uncovered three elite Moche **tombs**, one of which was associated with an equivalent miniature burial chamber. This simulacrum contained a small **copper** statue within a burial shroud surrounded by offerings of ceramics and a **llama** skull. The miniature is a remarkable representation of the adjacent Tomb 3, holding the remains of a high-status lord. The three principal tombs appear to have been built around the same time and were dedicated to three males aged 18–22. These figures were probably related and stood a remarkable 1.75–1.80 meters tall. They would have towered over the average north coast male. These men may have suffered from a disease similar to Marfan syndrome, a genetic disorder that causes thin, elongated bones, and the individuals were possibly siblings or first cousins. The individual of Tomb 2 was interred with the largest quantity of high-quality gold, copper, and ceramic objects, and he evidently wielded considerable authority. He is buried with gold ornaments, **weapons**, textiles, and eighteen different metal headdresses, sixteen of which are unique to Dos Cabezas. This noble was also adorned with realistic bat representations, including a molded ceramic bat figure, a solid gold bat nose ornament, and a headdress of numerous bat motifs manufactured from gilded copper. In Moche iconography, bats were symbolically evocative of **sacrificial** ideologies and ritual violence, and their numerous depictions in Tomb 2 might be an indication of the ceremonial, priestly role of the interred lord. Fine weaponry, including clubs, spears, spear-throwers, and gold-plated shields, are further symbolic of the individual's warrior status. All three burials were accompanied by subsidiary interments of usually females or children, who may have been **sacrificed** attendants. The molded Moche I ceramics found in the three tombs depict owls, condors, sea lions, crested (lunar) animals, felines, and birds. A whole llama offering also overlay the main figure of Tomb 2.

Excavations within a subsidiary adobe temple near the main **pyramid** uncovered a small, narrow chamber containing eighteen severed skulls. Osteological analysis revealed cut marks on extant portions of the upper vertebrae, indicating that the heads were placed in the room soon after their ceremonial decapitation. Moreover, on a higher **architectural** complex connected by a ramp to the subsidiary temple to the south, an elite interment was found buried with a copper gilded pectoral. A copper **tumi** knife was clutched in his left hand, and the head of a snapped face-neck jar accompanied the extended burial. Scholars suggest that this figure served as a high-status priest who presided over rites of ceremonial decapitation, and that this elderly priest may have been charged with the ritual execution of the eighteen victims found in the adjacent chamber. Furthermore, ceramic representations of supernatural decapitator animals have been excavated and looted from Dos Cabezas, and towering adobe friezes of fanged decapitators adorned the outer wall of the pyramid. It is evident that the central tenets of ritual violence underpinning Moche politico-religious ideology were well-established in the lower Jequetepeque by the Early Moche Period.

DOS PALMOS. **Nasca** settlement in the Pisco Valley, southern Peru. The site is formed by five plazas with sets of rectangular rooms densely packed around them. Dos Palmos is one of the northernmost Nasca sites.

DOUBLE-SPOUT BOTTLE. A type of vessel with two spouts connected by a handle, common in the valleys of central Colombia (**Calima**), coastal Ecuador (**La Tolita**), and on the coast of Peru, such as in **Lambayeque**, **Nazca**, and **Chimú ceramics**. *See also* SALINAR; TUMACO.

DÚHO. Wooden or stone bench used by chiefs and shamans of northern South America, the Caribbean, and Central America, as a symbol of power at the time of the European conquest. These benches were usually carved in the shape of four-legged creatures, most of them with a carved head at one end and an elongated tail at the other. The carved faces have been interpreted as animals (bats, dogs, turtles, and so on) or anthropomorphic creatures. All are considered to be representatives of the supernatural world and guiding spirits for the important men who sat on them. Most dúhos have been discovered in caves, attesting to their spiritual significance given that caves were sacred places used for ceremonies and sometimes burials.

– E –

"EAGLE" PECTORALS. Gold pendants manufactured by the **Sinú** and other groups of present-day Colombia. These pectorals probably represented birds that were important in shamanistic rituals, common in northern South America and southern Central America at the time of the European conquest. Most of the eagle pectorals were **looted** from **tombs** and thus have no provenience.

EL ABRA. **Hunter**-gatherer rock-shelter site in the Sabana de Bogotá, Colombia. The earliest occupation of El Abra dates to the Late Pleistocene. Its stone tool industry consists of unifacially retouched flakes. No projectile points were found at El Abra. See also CUMBE CAVE; SUEVA I; TEQUENDAMA; TIBITÓ.

EL ALFARCITO. Large **agricultural** site with **pirca** constructions in Jujuy, northwest Argentina. There are several cemeteries with infant **funerary urns**. **Trophy heads** were also found.

EL CEIBO. Cave site located in Santa Cruz, southern Argentina. It was occupied since the Late Pleistocene. The earliest stone tool industry is similar to level 11 of **Los Toldos**. It has important **rock art** including a large feline. The faunal remains recovered at the site include horse and **guanaco**.

EL INDÍGENO. **Hunter** and gatherer site in a high valley of Mendoza, Argentina, situated between 3,200 and 3,400 meters above sea level. After AD 500 and continuing into historical times, hunters moved to this upper valley site in the summer and lived in circular **pirca** shelters with stone foundations; 116 of these structures were recorded along the Indígeno River ranging in size from seven to ninety square meters. A few constructions are rectangular. Among the excavated materials are painted, polished, and **incised ceramics**; projectile points and other stone tools of **basalt** and chalcedony; and **camelid** and bird bones. Some of the painted ceramics are **Llolleo** and **Diaguita chileno** in style.

EL INGA. Open-air **hunter**-gatherer site in Pichincha, highland Ecuador. **Fishtail projectile points** were used in large numbers at El Inga. **Obsidian** was one of the main raw materials used for tool manufacture at the site. Obsidian from El Inga was provenienced to the nearby sources of **Yanaurco-Quiscatola** and **Mullumica**.

EL JOBO. Preceramic stone tool industry of northern South America characterized by large lanceolate bifacial points, known as El Jobo points. The site type of El Jobo is located on the western coast of Venezuela, close to **Taima-Taima**. *See also* MANZANILLO; MUACO.

EL MOLLE COMPLEX. Early **ceramic** period culture that extended from the Salado River in the north to the Choapa Valley in the south in north-central Chile, the *Norte chico* region, dating to AD 50–700. El Molle culture was based on **agriculture** and herding, and settlements can be differentiated by these two modes of economic practice. In these sites there are stone hoes. Stone hoes and **tembetá** of different shapes and stone types are very common in El Molle contexts. **Las Animas Complex** represents the later continuation of El Molle material culture.

EL PARAÍSO (OR CHUQUITANTA). Large preceramic site with monumental constructions in the central coast of Peru. It covers nearly sixty hectares and is located along the low Chillón River. El Paraíso was inhabited around 1600 BC and later (both preceramic and **ceramic**). There are eleven monumental structures, the largest two consisting of parallel structures four hundred meters long. One of the units has been excavated and restored. It is contemporaneous with the site of **Las Haldas** in the Casma Valley.

EL PEHUENCHE. Obsidian quarry located in a high valley in southern Mendoza, central Argentina. The obsidian source of **Laguna del Maule** is located several kilometers away. Groups living on both sides of the Andes used obsidian quarried from El Pehuenche. Pehuenche is also the name of an indigenous group of the region; one of their main staples was pine nuts (*pehuen* is a local pine tree; *che* means people).

EL VERGEL COMPLEX. Late **ceramic** period culture of southern Chile located between the Bíobío and Toltén rivers. El Vergel dates to around AD 1100–1300. Members of this culture were **hunters** and gatherers who had **domesticated llamas** (*chiliweke* in **Mapuche** language). The ceramic style of El Vergel is known as **Valdivia**. Burials were placed in cists or **funerary urns**.

EMERALDS. Precious stones extracted by South American people along the coasts of Ecuador and Colombia and **traded** throughout that region. Emeralds have been found at the **Inka** site of **Tomebamba** (highland Ecuador). *See also* MARKETS.

ENGLEFIELD. Site type and group of sites that date to around 4700–3100 BC in the Seno de Otway, Magallanes, southern Chile. These sites (Englefield 1, **Bahía** Colorada, Bahía Buena, and Punta Santa Ana) are identified by an elaborate **obsidian** industry of bifaces, leaf-shaped and triangular projectile points, scrapers, and knives. Tools were also made from the bones of marine mammals (seals). Bahía Buena and Punta Santa Ana are among Chile's national monuments. *See also* LANCHA PACKEWAIA.

ESPERANZA TRADITION. A tradition developed in the central plains of Argentina, mostly in the province of Santa Fé. Esperanza I is preceramic, while Esperanza II is defined by the presence of **ceramics**. The tradition dates to 400 BC–AD 1500. Esperanza II ceramics are mostly undecorated or have negatives of basketry and nets. The sites are small, suggesting group mobility.

– F –

FALDAS DE SANGAY. A very large site containing numerous earth **mounds** located in the Ecuadorian Amazon, dated to AD 1000–1500. It is estimated to occupy a surface of twelve square kilometers and is characterized by several large figurative mounds that represent anthropomorphic and feline creatures. Smaller residential mounds are also common at Faldas. Faldas de Sangay is one of the few well-known *terra firme* sites of the **Incised and Punctate Horizon**.

FALDAS DEL MORRO. One of the type sites of the **Azapa Phase** (1400–500 BC) in the city of Arica, northern Chile. The Azapa Phase is the Early **Formative Period** in the northern coast of Chile.

FAMILY. *See* KINSHIP.

FANGED DEITY. One of the representations of supernatural creatures in **Chavín** and **Moche** art. The fanged deity is also known as the god of the mountains (*dios de las montañas*) and is distinguished by snake hair and a snarling mouth. *See also* DEITIES; HUACA DE LA LUNA; HUACA EL BRUJO; SACRIFICE CEREMONY OR SCENE; SAN JOSÉ DE MORO.

FARFÁN. Chimú provincial capital in the Jequetepeque Valley, north coast of Peru. It was established around AD 1200 and was occupied until the Colonial Period. Farfán has six principal compounds. It extends for more than three kilometers along both sides of the Pan-American Highway north of the present-day town of Ciudad de Dios and is dominated by six monumental compounds arrayed on a linear axis, which exhibit architectonic canons characteristic of the large compounds or *ciudadelas* at **Chan Chan**. For example, Compound II, one of the largest and more elaborate precincts at Farfán, was embellished with typical pilastered doorway entrances, baffled corridors, carved wooden guardian figures, walled entry courts, niched audiencias, and a burial platform at the back end of the construction. The latter was used only once and is believed to have held the remains of General Pacatnamú himself. This mortuary structure within a ciudadela-like construction is the only one of its kind found outside of Chan Chan. Female dedicatory burials were excavated under the floor of the main *audiencia*, a practice also common at the **Moche** Valley capital. Subsidiary constructions including perishable domestic shelters, low platforms, canals, **adobe** walls, stone structures, and cemeteries surround the long line of compounds and a dense spread of material culture attests to a formidable residential population at Farfán.

Some scholars argue that the provincial capital was intrusive, similar to imposed **Inka** administrative centers, and that it was not built over a substantial earlier settlement. Moreover, the intrusive Farfán is interpreted as an "empty center," again resembling Inka provincial capitals; it served as the citadel of lords, officials, and immediate retainers supported by nonpermanent rotating populations that fulfilled *mit'a* (tribute in labor) obligations to the state. There is little evidence, however, that the lower classes residing at Farfán were necessarily impermanent, and no excavations to date have been conducted in domestic zones within the site. Perishable housing is by no means a direct signifier of a rotating workforce, and such residential structures were common throughout the valley both in prehistory and in recent times.

Archaeological analysis suggests that the Farfán storerooms cached small quantities of finished prestige items, the wealth objects of a few specific individuals. In fact, the reduced storage capacity and the site's location on the main coastal highway lead some scholars to argue that Farfán's main function was dissemination of state edicts and administrative information processing. Officials at the provincial capital collected information and coordinated activities related with labor and production of goods at the regional level. Staple resources were thus not stored at Farfán but were sent directly to Chan Chan in the Moche Valley through the coordinated efforts of administrators residing at the provincial capital. *See also* TALAMBO.

FELL CAVE. One of the earliest (1930s) stratigraphic finds of Late Pleistocene occupations in southern South America. Fell Cave is located in southern Chile along the Strait of Magellan near the **Palli Aike** Cave. One of the diagnostic elements of the earliest occupations is the **fishtail (projectile) point**. Similar points were used by other Late Pleistocene hunters in South America. Fell Cave is one of Chile's national monuments.

FIGURINES. Name given to **ceramic** artifacts with human shapes that were usually portable and not designed to carry materials such as comestibles. They represent females and males with **clothing**, ornaments, body painting, and other features (**cranial deformation**) that provide information about the customs of different South American peoples. Figurines are usually small (20–25 centimeters tall) and are common in many South American ceramic traditions. Some of the earliest examples were produced by the **Valdivia** culture. Cross-culturally, figurines often played an important role in religious ceremonies, such as fertility rites. *See also* CERAMIC MOLD; CHORRERA; GUANGALA; OSOIDE TRADITION; SAN FRANCISCO CULTURE; TABUCHILA PHASE; TOCUYANOID; VALENCIOID CULTURE; YURAJ MOLINO.

FIRST PAINTED HORIZON. This horizon includes all the early **ceramic** styles of Amazonia and Orinoquia that have painting. The earliest dates for this horizon are around 1000 BC. Ceramics were painted with red, black, and white. The earliest style is **Hokomo** in the Guajira Peninsula of western Venezuela. *See also* DABAJUROID; MOMIL; TOCUYANOID.

FISHTAIL POINT. One of the oldest types of projectile points manufactured and used by hunter-gatherers in South America (9000–7000 BC). Fishtail points are bifacial and stemmed and range in length from 3.5 to 7.2 centimeters. Some of the first stratigraphic finds of such points were made at the **Fell** and **Palli Aike** caves of southern Chile, which can be dated to 9000 BC and later periods. Points of this type were found along the Andes and in many regions of eastern South America. In eastern South America, they were first dated at **Cerro La China** to 8700 BC. Other fishtail points were found at **Cerro Los Burros** (Uruguay). In general, fishtail points have been found in surface collections or out of context, as a product of **looting**. Leaf-shaped (**Ayampitín**, **Lauricocha**) points become widely used after the disappearance of fishtails around 7000 BC. *See also* CERRO EL SOMBERO; CUEVA DEL MEDIO; EL INGA; LOS PINOS; PASO OTERO 5; PIEDRA MUSEO.

FORD, JAMES A. (1911–1968). American archaeologist who conducted research in several regions of the Americas. In South America, Ford conducted fieldwork in Colombia and Peru. Among his publications are *Excavations in the Vicinity of Cali, Colombia* (1944), *Cultural Dating of Prehistoric Sites in the Virú Valley, Perú* (1949), *Settlement Patterns in the Virú Valley* (1949), and *A Comparison of Formative Cultures in the Americas: Diffusion or the Psychic Unity of Man* (1969).

FORMATIVE PERIOD. This term describes early village life and subsistence based on **agriculture**, sometimes including **domesticated animals**, and the use of **ceramics**. Villages vary in size, complexity, and chronology. Formative societies were found throughout most of South America, both in the lowlands and in the highlands. *See also* CERRO NARRÍO; CHIRIPA; CHIVAY; CIÉNAGA; CONDORHUASI; ISLAND OF THE MOON; ISLAND OF THE SUN; JISKAIRUMOKO; KALASASAYA; LA CHIMBA; PALERMO; PIRINCAY, PITRÉN PHASE OR COMPLEX; PUKARA; QALUYU; QEYA; SUKAKOLLO; TAFI; TECOMATE, TELARMACHAY; TILOCALAR PHASE; TITIMANI; VALDIVIA;

WANKARANI; YURAJ MOLINO; ZONE HATCHURED HORIZON.

FORTIFICATIONS. Sites with high walls and military features or located in defensible locales can be considered as fortifications. The presence of baffled entrances, embrasures, fortified towers, **weaponry**, and other defensive elements would support the labeling of sites as fortifications. *See also* CARAJUANA; CERRO BAÚL; CERRO CHEPÉN; CERRO GRANDE DE LA COMPAÑÍA; CERRO MEJÍA; KILLKE; MALLKU CHIEFDOM; MONTAGNES COURONNÉES; PAMBAMARCA; POTRERO DE PAYOGASTA; PUKARA; PUKARA DE ANDALGALÁ; PUKARA JULI; SALINAR; TANKA TANKA; TUPURAYA; WARFARE.

FUNERARY URN. Many South American groups from different regions, time periods, and cultural traditions buried their dead in **ceramic** vessels called funerary urns. These urns could sometimes be closed with ceramic lids. Usually, funerary urns are found in cemetery areas (not under house floors). Among the groups that used funerary urns are the **Santa María**, **Belén** (infants), **El Alfarcito** (infants), **Guaraní** (adults and infants), **Candelaria**, **Padre Las Casas** (**Mapuche**), **Llolleo** (central Chile), **Hokomo**, **Valencioid**, **Rancho Peludo** (Ranchoid) (the last two in Venezuela), **Omereque**, **Mojocoya**, **Velarde** (the last three in Bolivia), **Manteño** (Ecuador), **Amazonian Polychrome Horizon** (**Marajoara**), **Las Mercedes**, **Tairona**, **Calima Complex**, Tolima, **Quimbaya**, **Tierradentro**, and **San Agustín** (the last six in present-day Colombia). Some Venezuelan indigenous groups buried individuals in funerary urns during the sixteenth to twentieth centuries. *See also* DABAJUROID; EL VERGEL COMPLEX; MARCELINA KUÉ; SAN FRANCISO CULTURE; SAPUCAÍ; VALENCIOID.

– G –

GALINDO. Very large Late **Moche** site located in the Moche Valley, north coast of Peru. From AD 500 to 700, Galindo occupied six square kilometers and contained four **adobe** platforms surrounded by walls (*cercaduras*). The residential area includes storage facilities, benched rooms, and kitchens. Elites and commoners lived in separate areas of the site with the elite in the center, separated from the commoners by a wall and ditch. *See also* PAMPA GRANDE.

GALLINAZO. The Gallinazo were first identified in the Virú Valley, north coast of Peru, which is considered to be the demographic and political epicenter of this cultural phenomenon. Excavations in Virú demonstrated that Gallinazo material culture stratigraphically overlay **Salinar** materials, while in Chicama research suggests that the two material assemblages were at first contemporaneous, with the eventual disappearance of the Salinar sequence. Significantly, many dimensions of **Moche** corporate **architecture**, city planning, **irrigation** technology, mortuary ritual, and **ceramic** production were first evident among the Gallinazo. Settlement mostly shifted from **fortified** positions in the mid and upper valley to the more expansive lower plains. In Virú, settlement was identified on both banks of the river, while in Moche, Gallinazo sites (though found throughout the lower valley) clustered in the south midvalley, thus reminiscent of settlement patterns documented for the earlier Salinar Phase.

Poured or pounded **tapia** (Early Gallinazo) and cane-mold **adobe** brick (Middle and Late Gallinazo) become the predominant building material, and monumental construction, consisting of lofty adobe platforms or **pyramids**, was built throughout the north coast, thus setting the precedent for later Moche ceremonial architecture. For instance, Huaca Gallinazo, a site among the Gallinazo group in the Virú Valley, measures approximately 75 by 60 meters and 25 meters high and was constructed of millions of adobe bricks. Castillo Tomoval in Virú is another pyramidal structure which required a formidable investment of labor, time, and planning. Indeed, the Gallinazo platforms were built using the same segmentary building techniques employed later by the Moche, suggesting an organized, multigroup labor force coordinated by a centralized power whose political and religious authority was ultimately materialized in the towering pyramids. Dwellings were constructed around adobe platforms, which formed the core of civic-ceremonial centers. Population increase, expansion of hydraulic networks, and the proliferation of undefended hamlets, as well as intensified sociospatial aggregation in the Moche, Virú, and Chicama valleys, indicate a relatively productive and peaceful era (especially in comparison to the preceding Salinar Period) characterized by the probable consolidation of centralized political systems. *See also* CERRO ARENA; CERRO OREJAS; GALLINAZO GROUP; PAMPA GRANDE.

GALLINAZO GROUP (HUACA GALLINAZO). The **Gallinazo** group on the north bank of the lower Virú Valley, northern coast of Peru, represents one of the largest clusters of sizeable settlements dating to the pre-**Moche** Early Intermediate Period. It is comprised of thirty sites that cluster in an area of thirteen square kilometers approximately three kilometers from the sea. The eight largest settlements and subsidiary satellites, interspersed with pyramids (5 km^2), are estimated to have once contained thirty thousand rooms by the time of the Late Gallinazo Phase. Agglutinated irregular rooms, usually rectangular in plan and built of **adobe**, constitute the characteristic urban dwelling within the Gallinazo group. They are associated with dense domestic debris and were often adorned with paintings. These numerous structures are thought to have housed nuclear and extended families and experienced multiple episodes of remodeling. The aggregation of honeycombed, labyrinthine domestic structures (lacking segmentation) surrounding **pyramids** could represent evidence of social differentiation grounded ultimately in **kinship** ideologies. The Gallinazo group probably served as the capital of a centralized polity coordinating **Vicú** defense and **agricultural** production. The greatest population and agricultural expansion ever achieved in the prehistoric Virú Valley occurred immediately before the violent conquest by the Moche.

GARAGAY. Large **Cupisnique** site in the Rimac valley, central coast of Peru. **U-shaped platforms** surrounding sunken plazas constitute the religious **architecture** of this ceremonial center. The central **mound** at Garagay has a mud-brick frieze that illustrates a supernatural being in the shape of a spider, in blue, red, yellow, and white.

GAVÁN. A very large site for the region located along the Canaguá River in the Venezuelan western lowlands or *llanos* of the Orinoco basin. Gaván is dominated by two large **mounds** on both ends of a

500-meter-long plaza. Smaller mounds, **calzadas**, encircling earthwork, and house mounds are also present at Gaván. The sequence is divided into an early phase (AD 300–550) and a late phase (AD 550–1000). *See also* OSOIDE TRADITION.

GEOGLYPHS. Geoglyphs are very large figures erected with rocks on the slope of hills or mountains that could be seen from several kilometers away. They are found from the upper Zaña Valley in northern Peru to **Nasca** in southern Peru and even farther south in northern Chile and to San Juan, Argentina (**Angualasto**). Some could have been astronomical calendars (**Nasca**) and others were probably related to directing **llama** caravans (northern Chile and central Argentina). The largest and most famed geoglyphs are the **Nazca lines**. *See also* CERRO SOMBRERO; VENTILLA.

GODS. *See* DEITIES.

GONZÁLEZ, ALBERTO REX (1918–). An important figure in Argentine archaeology. Gonzalez conducted field work in several regions of Argentina and abroad (for the Aswan Dam in Egypt). Among his numerous publications are *La caza pozo en el N. O. argentino* (1954); *Excavaciones arqueológicas en el yacimiento de Ongamira, Córdoba (Rep. Argentina)* with **O. F. A. Menghin** (1954); *Contextos culturales y cronología en el area central del N. O. argentino* (1955); *La estratigrafía de la Gruta de Intihuasi (Prov. De San Luis, R.A.) y sus relaciones con otros sitios precerámicos de Sudamérica* (1960); *Cultural Development in North Western Argentina* (1963); *Cronología del Valle de Hualfín, provincia de Catamarca, obtenida mediante el uso de computadoras*, with G. Cowgill (1970); *Argentina Indígena. Vísperas de la Conquista*, with José A. Perez Gollan (1973); *Arte, estructura y arqueología. Análisis de figures duales y anatrópicas del N. O. argentino* (1974); *Arte precolombino de la Argentina. Introducción a su historia cultural* (1977); *Pre-Columbian Metallurgy of Northwest Argentina: Historical Development and Cultural Process* (1979); *Notas sobre religión y culto en el N.O.A. prehispánico* (1983); *Las placas metálicas de los Andes del Sur. Contribución al estudio de las religiones precolombinas* (1992); and *Cultura La Aguada. Arqueología y diseños* (1998).

GOVERNMENT. *See* POLITICAL ORGANIZATION.

GRADIN, CARLOS J. (1918–2002). Argentine archaeologist who focused on **rock art** research, particularly in Patagonia. He published several articles and books on rock art. He coauthored with H. Schobinger the book *Cazadores de la Patagonia y Agricultores Andinos* (1985). Among his articles are "L´art rupestre dans la Patagonie Argentine" (1994); "El Arte rupestre de la Cuenca del Río Pinturas, Provincia de Santa Cruz, República Argentina" (1985); "El Alero de las Manos Pintadas (Las Pulgas, Pcia. de Chubut, Argentina)" (1973); and "Parapetos habitacionales en la meseta de Somuncura, Provincia de Río Negro" (1971).

GROUND SLOTH (*MYLODON DARWINII* AND OTHER SPECIES). Extinguished Pleistocene mammal hunted by South America's early human settlers. Among the sites where remains of ground sloth were found in archaeological contexts is **Fell Cave**.

GRUTA DEL INDIO. Large cave located along the Atuel River, Mendoza, central Argentina. Gruta del Indio is situated in the southernmost area of **maize agriculture**. The cave is very dry, allowing the conservation of organic remains. There are several occupations; the earliest one is pre-Atuel III (pre–2500 BC). Atuel III (2500–250 BC) is characterized by primary and secondary burials wrapped in mats made with vegetable materials. According to the material culture and the dating, Atuel III is related to **Los Morrillos**. Atuel II (post–250 BC) is marked by the first evidences of domesticated plants: **maize**, squash, beans, and **quinoa**. **Hunting** and gathering remained important features of Atuel II daily life and provided an important part of the diet. Triangular projectile points were widely used. Another element of Atuel II culture is **rock art**, which is found along the walls of the cave. Burials in this level are wrapped in leather. The Atuel II contexts are related to the **Ansilta** culture. The first **ceramics** are present in the most recent level (Atuel I).

GRUTA DO GENTIO. Cave site in Minas Gerais, central Brazil. There is significant evidence of plant collecting here. By 1900 BC, domesticated plants (**maize**, squash, gourd) appear in the Unaí Phase.

GUADALUPE PHASE (TIERRA DE LOS INDIOS STYLE). Culture that emerged in the Quíbor valley in northwestern Venezuela after AD 1000. People lived in villages comprised of houses on **mounds** or artificial oval embankments that were configured around a plaza or grouped in pairs, which could indicate that the society was divided in halves or moieties. Large grinding stones possibly used to prepare **chicha** were found throughout the site. Cremation and direct primary burial were common in the Guadalupe Phase. Houses are rebuilt on top of the remains of the previous dwellings, suggesting a long temporal continuity in settlements of this phase. Houses had smaller grinding tools. The main botanical and faunal resources were **maize**, papaya, deer, rabbit, **guinea pig**, iguanas, and fish. Differential access to animal protein signals the presence of social inequality. Guadalupe-phase **pottery** is characterized by **polychrome** vessels with geometric decorations, some representing a bat, called the Bat God.

GUANACO (*LAMA GUANICOE*). A wild **camelid** which has a much wider distribution than the wild **vicuña**. The guanaco was one of the most **hunted** mammals in western and southern South America. Guanaco skin was used to make **clothing** and tents, among other uses. Its blood was also used in rituals (Patagonia). *See also* AGUA DE LA CUEVA; ARROYO MALO-3; CERRO TRES TETAS; CHOROQOLLO; CUEVA CUYÍN MANZANO; CUEVA DE LAS MANOS PINTADAS; CUEVA DEL MILODON; CUEVA EPULLAN; CUEVA TIXI; EL CEIBO.

GUANE. Late Period culture (AD 900–1500) in the region of Santander, Colombia. Guane people were a part of the **Chibcha** linguistic family. The Guane formed **chiefdoms** and cultivated **maize**, **cotton**, and tobacco. One of the characteristics of Guane culture is that burials were placed in caves of the region.

GUANGALA. Culture that occupied the coastal region of Ecuador from the border with Peru to southern Manabí province from 200 BC to AD 600. **Agriculture**, fishing, and **trade** were important elements of Guangala economy. Guangala people worked with **copper metallurgy**. Iridescent painting represents an important feature of Guangala **pottery**. Human clay **figurines** are common; some show **coca** chewing.

GUANÍN. Arawak term used in northern South America for **tumbaga**.

GUANO. Bird dung was used as fertilizer since prehistoric times, at least since the time of the **Moche**, and was found in large quantities on islands along the southern, central, and northern coasts of Peru. Andean people also brought offerings to the guano islands, including wooden **figurines**, necklaces, and ***Spondylus***. In the sixteenth century AD the guano islands were also related to ancestor cults.

GUARANÍ. A branch of the **Tupiguaraní** linguistic group that occupied most of the tropical and subtropical forests of southeastern South America at the time of the Spanish conquest. The earliest sites date to the first centuries AD. Archaeologically, they are identified by their carinated **ceramics** decorated by brushing, corrugation, or **polychrome** painting. They lived in villages with several **malocas** around an open area. These villages moved on a regular basis after a short number of years. The Guaraní were horticulturalists or slash-and-burn **agriculturalists**: they planted **maize**, beans, **manioc**, sweet potato, tobacco, and **cotton**. Due to this system, also called **swidden agriculture**, every few years when the soils lost their nutrients the Guaraní had to move their village to a new location. **Hunting** and fishing were important sources of protein. One of their characteristic vessel types was large **funerary urns**.

GUATACONDO-1. Formative (Early Intermediate Period) village in the Quebrada of the same name, northern Chile. Guatacondo-1 has circular **adobe** houses, some interconnected, with totora roofs and storage areas. Circular patios are also common at the site. An oval-shaped central plaza formed the crossroads and main axis of traffic in the settlement. The inhabitants of Guatacondo-1 cultivated **maize**, squash, and beans and collected **algarroba** seeds. Among the archaeological remains excavated at Guatacondo-1 are undecorated **ceramics**, textiles, and a **ñandú**-feather headdress. The village was settled around AD 50–100 at the end of the **Formative Period**. *See also* TULOR.

GUIDON, NIÈDE (1933–). Brazilian archaeologist born in the state of São Paulo. Guidon conducted research in northeastern Brazil and Uruguay and concentrated on the earliest settlers of South America. Among her many publications in several languages are *Missao arqueologica no sudeste do Piauí, Brasil. Relatorio final* (1978); *Rescate arqueológico de Salto Grande* (1978) with several coauthors; *Las unidades culturales de São Raimundo Nonato, sudeste del Estado de Piauí* (1981); and *Inventaire des sites sud-américaines antérieurs à 12.000 ans* (1985) with G. Delibrias. She has directed the Franco-Brazilian Archaeological Mission to Piauí since 1973. Her work supported the creation of the Serra de Capivara National Park and **World Heritage Site of UNESCO**, and of the Fundacao Museu do Homem Americano, São Raimundo Nonato, Piauí, northeastern Brazil.

GUINEA PIG OR CUY (*CAVIA PORCELLUS*). Also known as *acurito*, *curi*, *jaca*, *wanku*, and *conejo peruano*, the guinea pig is a small mammal (rodent) that was **domesticated** in South America. There are three species, and only one has been domesticated. Guinea pigs were raised in the north, central, and south Andes. The earliest sites with guinea pig remains are **Tequendama**, **Sueva I**, **El Abra**, and Nemocón (9000–8000 BC), all found in Colombia, and **Cumbe** in Peru. During the Holocene Period, guinea pig became more common as a source of protein, especially after 500 BC. In the preceramic site of **Aguazuque** (central Colombia), it was the second most frequent mammal in the diet. A guinea pig hutch, or *cuyera*, was found at the **Wari** site of Hatun Cotuyoc in the Huaro valley (**Cuzco** region), suggesting that guinea pigs were raised in residential areas. In **Formative Period** occupations (1500 BC to AD 400) around **Tiwanaku**, guinea pig was an important source of protein, but its role declined with the emergence of the Tiwanaku state. In many areas of the Andes it was and continues to be the main source of protein as well as an important offering or **sacrifice** in ritual events. *See also* CULEBRAS; GUADALUPE PHASE; HACHA; LA FLORIDA; PAMPA GRANDE.

GUITARRERO CAVE. Cave with a long preceramic and **ceramic** sequence in the Callejón de Huaylas in the central highlands of Peru situated at 2,580 meters above sea level. The cave has a very long sequence dating to 10,500 BC and has excellent preservation of perishable remains. The main occupation, or Complex II, took place around 8000 BC and is characterized by several domesticated plants, such as beans, chili peppers, and gourds, which are among the earliest evidences of domesticated plants in the central Andes.

– H –

HACHA. Initial Period site located on the Acarí River on the south coast of Peru. The site covers 800 by 200 meters and dates to between 1000 and 700 BC. **Wattle-and-daub** structures are present along with five **adobe** structures that are among the earliest ceremonial **architecture** on the south coast of Peru. Many domesticated plants, including **maize**, beans, squash, peanut, sweet potato, and ají, as well as marine fish and shellfish, **camelids**, **guinea pig**, and probably deer, were recovered from this site. A large quantity of stone hoes were also encountered here. **Obsidian** from Hacha derives from four different sources, the majority having been procured from **Quispisisa**. A group of obsidian artifacts belonging to the Acarí type and extremely rare at other Andean settlements constituted one of the four identified sources.

HALLUCINOGENIC SUBSTANCES. Many lowland and highland South American people consumed hallucinogenic substances in ritual ceremonies, usually of a shamanistic nature. The discovery of **pipes**, **snuff trays**, remains of plants, and iconographic representations provide archaeological evidence for the use of psychotropic agents in ancient South America. The variety of substances used suggests a deep knowledge of plant properties. These substances were usually consumed orally or through the nose either as powder or liquid. One of the most widespread hallucinogenic substances in South America was **vilca** or cebil, *Anadenanthera colubrina* (Leguminosae), and the earliest evidence of its use dates between 2130 and 2080 BC at the site of **Inca Cueva 4** (Jujuy, Argentina) at 3,860 meters above sea level. *See also* LAS CONCHAS; MONTE GRANDE; PIPES; SNUFF TRAYS; TAFÍ; ZOOLITHS.

HANAN. Name given by the **Inka** and later **Quechua**-speaking groups to the upper half of the **kinship** moiety systems. The term also referred to the upper half of the city of **Cuzco**, which was spatially divided according to dualistic and quadripartite principles. The lower part of Cuzco was called **Hurin**. Other dual spatial-social categories in the central Andes that parallel the **Hanan/Hurin** divide include **Aymara** *allasa/masaa* and *uma/urco*. *See also* TOMEBAMBA.

HATUN XAUXA. One of the most important Wanka and **Inka** provincial centers in the fertile and productive upper Mantaro Valley in the central highlands of Peru. The present remains cover about forty-eight hectares, much less than its original size. The archeological site is mostly covered by the modern city of Jauja. In the center of the site there is a plaza with an **ushnu**, although elaborate Inka masonry is lacking. The Spaniards reported that there were numerous **qolcas** in the northern part of the valley.

HATUNQOLLA (ATUNCOLLA). Large **Inka** site on the western shores of Lake Titicaca (Peru). It was a regional provincial capital at the time of the Spanish conquest, constituting the largest Inka site in the Collao and one of the four regional administrative centers in the Inka empire. The other three provincial centers were **Hatun Xauxa**, **Pumpu**, and **Huánuco Pampa**. This site was a major center complete with a state temple, storehouses, and residences for Inka administrators. Hatunqolla covered approximately fifty to eighty hectares. *See also* CHUCUITO.

HIGH-ALTITUDE SANCTUARIES. High mountain peaks were (and are) considered sacred in the Andes. The **Inka** and local inhabitants prior to Inka conquest built precincts or left offerings on the summit of several mountains from southern Peru to central Chile and Argentina. Mountain sanctuaries were usually built above 5,200 meters above sea level, connected to rods and other installations at lower altitudes. Young individuals (children of both sexes) were often **sacrificed** at these shrines, especially during the Inka era. They were accompanied by offerings of gold and silver human and **camelid** figurines, fine textiles, ***Spondylus*** shell, **coca** leaves, **turquoise** bead necklaces, and other valuable items of a ritual nature. Some of the most well-preserved corpses were found in the **Llullaillaco** shrine. One of the northernmost of these sanctuaries was found on the summit of the **Ampato** mountain (6,300 meters above sea level) in Arequipa's Cailloma province. Several young sacrificed individuals were discovered here together with multiple offerings of wealth items (silver and gold, textiles, *Spondylus* shell, coca leaves, feathers, **maize**, and so on). Base camps at several altitudes, distinguished by corrals, dwellings, and platforms, were found associated with Ampato, as at other sites. The southernmost sanctuary is at the **Aconcagua**, while other high-altitude sanctuaries include **Cerro El Plomo** and the Licancabur volcano. *See also* ALTIPLANO; CLOTHING; NEVADO DEL ACONQUIJA; SHOBINGER, JUAN.

HOKOMO STYLE. Hokomo **ceramics** are probably the earliest **polychrome pottery** in northern South America (1000 BC). These ceramics are found in villages around the Maracaibo basin in Venezuela. Hokomo people based their subsistence on fish and shellfish, and they also cultivated **maize**, as suggested by the presence of **manos and metates**. Large **budares** also indicate that **manioc** was part of the Hokomo diet. People were buried in **funerary urns**.

HOSSORORO CREEK. Shell-midden site, one of the earliest sites in Guyana with evidence of **manioc** cultivation, as suggested by the presence of **budares**. Hossororo Creek is located on the southern basin of the lower Orinoco and dates to around 2000 BC. **Ceramics** appear in this site at 1550 BC, and they are similar to ceramics of the **Alaka Phase** of Guyana.

HUACA. Andean shrine or entity suffused with the sacred. Huacas include anything from double-yolked eggs and portable elements to prominent features of the natural landscape such as a boulder, cave, mountain, or spring or a religious monument of the built environment. The latter include the **Koricancha**, the Temple of the Sun in **Cuzco**, and others. In Cuzco and the surrounding valley, there was a network of huacas associated with specific **ayllus** or **panaqas** that formed a system called **ceque**. In the coast of Peru, all **pyramids** are traditionally called huacas. *See also* CHOKEPUKIO; HUACA DE LA LUNA; HUACA DE LOS REYES; HUACA DEL SOL; HUACA EL BRUJO; TÚCUME.

HUACA (WACA) DE LA LUNA. Large **adobe** pyramid in the **Moche** site, situated at the opposite end of the urban sector 500 meters to the east of **Huaca del Sol**. It is comprised of an integrated **architectural** complex of six monumental plazas and three principal platforms of varying size built adjacent to the south side of **Cerro Blanco**. In total, the edifice measures 290 meters from north to south and 210 meters from east to west and extends 32 meters off the pampa floor. Important discoveries made here recently have been instrumental in improving the understanding of Moche ceremonial space. The ample Plaza 1 (the "Great Plaza"), once surrounded by adobe walls decorated with **polychrome** murals and fronting the largest Platform I, could have held up to ten thousand people. It is connected to the elevated platform by a long ramp contiguous to the east wall of the plaza. However, as one ascends to the chamber and patios of the most ample platform, architectural space becomes progressively more restricted. The notable exclusivity of the principal, higher confines of the **pyramid** have led archaeologists to propose that the Huaca de la Luna served as the palace and temple of the highest echelon of Moche elite. Vibrant murals dating from the Early Period to Phase V adorned the walls of the main platforms and plaza perimeters and multiple building episodes, six of which have been identified, point to deliberate structural entombment, possibly related to dedication or termination rites.

The murals often depict various permutations of the principal **fanged deity** (referred to as *Dios de la Montaña* or "Deity of the Mountain") distinguished by snake hair and a snarling mouth and often repeated in checkerboard arrangements. Moreover, low-relief murals depicting snakes and rows of warriors carrying war clubs were sculpted on the stepped northern face of Platform 1 overlooking the Great Plaza. Such representations were replicated at **Huaca El Brujo** at Cao Viejo in the Chicama valley. The most striking and best-preserved polychrome reliefs consist of repeated disembodied faces bearing fangs situated in interlocking rhombuses. These murals were sculpted on the walls of the lower level of Platform I and perdured through several remodeling episodes. Murals depicting narratives popular in Moche ceramic art, such as the "Revolt of the Objects," were also uncovered in the temple.

Burials, dating mainly from the Middle Moche Period but also including later **Chimú** interments, have been uncovered in Platform 1. Several of the graves were associated with exquisite molded **ceramics** of warriors and **copper** cups similar to those depicted in the Presentation Theme. The associated offerings point to the high status and priestly affiliation of the interred individuals. Little to no domestic debris has been identified in the intensely excavated Platform I, indicating that specialized ritual activities, different from those performed at Huaca del Sol, occurred within this complex. Recent excavations in the smaller Platform II and the tripartite Plaza 3, situated to the east of Platform I, demonstrate that Huaca de la Luna functioned as the principal temple for the paramount cult of ritual human **sacrifice** that defined elite political relations and religious programs. A natural rock outcrop was incorporated into the construction of Platform II and the adjacent Plaza 3A. It probably symbolized the sacred power and divine properties of the towering coastal hill. Excavation in this plaza unearthed more than seventy sacrificed individuals, placed to the north of the rock outcrop and deposited in at least five separate episodes. The skeletal remains were those of young men and were often found disarticulated, suggesting dismemberment. Around fifty smashed and unfired clay effigies of naked prisoners with bound necks were deposited with the remains. Recently defleshed and decapitated sacrificial victims have also been uncovered in the adjacent Plaza 3C.

HUACA DE LOS REYES. Early **ceramic**-period compound on the **Moche** Valley of the north coast of Peru. Huaca de los Reyes is part of the **Caballo Muerto** Complex. Among the **architectural** features made of stone and clay are **U-shaped mounds**, porch arcades, colonnades, friezes, and formal paired elements. There are also anthropomorphic sculptured figures.

HUACA (WACA) DEL SOL. One of the largest **adobe pyramids** of the Americas, located at the **Moche** site in the Moche Valley, northern coast of Peru. Close to it is the **Huaca de la Luna**. Huaca del Sol consists of four ascending platforms and contiguous terraces built with an estimated 143 million adobe bricks. The core platform measures 380 meters long by 160 meters in width and stands 40 meters high. Juxtaposed columns of bricks exhibiting the same makers' marks, mold shape, and construction matrix indicate that multiple, segmentary labor parties were mobilized from throughout the region to construct the imposing edifice. Huaca del Sol and Huaca de la Luna attest to the centralized political and economic power of the Moche elite, who successfully controlled a large, regional labor force. The identification of burials, domestic debris, and organic remains from extant portions of Huaca del Sol suggests that varied ceremonial and administrative activities, including elaborate feasting rites, occurred here. The massive pyramid was no doubt the focus of preeminent state political and religious ceremonies. *See also* CERRO BLANCO; PAMPA GRANDE.

HUACA EL BRUJO (CAO VIEJO). The ceremonial center of Huaca Cao Viejo in the El Brujo Complex, located on the south bank of the Chicama valley near the shoreline on the north coast of Peru, is one of the most magnificent **Moche** sites ever excavated. It is comprised of six terraced platforms and a monumental plaza measuring 170 by 130 meters and 30 meters tall, similar in layout and configuration to **Huaca de La Luna**. Some of the best examples of well-preserved **polychrome** friezes in the north coast have been uncovered here. The perimeter wall of the plaza and the principal façade of the main platform towering above the monumental space were covered in bright murals depicting common themes of Moche religious and political iconography. A procession of naked prisoners with ropes tied around their necks, under the surveillance of warriors in full regalia, covered the interior walls of the main plaza. Other figures in frontal view were sculpted in an upper tier of the platform. Here, human femurs were placed within the stylized legs of the shamanistic figures. The remains of an arachnid decapitator and a complex cosmological scene were also uncovered, along with the **fanged deity** that was also commonly portrayed at Huaca de la Luna, here repeated in rhombus motifs. Mass graves of **sacrificial** victims and deliberate temple entombment at Cao Viejo demonstrate other parallels with the architectural history and ceremonial function of Huaca de la Luna in the Moche Valley. The presence of neighboring Huaca Chotuna indicates a dyadic configuration of ceremonial space at El Brujo, which is also evident at **Cerro Blanco**.

Indeed, a dualistic organization of ceremonial **architecture** is further apparent at **Licapa** and **Mocollope** in the Chicama valley. This conformity to architectonic conception and hence liturgical practice has led scholars to interpret that the core Moche area was highly centralized and politically integrated. Nevertheless, the data from Cao Viejo suggest the great authority and perhaps semiautonomous status of the Chicama elite, who appear to have conducted the full sequence of the preeminent **sacrifice ceremony**. It seems possible that cycles of ritual **warfare**, within a shared ideological framework and possibly state administration, were orchestrated between interacting elites based in the Moche and Chicama valleys. Later **Lambayeque** Period burials have also been excavated at this site.

HUACA PRIETA. Preceramic shell residential **mound** site on the coast near the mouth of the Chicama River, north coast of Peru. Remains of seafood and several domesticated crops, including beans, squash, **achira**, and peppers, were recovered here in excavations conducted by **Junius Bird**. Reeds and pyroengraved gourds used to make containers were also common.

HUACALOMA. One of the earliest sites with ceremonial **architecture** recorded in Peru's northern highlands. Huacaloma is located in the **Cajamarca** basin and dates to the Early Initial (Ceramic) Period. The early phase dates to 1500–1000 BC and the late phase to 1000–500 BC. Huacaloma has the rectangular platform **mounds** and ceremonial chambers of the **Kotosh Religious Tradition**. Huacaloma-style **ceramics** were found in the **Cumbe Cave**. *See also* NORTH PERUVIAN HIGHLANDS FORMATIVE PERIOD.

HUACHICHOCANA. Cave site located at 3,400 meters above sea level in Jujuy, northwest Argentina. The earliest occupation dates to between 7500 and 6500 BC. Huachichocana has early evidence of plant domestication in the region. The stone tools of the early occupation are **Ayampitín** in style, consisting of triangular points as well as flake tools. Many pieces of basketry and items made of wood were also recovered from the site.

HUACO (WACO). Name given in the Andes to ancient objects such as **ceramic** vessels. The name derives from the **Quechua** word *huaca* (waca), which denotes a sacred site or object. **Huaco retratos**, or **portrait vessels**, refer to ceramics molded in the shape of realistically rendered human faces. They are particularly well known among the **Moche**. The Spanish term ***huaquero*** (someone who looks for huacos) applies to individuals who are **looters** of prehistoric artifacts.

HUACO (WACO) RETRATO. Spanish name for **portrait vessels**: a **ceramic** vessel modeled in the form of a human head. Examples come from the **Moche** and **Tiwanaku** cultures. They usually represent prominent (male) individuals, often with large circular ear ornaments or earplugs (likely representing what the Spanish chroniclers called ***orejones*** or "long ears") or lip ornaments (**tembetá**) and headdresses, in Moche and Tiwanaku ceramics. *See also* TUPURAYA.

HUAJJE. Middle **Formative** political unit on the northwestern shores of Lake Titicaca, Peru, in the area of the present-day city of Puno.

HUÁNUCO PAMPA. Large **Inka** site in the Peruvian highlands. Huánuco Pampa was built by the Inka along the main highland road to serve as an administrative center. The site has hundreds of **pirca** enclosures grouped in neighborhoods. In its surroundings there are hundreds of **qolcas** for storage of tribute goods. The site is dominated by a huge plaza, which contains an **ushnu**.

HUAQUERO. Spanish term for **looter**. *See also* HUACO.

HUARGO CAVE. Late Pleistocene site located at approximately 4,100 meters above sea level in Huánuco in the central Peruvian highlands. Faunal remains of horse, paleolama, and *Scelotherium*, all extinct, were found associated with the material evidence of human occupation.

HUARICOTO. Early ceremonial center of the **Kotosh Tradition** in the Callejón de Huaylas in the central highlands of Peru. The site is situated at 2,750 meters above sea level and was a ritual center for nearly two thousand years, beginning in the Late Preceramic around 2200 BC. Its **architecture** consists of one-room structures, plastered floors, and a central hearth. This suggests that the rituals were limited to small groups of people and focused on fire and burning of offerings. In the site there are remains of maritime elements (shells and fish bones).

HUARPA. Early Intermediate culture of the Ayacucho valley, southern Peru. Huarpa groups inhabited the valley prior to the emergence of the **Wari** state, from AD 200 to 600. They formed a **señorío** with a strong **agricultural** basis. The Huarpa constructed numerous terraces in the Ayacucho area.

HUENTELAUQUEN. Archaic culture of the central coast of Chile dated to 4500–2500 BC. In the southern sector of its occupation, it continued after 2500 BC. The typical sites are **shell middens** (**concheros**), such as Huentelauquén, El Teniente, and **Bahía** Obispito. Apart from collecting shells, they were **hunters** of **guanaco** and other terrestrial animals. One of their characteristic elements are polished stone artifacts with geometric forms (squares, pentagons, and so on).

HUMAITÁ. Early Holocene tradition from the upper La Plata basin (southern Brazil and northeastern Argentina). It is referred to as Altoparanaense in northeastern Argentina and Cuareimense in northern Uruguay. The earliest Humaitá occupation dates to 6500 BC. Humaitá characteristic stone tools are large bifaces and scrapers, while projectile points are lacking. Among its polished stone artifacts are **zooliths**. In more recent times, Humaitá groups adopted the use of pottery while preserving their stone tool industry. This **ceramic** tradition is called Taquara (Brazil) and Eldoradense (northeastern Argentina). The **Tres de Mayo Cave** represents a site with both Altoparanaense and Eldoradense occupations. *See also* PLANÁLTICA TRADITION.

HUNTING. In many South American societies, hunting was an important means of subsistence. The earliest inhabitants relied on the hunting of species of animals that have long been extinct (*see* **megafauna**). In more recent times, **guanaco** and deer were among the most common hunted terrestrial mammals. South American people utilized several hunting techniques and **weapons**. One of the hunting techniques described by the Spanish is the **chaco**. *See also*

BOLA; CAMELIDS; INCA CUEVA 4; ÑANDÚ; TEQUENDAMA; YURAJ MOLINO.

HURIN. According to Spanish documents, the city of **Cuzco** was divided into two parts, halves, or moieties. Hurin, a **Quechua** word, is the name that the **Inka** gave to the lower half of the city of Cuzco, following the Andean dual division system. It also refers to the lower or "left" half of the Andean moiety system. The term for the other half was **Hanan**. *See also* TOMEBAMBA.

HURT, WESLEY R. (1917–1997). After doing early research in North American sites, in 1956 Hurt led an expedition to investigate sites in the **Lagoa Santa** region of Brazil. In 1958–1959 he taught at the University of Paraná in Brazil and conducted collaborative investigations of **sambaquís**, which marked the beginning of Hurt's practice of working and publishing with international scholars. He organized projects in Brazil, Colombia, and Uruguay, concentrating on preceramic occupations. Hurt published *O Sambaquí do Macedo* with Ondemar Blasi (1960); *Tradition Itaparica* (1969); *The Interrelationships Between the Natural Environment and Four Sambaquís, Coast of Santa Catarina, Brazil* (1974); and *Preceramic Sequences in the El Abra Rockshelters, Colombia* (1976). In 1985, Hurt was awarded the Society of American Archaeology 50th Anniversary Award for Outstanding Contributions to American Archaeology.

– I –

ICHMA POLITY (SEÑORÍO DE ICHMA). This polity extended over the Rimac and Lurín valleys in the central coast of Peru. It was based at the important ceremonial center of **Pachacamac** from the Middle Horizon to the time of the Spanish conquest.

IGLESIA DE LOS INDIOS. *See* LA RINCONADA.

ILLAPA. Andean thunder or lightning god associated with the south-central highlands. This **deity** controlled all celestial forces, such as thunder, rain, hail, and the rainbow. In his representations he is pictured using a sling. During Colonial times, Illapa was associated with Saint George.

INCA CUEVA 4. Cave site located on the limit between the **puna** and the upper Andean valleys (Jujuy, Argentina) at 3,800 meters above sea level. Inca Cueva 4 has occupations dating to the Late Pleistocene and Early Holocene. The earliest occupation was dated to between 8600 and 7200 BC and includes postholes, refuse pits, and hearths. Inca Cueva 4 served as a station in the nomadic cycle of highland groups. **Hunting** focused mainly on *vizcacha de la sierra* (*Lagidium* sp.)—a large rodent—which was the animal most commonly consumed at the site, followed by **camelids** and deer. Inca Cueva 4 is also characterized by preserved **rock art** consisting of paintings in red, ochre, yellow, and black. Inca Cueva 4 has the earliest evidence of the use of **hallucinogenic cebil** (*Anadenanthera* sp.), around 2130–2080 BC.

INCISED AND PUNCTATE HORIZON. Ceramics decorated with modeled ornaments, incision, and punctation are found in archaeological sites in a vast area of the northern lowlands of South America in sites that date after AD 500. Sites of the Incised and Punctate Horizon are large villages with **terras pretas**. The last two phases of the **Arauquinoid** sequence correspond to this horizon, as does the **Valloid** series. **Santarem** in the lower Amazon is an important representative of this horizon. *See also* FALDAS DE SANGAY.

INDIA MUERTA. Oldest **cerrito** in the Laguna Merin basin of eastern Uruguay. India Muerta dates to 3400 BC. The oldest occupations are associated with the **Umbú Tradition**. Two other radiometric dates obtained for the site are 1500 BC and 700 BC.

INGAPIRCA (HATUN CAÑAR). Large **Inka** settlement in the southern highlands of Ecuador, located at 3,200 meters above sea level. The Inka built this settlement on a preexisting Cañari town. The most important building is the so-called Temple of the Sun, which is of elliptical form.

INKA (ALSO SPELLED INCA). Name of the largest empire in pre-Columbian America and of its maximum leader (Sapay Inka). The

Inka empire was the last of the great states and/or empires that extended through the highlands of Peru in pre-Columbian times. Many of the organizational features can be traced to earlier societies. Inka government was based in the capital city of **Cuzco**, and included a population of several million inhabitants. When the Spaniards arrived to Peru in 1532, they were deeply impressed by the socioeconomic and **political organization** of the Inka and compared them to the Roman Empire. The Inka expanded during the Late Horizon, dated approximately from 1470 to 1532 AD, conquering other states including the **Chimú** and smaller political units of agriculturally-based or **pastoralist** groups of the Pacific coast, mountain valleys, and highlands. The Inka controlled the region that extends from central Chile and central Argentina to southern Colombia, some 4000 kilometers long, which was united by an extensive road system (**Inkañan**).

The empire was known as the **Tawantinsuyu**, which in **Quechua** means "the four parts" (tawa [four], suyu [part]). The Inka built administrative centers along the main roads, including **Huánuco Pampa**, **Inkallajta**, **Tumipampa**, and **Hatun Xauxa**. They also transformed mountainous regions into a vast agricultural domain with terraces and **irrigation** canals. Conquered people were integrated into the empire through taxation in labor, either in **agriculture**, textile manufacture, mining, construction, or military services. Tribute goods were stored in warehouses (**qolca**) located in different parts of the empire and were used to provide welfare for the local populations, the army, and the elites. Inka society was based on traditional Andean principles of reciprocity and redistribution. After conquest, lands were divided between the state, state and local **religion**, and the community, and new leaders known as *kurakas* were placed in order to reorganize the local society. Inka state religion was centered around **Inti**, the sun god, and the cult of major **wacas** such as the **Island of the Sun**, **Koricancha**, and **Pachacamac**. The frontiers of the empire were protected with **fortifications**, which were usually located along the eastern flanks of the Andes. The largest Inka fortifications are found at **Pambamarca**.

One of the Inka elements that is most known is the **architecture**, characterized by the presence of massive masonry walls and trapezoidal doorways that have survived earthquakes. Walls usually have niches, in some of which **mummy** bundles were displayed on ceremonial occasions. Some of the most relevant Inka sites in the Cuzco area are **Kachiqata**, **Machu Picchu**, **Moray**, **Ollantaytambo**, **Pisaq**, **Rumiqolca**, **Sacsaywaman**, **Tampumachay**, and **Yucay**.

The arrival of Francisco Pizarro to the town of Tumbes in 1532 marked the beginning of the end of the Inka Empire. Pizarro and his army moved along the Inkañan to the city of **Cajamarca**, where they met the Inka **Atawallpa** and took him prisoner. They later judged him and executed Atawallpa in Cuzco. Some members of the Inka royal family escaped to the eastern Andean valleys, where they formed an independent state that lasted until 1571. *See also* ACONCAGUA; CAPACOCHA; CERRO AZUL; CERRO GRANDE DE LA COMPAÑÍA; CHENA; CHOTUNA; CHUCARIPUPATA; CHUCUITO; CORTADERAS COMPLEX; DIAGUITA; FARFÁN; INGAPIRCA; INTIHUATANA; KALLANKA; KILLKE; LA PAYA; LLAMA; LLULLAILLACO; MANCO CAPAC; MAPUCHE; MAUKALLAQTA; NEVADO DEL ACONQUIJA; ÑAMLAP; ONA; PANAQA; PEINE; POTRERO DE PAYOGASTA; PUKARA DE ANDALGALÁ; PUMPU; QOLCA; QUECHUA; QUISPISISA; RANCHILLOS; RAQCHI; SAMAIPATA; SANTA MARÍA; SHINCAL; TAMBERÍA DEL INCA; TAMBO COLORADO; TAMBO VIEJO; TASTIL; TILCARA; TOLOMBÓN; TÚCUME; USHNU; VIÑA DEL CERRO; WATUNGASTA.

INKALLAJTA. Large **Inka** site in Cochabamba, Bolivia. Cochabamba was an important **maize**-producing area for the Inka. This large site was an administrative center for the province, with important Inka-style constructions. One of the main **architectural** features in Inkallajta is a **kallanka**.

INKAÑAN. **Inka** road system that was extensive in breadth and an impressive engineering feat. It was based on preexistent roads but was expanded by the Inka on a much larger scale. There was one main coastal road and one main highland road, both of which were interconnected by secondary roads. Cities, smaller towns, **tampus**, and other Inka constructions were located along these roads. Usually, the roads passed through the middle of towns and cities and were instrumental in facilitating Inka rule and administration.

INTERMEDIATE AREA. In South America, the Intermediate Area includes the coast and highlands of Ecuador and Colombia as well as the westernmost part of Venezuela. It also includes the southern part of Central America. The term *Intermediate Area* was originally defined on the basis of a typological negation: there were no state societies in this region as there were to the north (Mesoamerica) and to the south (central Andes). Societies in the Intermediate Area share certain broad similarities, however, in sociopolitical organization: they were mostly organized as small-scale political units or **chiefdoms**; moreover, this region is distinguished by diversity in geography, climate, and cultural development. Even though there was a lack of political unity on a broad scale, there was extensive interregional communication in this zone, as demonstrated by roads and the presence of widely exchanged exotic elements and the presence of merchants known as **mindalá**. The main cultural patterns of the region emerged around 1500 BC. *See also* BAHÍA; GUANGALA; ISLA DE LA PLATA; ISLA DE PUNA; JADEITE; JAMA-COAQUE STYLE; LA CHIMBA; LA ELVIRA; LA EMERENCIANA; LA PALESTINA; LOS ESTEROS; MACHALILLA; MALAGANA CHIEFDOM; MALAMBO CULTURE; MANTEÑO CULTURE; MILAGRO-QUEVEDO; NORTHWESTERN LITHIC TRADITION; PANZALEO; PEÑA ROJA; PIRINCAY; PUEBLITO; PUERTO HORMIGA; QUIMBAYA; REAL ALTO; REGIONAL DEVELOPMENT PERIOD; SAN AGUSTÍN; SAN ISIDRO; SAN JACINTO 1; SAN LORENZO DEL MATE; SINÚ; TAIRONA; TIBITÓ; TIERRADENTRO; TOLA; VALDIVIA.

INTI. Andean sun **deity** that was an important element of **Inka** state **religion**. The Inka ruler was believed to be his descendant in what is a strong case of divine **kinship** in pre-Columbian America. Inti was venerated in important state shrines built throughout the empire, with its center in the **Koricancha**, where Inti was represented by a golden plate. Another important Inti shrine was in the **Island of the Sun**, where the sun was believed to have appeared. *See also* INTIHUATANA.

INTIHUASI. Quechua term that means "house of the sun." It also designates a large cave site with several occupations dating from 6000 BC to AD 1500 located in the hills of northern San Luis, central

Argentina. Intihuasi represents one of the first preceramic sites in South America to have been radiocarbon dated in the 1950s. At Intihuasi, there are a vast number of stone tools in all layers, particularly of leaf-shaped (**Ayampitín**) and triangular projectile points, mostly manufactured from local raw materials. Several elements have a north Patagonian origin (**obsidian** from **Cerro Huenul**, **incised** stone plaques), suggesting that the people living in the area had relations with others living several hundred kilometers to the south.

INTIHUATANA. **Architectural** feature related to the **Inka** cult of the sun (**Inti**). The intihuatana is a standing stone that was used to record astronomical observations and solar rituals. There is an intihuatana in **Machu Picchu** and there are others at other Inka sites.

IRRIGATION. Irrigation is the transfer of water by artificial means from a natural source to cultivated fields. Pre-Columbian irrigation in South America developed in coastal valleys and the highlands of the Andes. The **Chicama-Moche (La Cumbre) intervalley canal system** was the largest in the New World prior to the nineteenth century. The northernmost example is the Late Period **Tairona** of northern Colombia. *See also* CHIMÚ; OMEREQUE; U-SHAPED CENTERS.

ISKANWAYA. Late Period planned site of the **Mollo Culture** with stone **architecture** in the Llika valley northeast of Lake Titicaca, Bolivia. The total surface area of the site is around thirteen hectares. Rectangular houses with windows and niches are grouped around open areas or patios. Streets follow an east-west direction.

ISLA DE LA PLATA. An island along the coast of Ecuador which served as a port of **trade** for harvesting of seashells.

ISLA DE PUNA. Center of ***Spondylus*** production on the coast of Ecuador.

ISLAND OF THE MOON. An island in Lake Titicaca, Bolivia. The earliest archaeological sites date to the Middle **Formative Period**. Iñak Uyu is the main site found on the island. It is composed of a large rectangular patio with niched rooms around three of its sides with the open side facing north. There are some elaborate **Tiwanaku ceramics** and gold and silver objects, which suggest that Tiwanaku elites used the island for ritual purposes. Stepped-diamond motifs carved in stone on both islands are similar to those at the site of Tiwanaku.

ISLAND OF THE SUN. An important **Inka religious** and **pilgrimage** center in the southern sector of Lake Titicaca, Bolivia. According to Inka tradition, the sun had emerged from the lake on that island, where a rock outcrop—Titikala—is located (the main sanctuary). On the island, there are **Formative** to Inka settlements and a Tiwanaku ritual site (**Chucaripupata**), suggesting that the ritual importance of the island can be traced back hundreds of years before the Inka. Both the Tiwanaku and Inka made ceremonial offerings to the lake, including stone boxes and gold **keros**.

ITAIPÚ. Ceramic tradition from the region of Rio de Janeiro, Brazil.

ITAPARICA TRADITION. Preceramic tradition of central and northern Brazil. Sites of this tradition appear in lowlands and highlands of the Brazilian plateau in open air and caves as well as in rock shelters in Minas Gerais, Goias, Pernambuco, and Piauí. These sites date from 9000 BC to after 6000 BC. Some of the caves and rock shelters have paintings (**rock art**). Itaparica cultures used mostly unifacial tools while projectile points are rarely found in Itaparica sites. According to the recovered faunal and botanical remains, Itaparica groups exploited forest, riverine, and swamp environments. Stone tools include scrapers, perforators, knives, choppers, **bola** stones, and grinders. Some Itaparica assemblages resemble those of the **Caroní Tradition** in the lower Orinoco.

ITARARÉ. South Brazilian **ceramic** tradition that dates to the end of the first millennium AD. Sites are located mainly in the state of Santa Catarina and consist primarily of large village sites with roughly forty houses or less. Houses are circular and have hearths. Itararé groups were **hunters** of deer, peccary, anteater, capybara (a rodent), and armadillo. They also fished and collected mollusks. Itararé stone tools include scrapers, choppers, and ground tools, while projectile points were made of bone. Itararé ceramics were produced in four different colors and are rarely decorated. *See also* PLANÁLTICA TRADITION.

IVAÍ TRADITION. Preceramic tradition of the middle Uruguay and middle Paraná rivers (Brazil, Argentina, and Paraguay) that dates to between 5000 and 1500 BC. Sites are situated in the vicinity of forested areas and close to rapids or waterfalls. Ivaí subsistence was based on river fishing, **hunting**, and gathering. Flaked tools are large and unifacial, consisting of nonstandardized forms with limited retouch. Ground and polished tools such as **bolas** and grinding tools are present in some sites while bifacial points are entirely lacking. Pebbles with **incised** decoration known in Spanish as *placas grabadas* have also been recovered from Ivaí sites.

– J –

JADEITE. Together with shells, **obsidian**, rock crystals, blue stones, and other green stones such as **malachite**, jadeite was **traded** over long distances in South America. Jadeite is a sodium aluminum silicate and is rare in nature. In Ecuador, there are some potential sources of jadeite in the southern highlands. Jadeite artifacts, dating to between 1300 and 1000 BC, were found at a Catamayo site near Loja (Ecuador). Jadeite ornaments also characterize **Tairona** burials. *See also* LIMONCARRO.

JAGUAR (*FELIS ONCA*). The jaguar is the largest of the felines in South America and an important animal in South American pre-Columbian **religions**. Many indigenous groups of lowland and highland South America depicted jaguar figures in different artistic and iconographic media (**ceramics**, stone, textile, bone, **metallurgy**). Powerful human figures are often distinguished in South American religious iconography by jaguar elements (claws, teeth, and so on), or with jaguar masks. The prevalence of jaguar imagery in Andean art is evident in **Chavín**, **Tiwanaku**, **Aguada**, and **San Agustín**. The jaguar appears to have been related to shamanistic forms of ritual activity. *See also* MARKETS; TUMACO.

JAMA-COAQUE STYLE. Important artistic style from the Manabí region of northern coastal Ecuador. Jama-Coaque developed from approximately 200 BC to AD 600 and is closely related to the **Bahía** culture. This style extended even later in some regions, lasting until the sixteenth century AD. Jama-Coaque society was organized as **chiefdoms** based in large ceremonial centers. **Warfare** played an important role in Jama-Coaque society and political economy. Jama-Coaque economy, as that of Bahía, was grounded in **agriculture**, **hunting**, and plant gathering. **Obsidian** from the Ecuadorian highlands is present in several Jama-Coaque sites. It could have been **traded** for ***Spondylus***.

JAMPATILLA. Obsidian source located in the province of Ayacucho, southern Peruvian highlands. It seems that its exploitation was local and limited to the Middle Horizon Period, AD 600–1000. Jampatilla obsidian was found in **Wari** sites but not at the capital itself.

JANABARRIU PHASE AND STYLE. Iconography associated with classic **Chavín**, 400–200 BC. In this phase, the site of **Chavín de Huantar** reached its maximum size (forty-two hectares) by including a small residential area. This residential area had sectors for different social groups, elites and commoners, and some sectors were inhabited by craft specialists. Janabarriu **ceramics** show strong continuity from earlier periods.

JAUJA. *See* HATUN XAUXA.

JEWELRY. A deep knowledge of source location and manufacturing techniques allowed South American indigenous groups to produce personal ornaments of socially accepted high value. In many cases, these objects were found associated to most segments of the society, without distinctions of gender and age. In other cases, as among the **Chibcha**, highly valued objects such as those made of gold were limited to members of the elite. Among the earliest settlers of South America, ornaments were made of shells. Among **agriculturalists**, we see numerous colored stones, some transparent, others opaque, and the use of metals, including gold and silver. *See also* AMBER; JADEITE; MALACHITE; METALLURGY; PLATINUM; SERPENTINITE; SODALITE; TRADE; TURQUOISE.

JINCAMOCCO. Large **Wari** settlement located in the Carhuarazo valley southwest of the modern city of Ayacucho and of the archaeological site of Wari. This site is adjacent to major roads and its importance was related to **maize** production. Large portions of the valley were terraced in order to increase **agricultural** production during Wari times. Jincamocco was established around AD 650, apparently by bringing dispersed rural populations to the valley floor. It occupied some 17–18 hectares and has a typical Wari rectangular enclosure that measures 130 by 260 meters.

JISKAIRUMOKO. Late preceramic/Early **Formative** site in the Ilave drainage in the Titicaca basin, Peru. During the late preceramic occupation, people consumed *Chenopodium* sp., but it is uncertain if these were domesticated or not. An important finding is a gold necklace that dates to 1740 BC, probably the oldest gold artifact discovered in the region.

– K –

KACHIQATA. Inka quarry located in the Urubamba Valley in southern Peru and exploited at the time of the Spanish conquest. Stone from Kachiqata was used to build the site of **Ollantaytambo** in the Urubamba Valley. Several large blocks were abandoned in the ramps and roads of the quarry, probably after the first arrival of the Spaniards to the site. Another important Inka quarry is **Rumiqolca**.

KALASASAYA. 1. **Aymara** term for precinct or platform built with carved stone (*kala* or *qala* translates to *stone*). These structures are located in large sites of the Titicaca basin and are associated with the Tiwanaku polity (**Tiwanaku, Khonko Wankane**). The largest example in Tiwanaku's civic-ceremonial center measures 135 by 130 meters. The walls are constructed of large stone slabs with smaller stones in between. 2. A **ceramic** style, also known as Tiwanaku I, originally found at the Kalasasaya of Tiwanaku and dating to the Middle **Formative Period** (800–200 BC). Similar ceramics were also found in elite areas of the contemporaneous site of **Pukara**.

KALLAMARKA. Formative and **Tiwanaku** site located in the Tiwanaku valley, Bolivia. The site is characterized by its stone walls, which include a **kalasasaya**.

KALLANKA. Inka architectural structure present in many sites distributed throughout the empire. These sites include **Tomebamba** (Ecuador), **Raqchi** (Peru), **Inkallajta** (Bolivia), **Nevado del Aconquija**, **Potrero de Payogasta**, **Shincal**, **Watungasta**, **Tambería del Inca**, and **Ranchillos** (one of the southernmost). The last five are in northwest and central Argentina. Kallankas are rectangular structures that were used as warehouses and textile workshops. They were also used for **religious** celebrations in **Cuzco** and other regional capitals. *See also* SAMAIPATA.

KARWA. Site located close to the Paracas Necropolis on the south coast of Peru. At Karwa, two hundred painted textiles with **Chavín** iconography were **looted**. Most of the textiles have representations of the **Staff God**, and some have a female **deity** associated with the **cotton** plant known as the **Staff Goddess**.

KERO (QUERO). Large beakers that were used in Andean ritual drinking, usually in pairs. Keros were made of wood, **ceramics**, stone, or metal and the exteriors were usually decorated. Kerus were found in northern Chile (**San Pedro de Atacama** and Arica), **Aguada**, **Pukara**, **Tiwanaku**, **Inka**, **Tupuraya**, **Viluco**, **Ansilta** (Ansilta keros have one handle), and highland Ecuador (**Tacalzhapa** I). In the central and southern Andes, keros date to after AD 700. In San Pedro de Atacama, keros usually have modeled animal or human figures attached to their upper body. *See also* BATÁN GRANDE; BENNETT MONOLITH; CHICHA; CONCHU PATA; PUQUISTYLE; QEYA.

KHONKO WANKANE. Large Late **Formative** and **Tiwanaku** site located in the Desaguadero River basin of the Bolivian highlands. The Desaguadero River valley is very flat and is presently dedicated to animal husbandry, with very little emphasis on **agriculture**. The site of Khonko Wankane is on an elevated spur. It was first identified by the presence of several **monoliths** and traces of surface **architecture**. Three stone-walled temples or **kalasasayas** dominate the civic ceremonial core of this site. Until recently, very little was known about the site due to the lack of systematic excavations.

KIDDER, ALFRED II (1885–1963). An American archaeologist with a long trajectory in North, Central, and South America, Kidder excavated in **Pukara** in 1939 and conducted a regional survey in the Titicaca basin in 1943. Among his published works on South America are *Archaeology of Northwestern Venezuela* (1944) and *Digging in the Titicaca Basin* (1956), in which he presented the first radiocarbon dates for the site of **Tiwanaku**.

KILLKE. Early pre-**Inka** and Inka Period (AD 1000–1400) **ceramic** style in the **Cuzco** valley. The Killke occupations represent the moment when the Inka were still a small local population, among others in the Cuzco valley, before their expansion outside of the valley. These sites were small villages. In the valley of Cuzco, Killke sites do not have **fortifications**, but forts on top of hills are common in Killke sites of the Lucre Valley and Urubamba. Killke ceramics are characterized by red and black geometric motifs.

KINSHIP. Individuals in all societies are related to others, their kin or relatives, with whom they are united by certain mutual rights and obligations. Kinship is the network of relatives. Compounds or residences around common areas or patios were the living quarters of extended families. In some residential areas, **tombs** were placed to connect the ancestors of the group with the living members, suggesting the concept of perpetuation of lineages and clans. DNA studies, chemical analysis, and the presence of ethnic markers including **cranial deformation** can help identify **family** relationships between members of multiple burials, as well as the presence of non-kin or foreigners.

KOANI PAMPA. Flat region on the southern shores of Lake Titicaca, Bolivia, north of **Tiwanaku**, where vast extensions of **sukakollos** (**raised fields**) and other **agricultural** features were constructed in pre-Columbian times. The largest settlement in the Koani Pampa is **Lukurmata**. There are several smaller sites among the sukakollos. These fields formed the basis of Tiwanaku's subsistence and political economy.

KORIABO. Cultural complex of the Late Prehistoric Period of coastal Guyane, Suriname, and Venezuela. Koriabo sites have been dated to between AD 1200 and 1750. One of its latest sites is located on a

1764 map. The Koriabo were good navigators and moved to the Caribbean islands. Koriabo sites are identified by a characteristic **incised-punctated ceramic**. Among the stone artifacts are zoomorphic pendants of polished green stones, which were produced and exchanged among many northern South American cultures. At the site of Kormontibo (Guyane), there is an abundance of polished stone axes, which suggests that the people there specialized in their manufacture.

KORICANCHA (CORICANCHA). Quechua name ("golden enclosure") for the temple of the sun in **Cuzco**, Peru, near the confluence of the city's two rivers. The Koricancha was one of the most important shrines in the **Inka** empire and formed the epicenter of the **Ceque system**. In its interior, there were representations of the main Inka gods, the sun and the moon, in gold, silver, and precious stones. Its wealth formed part of the ransom for **Atawallpa**. A portion of the original Inka temple has been incorporated into the Convent of Santo Domingo, and the finest surviving construction is a curved wall built of very carefully cut andesite blocks. *See also* RELIGION.

KOTOSH. Preceramic ceremonial center in the Huallaga Valley of central Peru. An important temple structure is the Temple of the Crossed Hands, built around 2000 BC. Sculpted clay panels with friezes of crossed human hands adorn a plastered wall of the temple. In the center of the temple is a shallow, stone-lined fire pit surrounded by large benches, connected to the outside of the structure by underground ventilation ducts. The fire pit was probably used in a highland rite that involved the burning of offerings, a common feature of the **Kotosh Religious Tradition**. These fire pits were found in highland sites on both the eastern and western slopes of the Andes. Charred remains include peppers, marine shells, bones, feathers, deer antlers, and rock crystal. A series of temples were built on top of the Temple of the Crossed Hands. *See also* MITO; SHILLACOTO.

KOTOSH RELIGIOUS TRADITION. Andean **religious** tradition that emerged in the central highlands of Peru during the Late Preceramic Period (circa 2000 BC). Two important sites were **Kotosh** and **La Galgada**. *See also* HUACALOMA; HUARICOTO; PIMAPIRU.

KROEBER, ALFRED L. (1876–1960). American anthropologist and archaeologist who conducted research in North and South America and other parts of the world and published books and articles on numerous topics including anthropological theory, linguistics, and ethnography. Among the publications based on his research in coastal Peru are *Archaeological Explorations in Peru* (1926), *Cultural Relations between North and South America* (1930), *Peruvian Archaeology in 1942* (1944), *Proto-Lima: a Middle Period Culture of Peru* (1954), and *Toward Definition of the Nazca Style* (1956). A posthumous book entitled *The Archaeology and Pottery of Nazca, Peru: Alfred Kroeber's 1926 Expedition*, coauthored with Donald Collier, was published in 1998.

KUÉLAP. Large site of the Chachapoyas culture dating to the Late Intermediate Period in the middle Marañón River in central Peru. The large, almost urban-scale, settlement is dominated by massive ramparts and is divided in two by a wall. Impressive circular towers (probably built for defensive purposes) and multistory stone buildings also characterize the **architectural** landscape of this large site.

KUNTUR WASI (LA COPA). Major ceremonial center located in the northern Peruvian highlands at 2,300 meters above sea level. Kuntur Wasi is considered an intrusion of the coastal **Cupisnique** and is renowned for its beautiful stone sculpture and gold artifacts. *See also* MONTE GRANDE; NORTH PERUVIAN HIGHLANDS FORMATIVE PERIOD.

– L –

LA BARCA. Formative Period site located thirty kilometers northwest of the city of Oruro in the highlands of Bolivia. With a date of 1735 BC, it is one of the earliest **Wankarani** sites. The La Barca **mound** is eight meters high and covers a surface of 0.60 hectares. The subsistence of La Barca inhabitants, as of those of other Wankarani sites, was based on herding, **hunting**, and fishing. **Camelids**, deer, birds, and fish were the main protein source for the inhabitants of this site.

LA CHIMBA. A multicomponent site in the highlands of northern Ecuador situated at 3,180 meters above sea level. The site was occupied during the **Formative** and post-Formative periods from 640 BC to AD 300: Middle Formative (640–390 BC), Late Formative (390 BC–AD 90), and post-Formative (AD 90–300). In the earliest occupations, **maize** and **potato** were cultivated, while **cotton** appeared in the middle part of the Middle Formative. **Oca** was first consumed in the Late Formative and the post-Formative. Botanical data, in general, were stable during the thousand years of occupation at the site.

LA ELVIRA. Late Pleistocene settlement located near the modern city of Popayán, Colombia. **Obsidian** from the **Río Hondo** source was used here, one of the earliest cases of obsidian use in South America.

LA EMERENCIANA. Late **Valdivia** ceremonial center in the province of El Oro on the southern coast of Ecuador. It was contemporaneous and similar in hierarchy spatial organization to **San Isidro** and **San Lorenzo del Mate**.

LA FLORIDA. One of the earliest **U-shaped ceremonial centers** of the central coast of Peru. La Florida is located in the Rimac valley. Its monumental **architecture** consists of clay and stone **pyramid** structures. The occupation began around 2000 BC, and the first **ceramics** appear in 1600 BC. The central **mound** is seventeen meters tall, framed by two wings or arms three to four meters high and some five hundred meters long. The open end of the U follows the same pattern as other temples: it faces northeast toward the Andean foothills. The subsistence of people living in La Florida was mainly of fish and shellfish, vegetables, and **guinea pig**.

LA GALGADA. Important ceremonial site of the **Kotosh Religious Tradition**. It is located at 1,100 meters above sea level on the Tablachaca River, a tributary of the Santa River, in central Peru. Most of the occupation (2400–1900 BC) dates to the Late Archaic or Late Preceramic. Two **mounds** and remains of some fifty domestic structures characterize the site: the residential **architecture** includes round and oval houses scattered around the mounds.

LA GRUTA. Open-air site located on an elevation on the left bank of the middle Orinoco, Venezuela. La Gruta is ten kilometers north of **Ronquín** and one kilometer south of **Corozal**. Layers of ash were found between 1 and 1.5 meters deep, including **budares** and **ceramics** of the **Zoned Hatchured Horizon**. *See also* CEDEÑOID.

LA MINA. The elaborate **tomb** of La Mina, situated at the foot of the peak of Cerro La Mina in the Jequetepeque Valley of northern Peru, was **looted** and subsequently salvage-excavated in the late 1980s. The tomb was found within a domestic settlement consisting of **shell middens**, hillside terraces, small constructions of **adobe** and cobbles, and dispersed cemeteries, dating to both the Preceramic and **Chimú** periods. The tomb consists of a spacious burial chamber (3.12 by 2.12 meters) dug into the bedrock of the hill and carefully built of thick walls of rectangular adobe bricks. Its interior walls were elaborately painted with **polychrome** murals consisting of interlocking volute motives within uniformly repeated squares. The chamber was roofed with cane, **algarroba** beams, and a capping layer of wide bricks. The tomb contained the jumbled remains of five men and **women** (a child, two adolescents, and two older women), but their rank and associations could not be determined due to the destruction wrought by looters. **Huaqueros** claimed to have looted a large number of Early **Moche** molded ceramics depicting supernatural beings, animals, and humans. Salvage excavations discovered an overlooked cache of fourteen vessels, six of which were exquisitely molded and finely painted. The fine artifacts and the high quality of the chamber point to the elevated status of the tomb's occupants.

LA MODERNA. Preceramic open-air site in the province of Buenos Aires, Argentina. Expedient flake tools of crystalline quartz and some curated tools of quartzite and **chert** were associated with **megafauna** (extinct giant armadillo). The dates for this occupation range from 5500 to 5000 BC.

LA PALESTINA. Preceramic (Late Pleistocene) open-air site in the municipality of Yondó, Middle Magdalena River, northeastern Colombia. It dates to 8400–8200 BC. Bifacial **chert** tools were recovered here.

El Fraile monolith, Kalasasaya, Tiwanaku (Bolivia). Martin Giesso.

Gateway of the Sun, Kalasasaya, Tiwanaku (Bolivia). Martin Giesso.

The Kalasasaya seen from the Akapana pyramid, Tiwanaku (Bolivia). Martin Giesso.

Mural, Huaca de la Luna, Moche, Peru. Edward Swenson, University of Lethbridge.

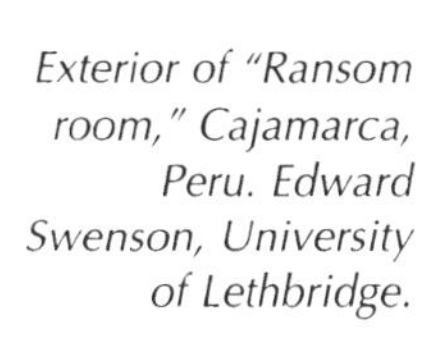

Exterior of "Ransom room," Cajamarca, Peru. Edward Swenson, University of Lethbridge.

Interior of "Ransom room," Cajamarca, Peru. Edward Swenson, University of Lethbridge.

Cerro Collor, Department of Cajamarca, Peru. Edward Swenson, University of Lethbridge.

Koricancha (Temple of the Sun), Cuzco, Peru. Martin Giesso.

Exterior wall of Koricancha (Temple of the Sun), Cuzco, Peru. Martin Giesso.

Koricancha (Temple of the Sun), Cuzco, Peru. Martin Giesso.

Sacsaywaman, Cuzco, Peru. Nora Bonnin, University of Illinois at Chicago.

Sacsaywaman, Cuzco, Peru. Nora Bonnin, University of Illinois at Chicago.

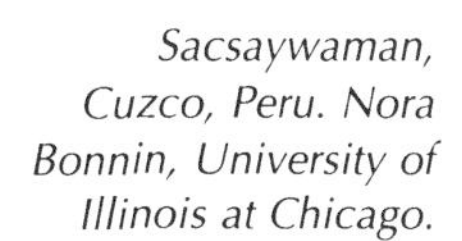

Sacsaywaman, Cuzco, Peru. Nora Bonnin, University of Illinois at Chicago.

Sacsaywaman, Cuzco, Peru. Nora Bonnin, University of Illinois at Chicago.

Fountain at Ollantaytambo, Peru. Martin Giesso.

Ollantaytambo, Peru. Nora Bonnin, University of Illinois at Chicago.

Central Axis, Ciudad Perdida, Colombia. Santiago Giraldo, Instituto Colombiano de Antropología e Historia–University of Chicago.

LA PALOMA. An Archaic fishing culture that emerged around 7000 BC and lasted until 3000 BC on the Pacific coast in central Peru. Inhabitants built small houses, round or oval in shape, with perishable materials and shallow foundations. Hearths were located inside the dwellings, although cooking also occurred outdoors. Storage areas and the practice of salting fish suggest that inhabitants lived permanently at La Paloma. Subsistence was based on seafood, mainly fish and sea mammals, although tubers (**oca**), fruits, and **algarroba** also constituted a portion of the diet. The overall health of the population was good, and individuals were relatively tall. Nevertheless, life expectancy was short: twenty-five years. Burials were flexed and tied in mats underneath the houses, accompanied with some grave goods. Communal **architectural** projects or monumental constructions appear to be lacking at this site. La Paloma is contemporaneous with and shares numerous traits of maritime adaptation with **Chinchorro**.

LA PAYA. Large Late Intermediate Period and Late Horizon site in the Calchaquí Valley, Salta, northwest Argentina. The **Inka** built an administrative center (Casa Morada) at La Paya in the middle of the existing town with numerous **pirca** walls. There is a niched hall built with unquarried stones at this site. Several high-status elements were found in **tombs**, suggesting that it was the residence of an Inka administrator.

LA PLATA ISLAND. Important sanctuary located along the central coast of Ecuador. This mountainous island, now a national park, was the focus of **pilgrimage** during the **Regional Development Period** (500 BC–AD 500).

LA RINCONADA (IGLESIA DE LOS INDIOS). Aguada ceremonial center located in the **Ambato** Valley, Catamarca, northwest Argentina. The site occupies 120 by 130 meters and is divided into three zones: **mound**, plaza, and residential areas. La Rinconada's main structure is a 23 by 13.5 by 3.60 meters high rectangular mound with masonry walls, oriented 10 degrees to the north as with the rest of the main constructions of the site. There are access ramps on the northern side of the settlement where the plaza (75 by 75 meters) is located and on its western side. La Rinconada is one of the most important Aguada cultic centers.

LA TOLITA. Large ceremonial center in coastal Ecuador characterized by dense residential structures configured around a series of **mounds**. Around AD 1, the site reached a size of approximately one square kilometer and consisted of forty **tolas** that reached up to five meters high. La Tolita was one of the main goldsmith centers in pre-Columbian Ecuador beginning around 400 BC.

LAGOA SANTA. Late Pleistocene site in Minas Gerais, Brazil. Some of the first findings of Pleistocene human remains in South America were made here in the mid nineteenth century. *See also* HURT, WESLEY R.; LUND, WILHELM PETER.

LAGUNA DEL MAULE. Main **obsidian** quarry area in central Chile exploited by groups from both sides of the Andes since at least AD 1. Numerous quarries are located on the eastern side of the Andean cordillera, with several large outcrops at high altitudes in Laguna del Maule (Chile). The obsidian quarry of **El Pehuenche** (Argentina) is at a short distance from this site.

LAMBAYEQUE. Also referred to as **Sican**. Culture that developed on the north coast of Peru after the collapse of **Moche** civilization: Early Sican (AD 700–900), Middle Sican (AD 900–1100), and Late Sican (AD 1100–1350). The major Lambayeque sites are **Batán Grande**, **Chotuna**, Apurlec, Jayanca, and **Túcume**. The end of Lambayeque or Sican is followed by the **Chimú** expansion.

Massive **pyramidal adobe** monuments, dominating large centers such as Túcume, Batán Grande, Apurlec, and Chotuna, exhibited certain continuities with the Late Moche Tradition and signal a comparable level of politico-religious specialization. Indeed, construction techniques such as marked adobes, first evident at **Pampa Grande**, were adopted from Late Moche architectural traditions. Moreover, settlement patterns, elite burials, expanded intervalley hydraulic systems, and high-quality **ceramic** and **metal** artifacts indicate continued social stratification, political centralization, organized division of labor, and craft specialization during the Middle and Late Sican periods.

The mythodynastic account of King **Ñamlap**, recorded by the Jesuit Miguel Cabello Balboa, is believed to relate to the establishment of the Lambayeque dynasty. It recounts the founding of the kingdom by a "foreign" king who journeyed with an elite entourage and specialized retainers on a fleet of balsa rafts proceeding from the north (possibly Ecuador). Ñamlap and his wife Ceterni built their palace at Chot, often identified with Chotuna near the coast in the Lower Lambayeque valley, and enshrined their main **deity** figure: Yampellec, represented by a green stone statue. The name Lambayeque is thought to derive from the appellation of this divinity. The dynastic record lists a series of nine rulers, including the final lord Fempellec, who was punished by devastating rains for moving Yampellec from its temple in Chot and engaging in sexual intercourse with the devil; he was executed by his people for the transgression, thus ending the dynasty. Cabello Balboa records that at the death of Ñamlap and his immediate heir, Cium, their demise was concealed from the populace by tales of their immortality; it was proclaimed that the kings sprouted wings and flew away. Cabello Balboa's account suggests that the founders of the dynasty were considered semidivine, and archaeologists often correlate winged depictions of the Sican Lord on ceramic and metal artifacts with Ñamlap himself (see below).

The Lambayeque cultural sphere is renowned not only for its imposing pyramids but also for its sophisticated and specialized metallurgical traditions. More finely-crafted gold, **copper**, and **tumbaga** (gold-copper alloy) artifacts have been **looted** from the ceremonial/mortuary site of Batán Grande (located in the middle La Leche drainage) than at any other archaeological site in the world. Exquisite **turquoise**-inlaid **tumi** knives depicting the winged Sican Lord have practically become a cliché of Andean prehistory, gracing the covers of Peruvian travel brochures (usually anachronistically juxtaposed with **Machu Picchu**). The discovery of elite burials at Huaca Loro and Huaca Ventanas, interred with **sacrificial** victims and literally tons of ***Spondylus*** shell, conus, finely-craft gold, and precious stone artifacts, points to a high level of social stratification and politico-religious specialization in Middle Sican polities.

The Lambayeque era is divided into three main periods (based on changing ceramic and architectural styles) following the fall of Moche V **Pampa Grande** and preceding the Chimú conquest of the north. The Early Sican Period (ESP—AD 700–900) corresponds to the Late Middle Horizon (Middle Horizon Epoch 2). It is argued, however, that the Early Sican Period was a turbulent and socially unstable era, likely characterized by highland encroachment and bearing the stamp of significant foreign influence, mainly **Wari**. On the basis of settlement data, the Lambayeque/La Leche heartland appears to have been in "political disarray," lacking a centralized authority and an organized regional economy. No large-scale corporate constructions were commissioned or built during this time, other than the Huaca La Merced pyramid in the Sican precinct of Batán Grande.

The Middle Sican Phase (AD 900–1100) is characterized by population increase, social agglomeration, intensified **bronze** smelting (arsenical copper), and the wide-scale construction of **religious architecture** at sites throughout the La Leche/Lambayeque region. Batán Grande emerged as the premier cult center of the Sican culture and towering adobe pyramids were built there. The reduced Sican Lord bottles ("Huaco Rey vessels"), depicting a stylized masked visage with comma-shaped eyes, were mass-produced during the Middle Sican era. The ubiquity of this representation makes obvious that the Sican Lord was the preeminent cult figure and symbol of the Middle Sican religious system. Huaco Rey probably symbolizes a revered, possibly semidivine architect of a "revitalization" or "messianic" movement that deliberately engineered the religious, cultural, and political changes marking the appearance of the Middle Sican symbolic repertoire and polity (thus "delivering" the populace from the instability of the preceding period).

The adobe temples of the Middle Sican Period excavated at Chotuna, Chornancap, Ucupe, and Batán Grande are visually arresting, distinguished by multiple painted columns, banks of **polychrome** wall murals, and large commanding platforms. They assume a characteristic T-shaped configuration dominated by a massive axial ramp, a shape somewhat common in much reduced scale at earlier Late Moche sites in the Jequetepeque Valley. Makers' marks on bricks do not suggest a *mit'a*-based form of labor mobilization, wherein mold shape, mark, and brick location directly correlate. Other scholars suggest a "sponsor model" wherein sponsors (elites, lineages, small polities) donated bricks bearing emblems of their identity ("logographic marks"), which served as testaments of the benefactor's religious devotion and respectable status.

Economic specialization is evident in the Middle and Late Sican, as exemplified by the production of arsenical copper *naipes* and pure copper *moneda hacha*, which were uniformly manufactured I-shaped and axe-shaped ingots that appear to have served as a rudimentary currency. **Trade** was managed by specialists, and the great quantities of *Spondylus* shell found in Middle Sican burials and caches indicate intense long-distance exchanges with Ecuador. Economic growth appears to have been accomplished by patronage of craft production and establishment of trade partners and secondary shrines. This inference is based on the lack of **fortified** sites and iconographic signifiers of **warfare**, along with the dispersed, multicentric distribution of ceremonial monuments in the Lambayeque area.

Late Sican (AD 1100–1350) marks an era of abrupt change. Middle Sican temples exhibit signs of a violent conflagration and abandonment (strata of intense burning episodes separate Middle and Late Sican contexts at many sites), the characteristic Sican Lord bottle is supplanted by more geometrically stylized wares, and the focus of power and institutionalized ceremonialism shifts from Batán Grande in the mid La Leche drainage to the massive lower valley city of El Purgatorio or Túcume. These developments are interpreted as a "concerted effort" to remove all vestiges of the preceding political and religious leadership of the Middle Sican. Important ceremonial monuments, population centers, and productive zones also arose at Apurlec and Jayanca in the northern La Leche region, interpreted by Shimada as a polity independent from the southern "La Leche-agro-industrial" complex dominated by Túcume. *See also* SAN JOSÉ DE MORO; STIRRUP BOTTLE; TALAMBO.

LAMING-EMPERAIRE, ANNETTE (1917–1977). French archaeologist who worked in Brazil and southern Patagonia. Her husband, Joseph Emperaire, was also an archaeologist. Laming published several works on general archaeology and the prehistory of France and South America. The latter include *A jazida José Vieira, Un Sitio Guaraní e Precerâmico* with Joseph Emperaire (1959); *La Grotte Fell et Autres Sites de la Région Volcanique de la Patagonie Chilienne* with J. Emperaire and H. Reichlen (1963); *Guia para o estudo das industrias liticas* (1967); *Los sitios arqueológicos de los archipiélagos de Patagonia Occidental* (1972); *Pecheurs des archipels et chasseurs des pampas* (1972); and *Le site de Marazzi en Terre de Feu* with D. Lavallée and R. Humbert (1972). After her death, *Le problème des origines* *americaines: théories, hypothèses, documents* (1980) was published, and her students and other scholars published a volume in her memory: *Coletânea de estudos em homenagem a Annette Laming-Emperaire* (1978).

LANCHA PACKEWAIA. Site on the Beagle channel, Tierra del Fuego, Argentina, dated to 4200–2300 BC. With **Tunel**, it is one of the southernmost archaeological sites of the Americas. Both sites are similar to **Englefield** in their lithic industry, while maritime mammals (seals) constituted the main source of protein at both settlements as well. *See also* PONSOMBY.

LAPA DO BOQUETE. Large cave with Early Holocene occupations in the upper San Francisco River, Minas Gerais, Brazil. Dates obtained for this settlement range from 10,000 to 7000 BC. The food remains discovered here include riverine shellfish, pecari, and deer.

LAPA VERMELHA IV. Late Pleistocene site in Minas Gerais, central Brazil. Evidence of human occupation associated with **megafauna** in the cave dates from 10,000 to 9000 BC.

LAS ANIMAS CULTURE. Culture that inhabited north-central Chile (Norte Chico) from approximately AD 800 to 1200. Social status differences are reflected in burials excavated at sites of this period. Strong cultural continuity is evident between the Las Animas and the later **Diaguita** culture after AD 1200. **Copper** and silver **metallurgy**, manifest in recovered personal ornaments and tools, appears for the first time in the region during this period. Textiles of **camelid** wool, manufactured with stone and wooden **spindle whorls**, are also diacritics of the Las Animas culture. Stemmed and unstemmed triangular and leaf-shaped stone projectile points were also present. *See also* EL MOLLE COMPLEX.

LAS CONCHAS. Preceramic (Archaic) site on the north coast of Chile located in the vicinity of **Tiliviche**. The term Las Conchas also applies to other sites with similar characteristics. The earliest occupations were dated to 7700 BC and are associated with a great amount of maritime food remains. Fragments of a fish net of the same age make it one of the earliest in South America. Some of the earliest evidence in South America for the use of **hallucinogenic substances** (*Banisteropis* sp.) has been documented at Las Conchas.

LAS HALDAS. Late preceramic site in the Casma Valley, Peru, contemporaneous with **El Paraíso** and **Cerro Sechín**. Las Haldas is one of the earliest examples of corporate **architecture** in the Andes. Structure 1 was built using large standing slabs with smaller blocks in between, an architectural technique used in other monumental constructions of the coast and highlands in later periods. The site was abandoned rapidly and later reoccupied by people who built houses on top of the main **mounds**. The Las Haldas inhabitants subsisted on a diet based on marine products, including mollusks, sea mammals, birds, and shallow-water and deep-water fish. Cultivated plants such as **maize**, beans, squash, and avocado also supplemented the diet. **Cotton** and gourds were also cultivated.

LAS MERCEDES. Culture in the lowland valleys in Salta and Santiago del Estero, northern Argentina, which first appeared around AD 200 and developed until the Colonial Period. Their subsistence was based on a combination of **agriculture**, **hunting**, fishing, and gathering. The main elements of the diet were **maize** and squash, **guanaco**, **ñandú**, reptiles, amphibians, and fruits of the **algarroba** and **chañar**. Villages, including the type site of El Veinte (AD 800–1200), were built on top of *albardones* (mounds formed mainly by river deposits). Secondary burials (the body is defleshed and the bones are wrapped up in a bundle) placed in large **funerary urns** were common in settlements associated with the Las Mercedes ceramic style. This style exhibits Andean and tropical lowland cultural elements.

LAS PIRCAS CULTURE. This culture thrived in the Middle Zaña Valley of northern Peru and dates to between 6500 and 4500 BC. Low earth ceremonial **mounds**, semi-domesticated crops, and exotic elements are associated with this cultural complex.

LAS VEGAS SITE 80. One of the Las Vegas preceramic sites in coastal Ecuador. This site is located on a low hill and was inhabited from 6000 to 4500 BC. A cemetery was identified here. *See also* NORTHWESTERN LITHIC TRADITION.

LATHRAP, DONALD W. (1927–1990). An important and influential scholar of lowland South American archaeology. He published *The Upper Amazon* (1970), *Ancient Ecuador: Culture, Clay and Creativity 3000–300 BC* (1975), and numerous articles, such as "The Antiquity and Importance of Long-distance Trade Relationships in the Moist Tropics of Pre-Columbian South America" (1973); "Summary or Model Building: How Does One Achieve a Meaningful Overview of a Continent's Prehistory" (1973); "Más evidencias sobre el Desarrollo de la Cultura Selva Tropical en la Costa Norte de Colombia, durante el primer y segundo milenio antes de Cristo" with D. Foster (1975); and "Our Father the Cayman, Our Mother the Gourd: Spinden Revisited, or a Unitary Model for the Emergence of Agriculture in the New World" (1977).

LAURICOCHA. Cave sites around the Lauricocha Lake in the upper Marañón valley in central Peru. Leaf-shaped projectile points found here in stratigraphic contexts in the 1950s, and later in other parts of the Andes, take their name from this site. These caves were first inhabited around 8000 BC. Several **tombs** of adults and children excavated at Lauricocha indicate that its early inhabitants practiced **cranial deformation** and used necklaces with **turquoise** beads. The occupation of the Lauricocha caves extends until the early centuries AD. *See also* ANCON; PAIJÁN; PURIPICA-1; TILIVICHE; VISCACHANI.

LAYZÓN. 1. Culture that developed in the Cajamarca basin of the northern Peruvian Andes from 250 BC to AD 0. It is believed that **Cajamarca** kaolin **ceramics** (plates and bowls with geometric designs) derive from Layzón. 2. A large ceremonial site associated with elaborate stone masonry in the Cajamarca basin. *See also* MONTE GRANDE; NORTH PERUVIAN HIGHLANDS FORMATIVE PERIOD.

LICAPA. Licapa was an important **Moche** site distinguished by characteristic **adobe pyramid mounds** in the Chicama valley. Dualistic organization of ceremonial **architecture** is apparent here. *See also* HUACA EL BRUJO.

LIMA CULTURE (NIVERÍA CULTURE). Early Intermediate Period culture (AD 1–500) from the central coast of Peru. The main site is **Maranga**, which probably represented the center of the polity. Most of the Lima sites are covered by the modern city of Lima. Chamber-and-fill construction technique originated in Lima sites. Lima culture is also characterized by multiple ceremonial centers.

LIMONCARRO. Limoncarro is located in the Jequetepeque Valley of the north coast of Peru twenty kilometers inland on the lower south side of Cerro Calera. The principal surviving temple is built primarily of stone and mud mortar (once covered in fine plaster) as well as smaller quantities of conical **adobe** bricks. It consists of a three-tiered central platform, 5 meters high, which is flanked by lower **mounds** only 1.6 meters high. Together, the three platforms assume a characteristically **U-shaped** form and surround a rectangular plaza 500 square meters in area. Adobe friezes and the remnants of colonnades were further identified here, and recent excavations exposed monumental adobe friezes of felines in profile along the inner walls of the lower platforms. Moreover, beautifully carved **jadeite** artifacts and steatite bowls with complex iconography were uncovered from a subsidiary mound during road construction in the 1960s. One depicts a carved supernatural arachnid associated with vegetal attributes holding a decapitated head in its claw and at least ten ingested heads in its stomach. Limoncarro represents the most elaborate **Cupisnique** ceremonial center in Jequetepeque and is believed to have been a complex and varied settlement characterized by a large domestic zone and subsidiary ritual monuments (the majority which have been destroyed by the expansion of the **Cajamarca** roadway and **agricultural** development) that occupied an area of one by two kilometers. The elaborate temples probably served as the premier node of ritual and ideological production for much of the lower Jequetepeque Valley.

LITORAL (LITORALEÑA) TRADITION. This tradition is defined by **sambaquí** builders of the central and southern coasts of Brazil.

The Litoral Tradition represents an early form of adaptation to marine coastal environments. The first sambaquís can be dated to around 7000 BC, extending until the first century AD.

LLAMA (*LAMA GLAMA*). One of the two domesticated **camelids** in the Andes. Llamas were the main source of protein, wool, fuel, and **transportation** in the central and southern Andes. Llamas were probably domesticated in the central or southern Peruvian highlands and were introduced into highland Ecuador in the last centuries BC. The llama was introduced into central Chile by the **Inka** after AD 1450. Llama caravans were very important in the transportation of goods along the coast and between coastal and highland communities.

LLOLLEO. (Pronounced Yo-yeo.) Culture from the coast and valleys of central Chile dated to between AD 100 and 900. Llolleo **ceramics** were also found in Mendoza and Neuquén (Argentina). Settlements are small, suggesting that they were formed by a single extended **family**. Houses were constructed of **quincha** and **funerary urns** were buried in domestic areas. No evidence of domesticated plants or animals have been identified at Llolleo sites. Llolleo subsistence was based on a wide spectrum of **hunting**, gathering, and/or fishing activities. **Cranial deformation** was varied but limited to a small number of individuals. *See also* EL INDÍGENO.

LLULLAILLACO. (Pronounced Yule-yai-yaco.) A **high-altitude Inka** sanctuary site, Llullaillaco is the highest archaeological site in the world. It is situated on one of the highest Andean peaks and volcanoes in the world on the border between Argentina and Chile in the dry **puna**, where there is very little permanent snow. Several **pirca** constructions and three children with offerings were found on its summit. Other installations along the road to the summit were also present at this site. The offerings include textiles and **figurines** made of gold, silver, and ***Spondylus*** shell.

LOMA NEGRA. One of the northernmost **Moche** sites near the Piura River on the north coast of Peru. It is located in the **Vicús** region. The high quantities of beautiful gold, **copper**, and **tumbaga** objects discovered in the **shaft tombs** of Loma Negra, crafted with exceptional technical skill and nearly identical to the north coast artifacts recovered from **Sipán**, are interpreted as emblems of royalty, power, and status. Moreover, their production most likely necessitated an organized guild of retainers attached to an elite court. Such a court was probably located in the Nima/Loma Valverde (Tamarindo) Complex in the Piura valley near Cerro Vicús, a site associated with **tapia** and **adobe** platforms similar to **Gallinazo** and Moche **architecture** of the core valleys. In fact, there appears to have been a long history of contact, **trade**, and interaction (since the **Cupisnique** Period) between the inhabitants of Piura and the valleys of the north coast, and Gallinazo styles are closely related to earlier Vicús types.

Although much work is required to decipher the nature and significance of the enigmatic Moche-Vicús satellite, it appears that Piura lords were important intermediaries of Moche **trade** interests. The Cerro Vicús region is strategically situated between the north coast and the equatorial region, and elites and privileged groups appear to have prospered in the administered trade of ***Spondylus***, cinnabar, and other goods from Ecuador in exchange for metal objects and possibly comestibles from the north coast valleys.

Early research suggested that the Moche I style developed in the Cerro Vicús region, a small and distant enclave in the mid Piura valley. This Moche-related **ceramic** tradition, which also entailed alternate assemblages of local hybrids (often differentiated as Vicús-Mochica and Vicús-local), included molded vessels equal in quality to those from the Moche-Chicama region and nearly identical to pots **looted** from the tomb of **La Mina** in Jequetepeque. Some scholars argue that Vicús represented a small colony of Moche artists who served local elites but ultimately reported to power brokers in the south. Others contend, however, that the adoption and reformulation of Moche ideology at Cerro Vicús were local phenomena, engineered by a small group of elites who were never subjected to Moche polities in the south. The fact that the Moche-Vicús style was not widely disseminated elsewhere in the Piura-Tumbes region tends to support this interpretation. Other authors also propose that, in the Vicús area, the puzzling mix of diagnostic features of different Moche phases may be viewed as a reflection of frontier conservatism and limited contact with the Moche heartland. Indeed, the juxtaposition of Moche IV **metallurgical** styles with Moche I ceramic art would suggest a relatively later emergence or at least protracted continuity of the phase I and II styles in the mid Piura valley. Although it was also suggested that the stylistic canons of sheet metal representations were somewhat ahead of the fineline ceramic tradition, this is difficult to verify given the lack of crosscorrelation with radiocarbon dates and the dearth of sound excavated contexts in Piura.

LOMAS. Spanish term for partially or completely artificial **mounds** in areas subject to flooding, as in **Moxos** lowland Bolivia. Other local terms for lomas include *cerritos* or ***cerritos de indios*** (Spanish), and **aterros** (Portuguese). Along the coast of Peru, natural hills or lomas were residential sites for **hunters** and gatherers during the preceramic period.

LOOTING. Looting began with the arrival of the European conquerors—and maybe earlier—and has been going on for centuries. It continues today on a vast scale. One of the reasons for looting is the selling of prehistoric artifacts in the market, at present even on the Internet. The illegal trafficking of antiquities is one of the largest sources of wealth throughout the world. Sites with monumental **architecture** have been a major target of looters. National, regional, and local governments have been trying in the last decades to stop the looting of archaeological sites, with many countries having tough laws and/or enforcement mechanisms. Looting, due to the loss of precious artifacts, causes serious problems for archaeological work and historical research. There has been serious looting in urban sites such as **San José de Moro**, **Sican**, and **Tiwanaku**; in sites with **rock art**; and in cemeteries. *See also* CHANCAY; DOS CABEZAS; KARWA; LA MINA; LOMA NEGRA; PYRAMID; RECUAY CULTURE; SAN AGUSTÍN.

LORD OF THE SEA (MASTER OF FISHES). Deity portrayed in **Nasca** vessels. It is associated with **trophy heads** and other evidence of ritual violence.

LOS CATALANES CAVE. One of the few archaeological sites excavated in the Araucanian or **Mapuche** region of southern Chile.

LOS ESTEROS. Religious and civic center associated with several **tolas** and located in central Manabí in coastal Ecuador. This settlement dates from 500 BC to AD 600 or the early period of **Regional Development**. **Ceramics** recovered from the site correspond to the **Bahía** style.

LOS GAVILANES. Preceramic site in the north-central coast of Peru situated near the modern city of Huarmey. It occupied approximately two hectares and is characterized by three occupations dating to between 3000 and 1800 BC. During the second occupation (2500–2000 BC), the inhabitants of Los Gavilanes built storage rooms for **maize**. Other sites of the region contain similar silos.

LOS HELECHOS. Site with a Late Pleistocene-Early Holocene occupation in the province of Buenos Aires, Argentina.

LOS MORRILLOS. Culture from the Archaic Period in San Juan in central Argentina. Groups living in the cordilleran valleys of San Juan from 5900 to 2000 BC were related to this cultural complex. The Morrillos people were mobile hunter-gatherers who shared the higher valleys with groups who migrated from Chilean valleys in the summer. **Hunting** of **guanaco** was important, as well as gathering of **chañar** and **algarroba** seeds, cactus, bird eggs, and so on. Most of the projectile points of Los Morrillos were triangular and unstemmed, a tradition that differed from the contemporaneous **Ayampitín** groups. Numerous items made of wood, natural fiber, leather, and so on are preserved here, including complete skeletons with hair and skin, since the climate in this region is one of the driest of South America, with twenty-five millimeters of annual rainfall. **Clothing** and nets were made with guanaco skin. *See also* GRUTA DEL INDIO.

LOS PINCHUDOS. Late Intermediate Period site in the eastern Andes not far from **Abiseo** and **Pajatén**. Three main buildings distinguish this site. Funerary **chullpas** were also present, as in other regions of the Andes.

LOS PINOS. Rock shelter with occupations dating to 7500 BC located in the province of Buenos Aires, Argentina. Los Pinos is situated five kilometers from the **Cueva Tixi**, a site dating to the same period. Lithic artifacts including a **fishtail projectile point** were found in association with several hearths.

LOS TOLDOS. Name given to several cave sites in Santa Cruz, southern Argentina. The earliest occupations at Los Toldos, known as the *Nivel 11* (Level 11), date to the Late Pleistocene and contain only unifacial tools. The Nivel 11 dates to 10,600 BC. A stone tool industry similar to that of Los Toldos was found at the site of **El Ceibo**. The second-oldest occupation is designated the **Toldense** (9000–6700 BC), which is characterized by bifacial projectile points. A long hiatus separates the Toldense from the later occupation, the **Casapedrense** occupation (5200–2800 BC). The Casapedrense is identified by a distinct stone tool industry. The stone tools are made on blades and constitute one of the few blade industries of South America.

LOST-WAX TECHNIQUE. A technique used in South American **metallurgy**. Lost wax is a complex process that consists of forming a central mass with clay and charcoal and covering it with a thin layer of wax. The wax is then covered with another layer of charcoal and clay. Application of heat causes the melting of the wax, and liquid metal is poured into the empty space. This technique was independently discovered in several parts of the world. The Lafone Quevedo plaque from northwest Argentina represents an example of the successful application of this technique. Very few lost-wax casting molds have been preserved, such as the one recovered from a tomb in central Colombia. *See also* AGUADA; NORTHERN PERUVIAN COASTAL METALLURGICAL TRADITION.

LUKURMATA. Urban center on the southern shores of Lake Titicaca. It was continuously occupied for the last 2,000 years. A small village in its first centuries around AD 500, Lukurmata was incorporated into the expanding **Tiwanaku** state and became the main Tiwanaku center in the agriculturally productive **Koani Pampa** area. Lukurmata was constructed on an elevation overlooking the lake and consists of a central district (Wila Kollu) containing a semisubterranean Tiwanaku temple and elite residences. In the Wila Kollu sector the earliest occupations were found, dating to the first century BC. Several sectors have been excavated, including the Misiton, located outside of the civic-ceremonial area. Material evidence for the manufacture of **musical** instruments from **camelid** bones was recovered in this particular sector. **Obsidian** from several sources was found in Lukurmata, including some from **Quispisisa**, a quarry located some seven hundred kilometers to the north-northwest.

LUMBRERAS, LUIS G. (1938–). Peruvian archaeologist who has done extensive research and publishing. Lumbreras taught at several Peruvian universities as well as abroad. He wrote numerous articles and books including *Esquema arqueológico de la sierra central del Perú* (1959); *La cultura de Wari, Ayacucho* (1960); *De los Pueblos y Culturas del Antiguo Perú* (1974), which was translated into English; *Las fundaciones de Huamanga* (1974); *Arqueología de la América Andina* (1981); and *Chavín de Huantar en el nacimiento de la Civilización andina* (1989).

LUND, WILHELM PETER (1801–1880). Born in Denmark, Lund was one of the pioneers of paleontology and archaeology in South America. He discovered the association of humans and **megafauna** in **Lagoa Santa**, central Brazil, and the human origin of coastal **sambaquí**.

– M –

MABARUMA. Pottery style related to the **Barrancoid** Tradition of northern South America. Mabaruma is the oldest **ceramic** in Suriname and dates to 2000–1550 BC. One of the characteristics of Mabaruma pottery is the use of **cariapé**.

MACHALILLA. Middle **Formative** culture and **ceramic** style from the coast of Ecuador that dates from 1400 to 800 BC. The ceramics of this culture represent an outgrowth of the **Valdivia** style. These ceramics are found throughout the Ecuadorian coast. There is a presence of charred **maize** in some Machalilla sites. *See also* STIRRUP BOTTLE.

MACHU PICCHU. One of the most-visited and most-photographed archaeological sites in the Americas. This **Inka** palatial center is situated along the Urubamba River at 2,700 meters above sea level. Machu Picchu was built by the Inka along the road that leads from **Cuzco** to the lowland valleys. It is included in the list of the **World**

Heritage Sites of UNESCO and forms part of the Historic Sanctuary of Machu Picchu, a reserve of approximately 32,200 hectares that protect not only the archaeological site but also the environment that surrounds it. **Hiram Bingham III** "discovered" the site in 1911. The top of a mountain was completely razed and many residences and terraces were built surrounding a central plaza. An important construction is the Temple of the Three Windows.

There are several interpretations concerning Machu Picchu's primary function. For instance, it is thought to have served as the royal estate of Pachakuti's **panaqa** or possibly as a **religious** center. The **Inka** emperor Pachakuti is believed to have organized the city of Cuzco and begun the expansion of the empire. A large number of burials were found in Machu Picchu, including those of men, **women**, and children, most of whom were probably retainers of the panaqa. The skeletal remains suggest that most were in good health, and there is limited evidence of violence in the osteological remains. **Obsidian** from different sources found in Machu Picchu suggests that retainers came from different regions of the empire. *See also* CHOQE K'IRAW.

MAIZE (*ZEA MAYS*). One of the most important domesticated plants in the Americas. Maize was grown in warm and temperate areas below 3,500 meters above sea level and as far south as central Argentina and Chile. **Chicha**, a fermented drink made of maize, was a very important beverage consumed in rituals. Maize is represented in **rock art**, modeled **ceramics** (for example, **Moche** and **Chimú**), metals, and other media. In many indigenous societies of the Americas, maize is an important component of **religion** and religious symbolisms of fertility. In Moche society, there may be evidence of a **Maize god** as suggested by ceramic iconography. In the Amazon and Orinoco basins, maize became the main crop around AD 1000. *See also* COTOCOLLAO; CULEBRAS.

MAIZE GOD. Important element in **religious** iconography of the **Moche** society in the north coast of Peru. *See also* MAIZE.

MALACHITE. Greenish stone, a **copper** carbonate hydroxide, **traded** over long distances in Andean and sub-Andean regions of South America (for example, **Pitrén**). Malachite, like **turquoise** and other blue stones, was used by sedentary **agriculturalist** populations to manufacture beads and other ornaments. Not much is known about its sources and procurement systems. *See also* JEWELRY.

MALAGANA CHIEFDOM. Some evidence coming from findings of rich **tombs** in the Cauca Valley of southwestern Colombia indicates that around 200 BC to 100 AD the Malagana formed farming communities. **Maize** is one of their basic crops. Gold **metallurgy** was well advanced among the Malagana.

MALAMBO CULTURE. This culture had its origins around 1100–1000 BC in northern Colombia. Malambo people lived in simple villages and their subsistence was based on bitter **manioc**, evidenced by griddle fragments. The Malambo site is in the delta of the Magdalena River (Colombia). The **ceramic** style is a continuation of the **Puerto Hormiga** types and includes plastic decoration such as incisions, modelings, ornaments, and clay masks.

MALLKU CHIEFDOM. Late Intermediate Period political unit of the Lipez highland area of southwestern Bolivia. Sites are usually **fortified** and on hilltops. Mallku society was based mostly on **camelid pastoralism**.

MALOCA. Term used to refer to a communal house that formed the foundation of **agricultural** villages in the tropical forests of South America. Rectangular or ovoid in shape and made of wood, palm leaves, and other organic materials, malocas can be identified archaeologically by the dark coloration of the soil produced by the decomposition of organic materials (bones, plants, ash, and so on). In Venezuela, communal houses are called *churuata*. *See also* MARAJOARA; SAPUCAÍ; TUPIGUARANI.

MANCHÁN. Manchán, located in the Casma Valley of Peru, represents one the largest **Chimú** administrative centers south of **Chan Chan**. Manchán consists of nine contiguous **adobe** compounds, cemeteries, and large domestic zones. Some scholars argue that the salient differences in **architecture**, burial practices, and craft production between Manchán, the center of Chimú administration in

Casma, and the capital suggest that Chimú political might was exercised through power-sharing with local elites. In fact, the incorporation of Casma did not lead to a dramatic disruption in settlement except for the founding of three intrusive sites and population attrition at the former pre-Chimú center of **Túcume** (El Purgatorio). Despite the partnership with local elites (reflected in the incomplete imposition of Chimú architectural styles), there was still a fundamental transfer of power to Chimú nobility, which coopted and manipulated local authority despite deference to native lords and traditions.

MANCO CAPAC (MANKO QAPAQ). An **Inka** mythical figure, Manco Capac was the founder of Inka kingship (ruling dynasty). According to Inka traditions, Manco Capac traveled with his wife Mama Ocllo from Lake Titicaca toward the north and founded the city of **Cuzco** in a fertile valley. *See also* MAUKALLAQTA; ÑAMLAP.

MANICUAROID. Shell midden sites located along the Caribbean coast. A large Manicuaroid shell midden was excavated at Punta Gorda on Cubaguá Island in eastern Venezuela. Manicuaroid sites date from 2300 BC to the first century AD. Early Manicuaroid sites lack **ceramics**, but later occupations were found associated with pottery. Manicuaroid sites were found on Margarita Island and on the mainland of the Caribbean region. Some authors suggest that Manicuaroid people colonized the West Indies.

MANIOC (*MANIHOT ESCULENTA*). Important domesticated plant with starchy roots. It served as one of the main staples in the warm regions of South America. It is also known as *cassava*, *yucca*, or *tapioca*. Manioc is consumed boiled or ground as flour or fermented in alcoholic drinks. Among its earliest findings are in the coast of Peru dating to 4000 BC. Manioc can be cultivated in different types of soils (even in poor soils and in desert areas) and its roots can be kept underground for a long period without decomposing. Manioc is very rich in carbohydrates but poor in protein. *See also* AGRICULTURE; BUDARES; MALAMBO CULTURE; MOMIL; MONT GRAND MATOURY.

MANO AND METATE. A term designating grinding implements made of stone and used by many South American groups. Metate is a Nahuatl term used in Mexico and parts of Central America; it is not universally employed in South America, where other terms such as *conanas*, *molinos*, and *morteros* are more current. In South America, metates have assumed different shapes according to place and time. They were used to grind crops and/or minerals and were made of coarse volcanic rocks, sometimes as individual artifacts and other times carved in boulders. According to historical documents, grinding tools were traditionally employed by **women** in the ancient Andes and other parts of South America. *See also* SAMBAQUÍ; SAN JACINTO 1; SALADOID; TUMACO; UMBÚ TRADITION.

MANOS PINTADAS CAVES. *See* CUEVA DE LAS MANOS PINTADAS.

MANTEÑO CULTURE. This term refers to a multiregional Integration-period polity in the coast and interior of southern Ecuador. Manteño has also been referred to as Manteño-Huancavilca. Manteño culture dates to the Late Period (AD 900–1550). Large Manteño sites include ceremonial centers. Manteño people were involved in the procurement and exchange of ***Spondylus*** and practiced **copper metallurgy** along with the manufacture of axes, **axe monies**, and tools. Manteño **ceramics** represent a continuation of previous coastal traditions. Their surface is usually black with bright finish. Common ceramic forms are **compoteras**, jars, and **funerary urns**. **Spindle whorls** have decorations of everyday life scenes. Manteño people manufactured stone sculptures for the first time in the area including **U-shaped** seats or thrones and statues of mythological animals (felines and eagles). Manteños also worked gold, silver, and copper alloys. Wool and **cotton** textile production also distinguished Manteño culture. Shell, gem, and precious metal pendants were often woven into fine textiles, which served as important **trade** items.

MANZANILLO. Late Pleistocene-Early Holocene site near the city of Maracaibo (northwestern Venezuela) in the northwest sector of Lake Maracaibo. Stone tools were made with fossilized wood and belong to the **El Jobo** Tradition (11,000–9000 BC).

MAPUCHE. (*Che* [people], *mapu* [land]). Indigenous group that originally lived in southern Chile since AD 1000. During Colonial times, some Mapuche groups settled in southern Argentina. The Mapuche resisted the **Inka** and Spanish conquest and preserved their autonomy for several centuries. After the Spanish conquest of central Chile, some Mapuche groups moved into southern Argentina, where they continue to reside as well as in Chile. Mapuche buried their dead under burial **mounds**. These burial mounds form groups in open-area landscape. The Mapuche culture is also well known for its silver work. *See also* LOS CATALANES CAVE.

MARAJOARA. Elaborate **ceramic** style and culture from the Marajo Island situated in the mouth of the Amazon, Brazil. It represents one of the main styles of the **Polychrome Horizon** and dates from AD 400 to 1100. Marajoara sites consist of one or more earth **mounds**, which served as residential areas. Individual mounds occupy an area of two hectares or less and can reach a height of five meters. Houses were built for several families (**malocas**) and ceremonial activities took place in the open air and in cemeteries, where individuals were placed in **funerary urns**. The diet of the Marajoara people was varied and included domesticated plants, wild plants, and fish.

MARANGA. A major ceremonial and residential center in the Rimac valley, central coast of Peru. The site and polity developed from AD 200 to 800. The site consists of twelve platform **mounds**, the largest one being Huaca San Marcos. *See also* LIMA CULTURE.

MARAZZI. A small rock shelter which is one of the earliest sites in Tierra del Fuego, Chile, in southernmost South America. Marazzi is located along the seashore in **Bahía** Inútil. Unifacial tools, **bolas**, and **guanaco** bones dating to 7500 BC were recovered here. The site was occupied shortly after the glaciers receded. However, due to the limited number of artifacts associated with the site, it is difficult to establish its relations with other Patagonian sites. The **Tres Arroyos** rock shelter is situated nearby.

MARCA HUAMACHUCO. Large urban site in the northern highlands of Peru. It covers approximately 2.4 square kilometers and is located on an elevated plateau. The **architectural** features include multistory, circular, curvilinear, and rectangular buildings. Marca Huamachuco was built in the Early Intermediate Period (AD 200–600) and Early Middle Horizon (AD 600–800) and remained important during the **Wari** conquest of the area, which had its center in the site of **Viracochapampa**.

MARCAVALLE. Initial Period site in the **Cuzco** basin in the southern highlands of Peru. Its earliest occupations date to 1300 BC. **Adobe** walls delineated domestic residences at this early village site.

MARCELINA KUÉ. Preceramic and **ceramic** site in southeastern Paraguay close to the Paraná River and the city of Encarnación. The ceramic level is characterized by six **terras pretas** and a grouping of **funerary urns**. The site report describes excavations of the preceramic occupation. Most of the stone tools and debris of the preceramic level are of silicified sandstone. Among the stone tools were stemmed projectile points, endscrapers, and sidescrapers.

MARCOS, JORGE G. (1932–). Ecuadorian archaeologist born in Guayaquil. His doctoral research at the University of Illinois at Urbana-Champaign (1978) investigated the site of **Real Alto** and **Valdivia** culture. His recent published work includes *El proceso de neolitización en los Andes ecuatoriales (8.000–2.000 A.D.)* (1999); *Los Agro-alfareros Valdivia de Real Alto, en el Antiguo Ecuador: Un modelo para la "Revolución Neolítica" en el Nuevo Mundo* (1993); and *Real Alto, la historia de un centro ceremonial Valdivia* (1988).

MARKETS. Open markets were common in many settlements of the northern Andes, but were uncommon in most of the central Andes and in Venezuela during pre-Columbian times. In the northern Andes, products such as gold, **emeralds**, **salt**, **cotton** blankets, honey, **jaguar** pelts, **coca**, and other crops were exchanged in periodic markets in the **Chibcha** area. *See also* MINDALÁ; TRADE.

MASHWA OR MASHUA (*TRAPAEOLUM TUBEROSUM*). Also known as *añu*, *cubios*, and *isañu*, mashwa is a domesticated Andean tuber with edible leaves, flowers, and tubers. Mashwa is very high in protein and caloric yielding. It is frost tolerant and performs well in poor soils. Tubers can be eaten raw or cooked and are cultivated between 3,000 and 4,000 meters above sea level with a preferred range between 3,500 and 3,800 meters above sea level. Mashwa is cultivated from Bolivia to Colombia. *See also* PUNA.

MAUKALLAQTA. Inka palace and temple complex located in the province of Paruro in the southern **Cuzco** valley. Maukallaqta is thought to be related to the figure of **Manco Capac**.

MEGAFAUNA. General term used for large mammals that characterized the Late Pleistocene in the Americas and have been extinct since the Late Pleistocene or Early Holocene, between 11,000 and 7000 BC. In South America, the megafauna which were hunted by the early inhabitants include the glyptodont (*Glyptodon* sp., *Doedicurus* sp.), mastodon, giant sloth, sloth, horse (*Equus* sp., *Hippidion* sp.), and llama (*Paleolama* sp.). The horse and the llama resemble their modern counterparts. *See also* CUEVA DEL MEDIO; CUEVA DEL MILODON; CUEVA TIXI; EL CEIBO; HUARGO CAVE; LAPA VERMELHA IV; MONTE VERDE; PAIJÁN; PARANAÍBA PHASE; PASO OTERO 5; QUEREO; TAGUA-TAGUA; TAIMA-TAIMA; TIBITÓ.

MEGGERS, BETTY (1921–). American archaeologist who dedicated her career to the study of South America, particularly Brazil and Ecuador. Her main works include *Archaeological Investigations at the Mouth of the Amazon* with C. Evans (1957), *Early Formative Period of Coastal Ecuador: The Valdivia and Machalilla Phases* (1965) with C. Evans and E. Estrada, *Ecuador* (1966), and *Prehistoric America* (1972).

MENGHIN, OSWALD F. A. (1888–1973). Austrian prehistorian and a professor at the University in Vienna beginning in 1918. In 1938 he was named president of the university. He moved to Argentina after the end of World War II. Menghin conducted research in Pampa and Patagonia and in other regions of South America and published several articles. Among his works on South America are *Investigaciones prehistóricas en Cuevas de Tandilia (Pcia. De Buenos Aires)* (1950) with M. Bórmida,

Fundamentos cronológicos de la Prehistoria de Patagonia (1952), *Excavaciones arqueológicas en el yacimiento de Ongamira, Córdoba (Rep. Argentina)* with **Alberto R. González** (1954), *Un yacimiento en Ichuña (Departamento Puno, Perú) y las industrias precerámicas de los Andes Centrales y Septentrionales* (1957), with G. Schroeder, and *Estudios de Prehistoria araucana* (1962).

METALLURGY. The Andean region of South America is one of the centers of metallurgic production. Several prehistoric metallurgical traditions have been identified in South America, mainly in the Andes, and different techniques and alloys were discovered in the region. In general, metallurgy was closely related to ritual production. Among the **Inka**, gold was related to the sun and masculine principles while silver was associated with the moon and feminine qualities. When Francisco Pizarro captured **Atawallpa** in 1532, he requested a ransom of gold and silver objects, which were brought from different parts of the Inka empire. **Copper** was a prestigious element in the Andes and was often associated with **mummy** bundles. **Axe monies** were made of copper in various regions of the Andes including the **Lambayeque** drainage of the Peruvian north coast. Copper metallurgy appears in Ecuador in **Chorrera** sites of the Late **Formative Period**. **Platinum** objects were made in the **Intermediate Area** by **Tumaco** and **La Tolita** people. *See also* BRONZE METALLURGY; JEWELRY; LOST-WAX TECHNIQUE; MOJOCOYA; QUIMBAYA; SIPÁN; YURAJ MOLINO.

MIDDEN. Term that refers to accumulation of debris of human activity (food processing, cooking, discarding of broken objects, and so on) that form in and around human settlements. An example of midden is the **sambaquí**, formed by the accumulation of shells. *See also* CONCHERO.

MILAGRO-QUEVEDO. Late Period culture of southern coastal Ecuador which developed in the period of Regional Integration, from AD 900 to 1450. Milagro-Quevedo people formed a large political unit around the main site of Milagro. Burial in artificial platforms, elaborate **copper metallurgy**, and carved seals and stamps represent important material signatures of this tradition.

MINA PHASE. Group of **shell mounds** or **sambaquís** found on the Atlantic coast east of the mouth of the Amazon in Brazil. These sites date to 3500 BC and contain early **ceramics**.

MINDALÁ. Term that designates prehistoric merchants from Ecuador. They **traded** across the Andes and by sea with groups in Colombia, Central America, and Peru. Some of the items they traded in **markets** were gold, **salt**, and **cotton**.

MIRRORS. Some South American societies manufactured mirrors with various raw materials. They were made of **bronze**, pyrite, anthracite, **obsidian**, gold, silver, and other materials that can reflect images. Usually of circular shape, some are flat and others are concave; some have handles and others have suspension holes. Mirrors were used in ritual ceremonies.

MISTOL (*ZIZIPHUS MISTOL*). Also known as *mistol cuaresmillo* or *sacha mistol*. Tree of the family *Rhamnaceae* that grows in several regions of South America (central and northern Argentina and the **Chaco** region). It reaches nine meters high. In pre-Columbian times, its fruits were eaten and made into a drink called *arrope*. Mistol also has medicinal properties, can be made into a dye, and its wood was used for **architecture** and in the manufacture of **manos** and spears.

MITO. Name of a phase of the site of **Kotosh** and of a preceramic **architectural** style in the north-central highlands of Peru. Mito is dated to 2500–1800 BC.

MOCHE (MOCHICA). An Early Intermediate Period coastal state and series of independent complex polities, the Moche extended their control from the Huarmey River in the south to the Piura River in the north from 200 to 900 AD. The main site and capital of the state is Moche, with its two main monuments the **Huaca del Sol** and the **Huaca de la Luna**. Examples of Moche art are found in museums throughout the world in diverse media and forms: **ceramics**, metals, textiles, gourds, wood, bone, shell, and feather work. Moche ceramics are both modeled and painted and depict numerous elements of Moche daily life and ritual, including houses, **pyramids**, **religious**

scenes of **warfare** and **sacrifice**, portraits of important individuals (**waco retrato**), craft activities, erotic scenes, plants and animals (terrestrial and maritime), and others. Moche smiths were highly skilled and manufactured several metals, alloys except for the tin **bronze** which was developed in the southern highlands. Other large Moche sites include **Dos Cabezas** and Cao Viejo. *See also* GALINDO; HUACA EL BRUJO; LA MINA; LAMBAYEQUE; LICAPA; LOMA NEGRA; MOCOLLOPE; NORTHERN PERUVIAN COASTAL METALLURGICAL TRADITION; PACATNAMU; PAMPA DE LAS LLAMAS; PAMPA GRANDE; PAÑAMARCA; RECUAY CULTURE; SACRIFICE CEREMONY OR SCENE; SALINAR; SAN JOSÉ DE MORO; SIPÁN; TRANSPORTATION.

MOCOLLOPE (CERRO MAYAL). One of the largest **Moche** administrative and ceremonial centers in the Chicama valley, north coast of Peru. Recent excavations at Cerro Mayal, near the **religious** center of Mocollope in Chicama, have revealed that the extensive site specialized in the mass production of fine **ceramics**, which likely financed the religious and political programs of Chicama's elite residing at Mocollope and Cao Viejo. In fact, numerous **pyramidal** platforms and ceremonial loci were constructed in the Chicama valley during the Middle Period (AD 400–600), such as Cao Viejo, Mocollope, Licapa II, and La Campanilla, indicating a high concentration of elite officials and the power and influence of Chicama lords. *See also* HUACA EL BRUJO.

MOJOCOYA. A **ceramic**-producing culture of the southwest of Cochabamba and the north of Chuquisaca, Bolivia during the Early Intermediate Period (AD 200–600). The main ceramic vessels manufactured by the Mojocoya include **funerary urns** and tripod vases with spiral and stepped designs. Textiles, **metallurgy**, and basketry played an important role in Mojocoya society. **Tupuraya**, Quillacollo, and Cochabamba are contemporaneous ceramic styles of that region.

MOLLO CULTURE. A culture that developed in the valleys to the east of Late Titicaca (Bolivia) during the Late Period (AD 1000–1400). One of its most important sites is **Iskanwaya**, associated with numerous **pirca** constructions.

MOMIL. Early **agricultural** site in the Caribbean lowlands of Colombia. During its earliest phase, Momil I (1000 BC), **manioc** was the main domesticated plant. In Momil II, around AD 1, the disappearance of **budares** and the appearance of **manos and metates** suggest that **maize** replaced manioc as the staple crop. Momil II represents a manifestation of the **First Painted Horizon**.

MONOLITH. Stone sculpture manufactured from a single block. Several Andean cultures from northwestern Argentina (**Tafí**) to Colombia (**San Agustín**) made monoliths that represented mythical beings and other anthropomorphic and zoomorphic figures. The **Bennett Monolith** found in **Tiwanaku**'s semisubterranean temple represents an elaborate example of monolithic art. The "Lanzón" at **Chavín de Huantar** (Peru) provides another such example.

MONT GRAND MATOURY. Thémire Complex site located at 234 meters above sea level on one of the highest elevations of the Guyane coastal plain. This site dates to between AD 1220 and 1650. The presence of **budares** and microflakes suggest that people living in this site cultivated **manioc**. Most ceramics are decorated in the **Arauquinoid** style of Suriname, and small numbers are **polychrome**. Among the stone tools are ceramic polishers and polished axes.

MONTAGNES COURONNÉES. Sites with trenches and very limited domestic occupation in Guyane and eastern Suriname (Pondokreek site). They were tentatively dated to the Late Prehistoric Period, after AD 1000, and could have served as **fortifications**.

MONTE GRANDE. The extensive site of Monte Grande (1500–1100 BC) is perched on a mesa five kilometers from the modern town of Tembladera in the middle Jequetepeque Valley (north coast of Peru) and exhibits extraordinary architectural planning of both residential and ceremonial structures. The two monumental constructions (Huaca Grande and Huaca Antigua) in the center of the thirteen-hectare site were built of plastered stone and sculpted **adobe** decoration that resembled the **architecture** of the ceremonial centers of **Kuntur Wasi** and **Layzón** in the upper headwaters of the Jequetepeque Valley. A rectangular plaza flanked by niched walls is one of its more salient features, and structures are aligned with the flow of the river or nearby mountain peaks. More than one hundred residential structures built of cane and mud (not all occupied at one time) were clustered around open patios and oriented according to set configurations. The possible residence of elite **religious** specialists was identified, and the consumption of a **hallucinogenic** land snail seems to have been a common practice at the site. Monte Grande appears to have been one of the larger and more important of the middle-valley centers, supported by a substantial residential population. The majority of ceremonial structures in the middle Jequetepeque were associated with domestic areas and **agricultural** terraces.

MONTE VERDE. Late Pleistocene open-air site located near the city of Puerto Montt in southern Chile. Monte Verde is one of the most intensively researched sites in the Andes and represents one of the earliest settlements ever discovered in the Americas. It consists of two occupations: the earliest, Monte Verde I, dates to around 35,000 BC, and the following, Monte Verde II, to 13,000 BC. The earliest occupation, which lies 1.2 meters below Monte Verde II, is highly controversial, as there are few elements that clearly indicate human activity. Monte Verde II consists of a group of wooden structures, hearths, floors, and pits. The inhabitants of Monte Verde II were **hunters** and gatherers: there are remains of **megafauna**, including mastodon and paleolama, as well as plant remains, some deriving from different ecological areas. Among the stone tools are bifacial projectile point, **bolas**, and grinding stones. Monte Verde is one of Chile's national monuments.

MORAY. Inka site located near **Cuzco**. It is renowned for its beautiful circular and concentric terraces, possibly used to cultivate **maize** and other crops.

MORENO, FRANCISCO P. (1852–1919). Moreno was an Argentine geographer, explorer, and anthropologist. In 1872, he was one of the founders of the Sociedad Científica Argentina (Argentine Scientific Society). He conducted numerous expeditions to Patagonia, a territory which at that time few nonindigenous people had visited. There he conducted ethnographic and archaeological research. In 1879, he donated his collection of anthropological materials to the province of Buenos Aires, and the provincial government created the Anthropological and Ethnographic Museum (later Museo de La Plata) on this basis. Among his archaeological work is *Noticias sobre antigüedades de los indios del tiempo anterior a la conquista, descubiertas en la provincia de Buenos Aires* (1874), "Antropología y arqueología, importancia del estudio de estas ciencias en la República Argentina" (lecture given in 1881), and *Estudio del hombre americano*. On his last trip to Patagonia in 1912, he traveled with ex-president Theodore Roosevelt. A large glacier in the province of Santa Cruz takes his name.

MOSELEY, MICHAEL. Moseley conducted research in Peru, Bolivia, and Colombia. He published numerous articles and was editor and co-editor of important books on Peruvian archaeology. Among his published works are *Twenty-Four Architectural Plans of Chan Chan, Peru* (1974), *The Maritime Foundations of Andean Civilization* (1975), co-editor of *Chan Chan: Andean Desert City* (1982), *Trabajos Arqueologicos en Moquegua, Peru* (1990), *The Northern Dynasties: Kingship and Statecraft in Chimor* (1991), and *The Incas and Their Ancestors: The Archaeology of Peru* (1992, 2001).

MOSSAMÈDES. Earliest horticultural tradition along the upper Tocantins River, central Brazil. It emerged in the seventh or eighth century AD and later spread into Minas Gerais (**Sapucai**), **Bahía**, Piauí, and other states such as **Aratú**, and persisted until the Iberian conquest.

MOSTNY, GRETE (1914–1991). Mostny was an Austrian-born Chilean archaeologist and anthropologist. She studied at the University of Vienna and the Free University of Brussels. At the onset of World War II she left Europe and moved to Chile. Mostny began archaeological research in Chile in the early 1940s, focusing on the central and northern regions as well as on **rock art** traditions. Mostny served as director of the Museo Nacional de Historia Natural. Her most popular book is *Prehistoria de Chile* (1974), which was reprinted in several editions. In 1983, she published *Arte rupestre chileno* with **Hans Niemeyer**.

MOUND VELARDE. *See* VELARDE.

MOUNDS. Platform mounds are very common **architectural** features in many South American cultures. They are made of earth, **adobe**, stones, and other materials, depending on the region. These structures are locally known as **cerritos de indios**, **aterros**, or **huacas** (**wacas**). Some mounds are residential, cemeteries, **religious** constructions, or a combination of these. The largest mounds are found along the central and northern coasts of Peru. *See also* LOMAS.

MOXEKE-PAMPA DE LAS LLAMAS. One of the largest Initial Period sites in the Casma Valley, north-central coast of Peru. The site covers more than 2.2 square kilometers, and its origins can be traced to approximately 1800 BC. It was abandoned around 1400 BC. The two main **mounds**, Moxeke and Huaca A, are separated by a large plaza and surrounded by dwellings and satellite monumental **architecture**.

MOXOS. Lowland savanna region located in the Bolivian Amazon basin. Vast extensions of **raised fields** and associated features such as **calzadas**, artificial **mounds**, and dams were constructed from approximately 500 BC to the Spanish conquest. The raised fields were built in order to drain the excess of water of the rainy season. Similar structures were built in the Llanos de Barinas (Venezuela). At the time of the Spanish conquest, the region of Moxos was settled by the Baurés **chiefdoms**. *See also* VELARDE.

MUACO. Paleo-Indian (Late Pleistocene) site near the city of Coro in northwestern Venezuela. It is a **hunting** site situated by an ancient spring where animals—many now extinct—came to drink water. There are many bones of mastodon, giant sloth, and horse. Radiocarbon dates range between 14,900 and 12,800 BC. Tools of the **El Jobo** Tradition were found here along with other cutting tools. *See also* MEGAFAUNA.

MUISCA. Late Period (AD 900 to Spanish Conquest) culture from the plateau and slopes of the eastern Cordillera in the present-day departments of Cundinamarca and Boyacá, Colombia. Similar to the

Tairona, they were **Chibcha**-language speakers. The most important goods produced by the Muisca include **salt**, **cotton** blankets, **pottery**, gold objects, and **emeralds**. Salt was extracted from mines located at Zipaquirá, Nemocón, and Tausa. The Muisca combined gold with **copper** to produce the alloy **tumbaga**. *See also* TRANSPORTATION.

MULLU. *See SPONDYLUS.*

MULLUMICA. Important **obsidian** quarry in the northern Ecuadorian highlands. Mullumica was exploited since the Early Holocene (8000 BC). Sites with Mullumica obsidian in Ecuador are **Chobshi Cave** and **El Inga** and La Carolina on the coast. Obsidian from Mullumica was also found in coastal sites of southern Colombia. The term Mullumica implies a possibly interesting material and symbolic relationship between **mullu** and obsidian, two valuable goods in the Andes.

MUMMIES. Many South American cultures preserved the bodies of deceased individuals through various processes of mummification. Ancestor worship was an important component in many Andean **religions** and thus emphasis was placed on ritually preserving and manipulating the dead, who continued to play important roles among living social actors. The earliest mummification techniques were employed by the **Chinchorro** in northern Chile. Many other South American indigenous groups prepared the corpses for periodic ritual celebrations in which the mummy or bundle was brought to interact with the living. In some cases, mummification continued into the Colonial Period, as assessed by an eighteenth-century document from the Samacá valley of central Colombia. *See also* CERRO COLORADO; CERRO EL PLOMO; CHANCAY; CHIRIBAYA; HIGH-ALTITUDE SANCTUARIES; INKA; PANAQA; PARACAS.

MUSCOVY DUCK (*CAIRINA MOSCHATA*). Bird **domesticated** for its meat and common throughout pre-Columbian Central and South America. Muscovy ducks are the only domestic ducks that are native to South America. The original coloration of wild ducks is black and white, but domestication produced many more colors, including brown and blue. The males are large, weighing up to six kilograms, with the smaller females reaching only four kilograms. After the conquest, Muscovy ducks were taken to many parts of the world, but they are not as common as turkey, the other domesticated bird of the Americas. *See also* PAMPA GRANDE.

MUSIC. Music was an important part of the lives of indigenous people of South America, particularly in relation to feasts, rituals, and ceremonial events. Indigenous people of South America used a variety of percussion and wind instruments. Musical instruments were found in the context of several South American pre-Columbian cultures. They were made of a variety of materials. Wind instruments or aerophones were made of human or animal bones, **ceramics**, stone, canes, and so on. Percussion instruments, either membranophones (where the skin or leather vibrates) or idiophones (hard instruments such as rattles), were also made of several materials. Most of the prehistoric musical instruments found in museums lack their provenience, and in many cases it is difficult to determine their age. *See also* CHECUA; LUKURMATA; NORTHERN PERUVIAN COASTAL METALLURGICAL TRADITION; *STROMBUS PERUVIANUS*; TUMACO.

– N –

NAMANCHUGO. *See* CATEQUIL.

NANCHOC. An intensive Middle Preceramic occupation has been documented in the Zaña Valley of northern Peru (6000–2400 BC), which was concentrated in the thorn and tropical forests of the low slopes of the western Andes. The ceremonial site of Nanchoc (Cementerio de Nanchoc) is one of the more important settlements, dominated by two earthen **mounds** and subsidiary constructions two hectares in size. The site functioned primarily as a center of lime procurement and **religious** ceremonialism and was strategically placed in close proximity to different ecotones containing varied resources. The multicomponent site was divided into three spatial and functional sectors, which consisted of the pair of triple-tiered earth mounds, an open-air workshop (lime production), and a modified hill. The dual mounds were delineated with aligned stones with double entrances on their south sides.

NARIÑO (OR QUILLACINGA). Late Period culture in the southern highlands of Colombia, dated to between AD 700 and 1500. Nariño groups were organized in **chiefdom** political systems. Nariño groups cultivated **maize**, **quinoa**, and Andean tubers such as **potato**, **oca**, and **ulluku**. One of the characteristics of their burials was the placement in extremely deep shaft **tombs**, some forty meters deep.

NARRÍO. Artistic style from the highlands of Ecuador dating from 700 BC to AD 700. *See also* CERRO NARRÍO.

NASCA CULTURE. Regional entity whose center was located in the Nazca Valley, southern coast of Peru, during the Early Intermediate Period (AD 200–600). Nasca (written with *s* instead of *z* to distinguish the contemporary Nazca town and region) is known for its **polychrome** ceramics, fine textiles, and the **Nazca lines**, all of which project images of Nasca corporate art. **Ceramics** give us a panorama of Nasca life as they portray humans, animals, vegetables, and mythical figures and scenes of **warfare** and elites in action. Most textiles were made with **llama** and **alpaca** wool and continue the tradition of the **Paracas** textiles. The Nasca had a large ceremonial center at **Cahuachi**. **Trophy heads** were important in Nasca culture and **religion**. *See also* DOS PALMOS; PUKIO; TAMBO VIEJO; VENTILLA.

NAZCA LINES. Complex and massive series of petroglyphs made on the flat pampa of Nazca, which are only visible from high hills or from the air. They were made by **Nasca** people by removing rocks and desert pan to uncover the lighter-colored soil below. There are numerous figures of animals, humans, and geometric motifs. The Nazca lines are included in the list of the **World Heritage Sites of UNESCO**.

NEVADO DEL ACONQUIJA. Important **high-altitude sanctuary** in Catamarca in northwest Argentina, associated with several **Inka** constructions. These include a **kallanka**, **ushnu**, **qolcas**, and a plaza surrounded by a wall.

NIEMEYER, HANS WALTER (1921–2005). Chilean archaeologist who did research in the north, north-center, and center of Chile. He served as president of the Sociedad Chilena de Arqueología (Chilean Archaeological Society) for ten years. His published works include *Investigaciones arqueológicas en el valle del Huasco* (1955); *Investigaciones arqueológicas en las terrazas de Conanoxa, valle de Camarones (Provincia de Tarapacá)* with V. Schiappacasse (1963); *El yacimiento arqueológico de Huana* (1970); *Cultura El Molle del río Huasco. Revisión y síntesis* (1982); and *Culturas prehistóricas de Copiapó* (1998) with Miguel Cervellino and Gastón Castillo. Several of his published articles are on **rock art**. Recently, a book on Niemeyer was published in Chile: *Hans Niemeyer y la arqueología científica en Chile* (2003).

NORDESTE TRADITION. Group of Early Holocene sites in Piauí, northeastern Brazil, which date from 10,000 to 1500 BC. Subsistence was based on the **hunting** of small animals and gathering of fruits and other vegetable products. Stone tools were made of quartz, quartzite, and rarely, **chert**. Polished stone tools were dated to 7200 BC at the site of Toca do Sítio de Meio. This site also contains early **ceramics** dating to 6500 BC. **Rock art** is associated with Nordeste Tradition sites, and the paintings were dated to 10,000–4000 BC.

NORTH PERUVIAN HIGHLANDS FORMATIVE PERIOD. Some of the most extraordinary Initial Period and Early Horizon ceremonial centers were built in the upper Jequetepeque River and adjacent **Cajamarca** basin to the east. **Kuntur Wasi** (upper Jequetepeque—2,300 meters above sea level) and **Layzón** (Cajamarca basin), for instance, are characterized by high platforms built of fine masonry, monumental staircases, and exquisite stone sculpture and stelae of supernatural figures. Beautiful gold artifacts have recently been discovered in burials at Kuntur Wasi, and the ceremonial hydraulics and stone works of sites such as Agua Tapada (Cajamarca basin) further attest to the remarkable sophistication of artistic production and presumably the religious ideologies they supported. Archaeological data indicate that societies in the Cajamarca basin developed strong ties with **Cupisnique**, Tembladera (mid-Jequetepeque

Valley), and communities in the tropical lowlands to the east; indeed, the north highlands of Peru emerged as one of the more important panregional **religious** spheres in the Andes during the Initial Period. Large and prominent ceremonial centers such as **Pacopampa** (north highlands), **Huacaloma** (Cajamarca basin), Kuntur Wasi, and **Layzón** appear to have been interconnected in terms of religious observance, ideological prescriptions, and possibly intersocial **pilgrimage** and devotion.

NORTHERN PERUVIAN COASTAL METALLURGICAL TRADITION. This tradition is defined based on gold artwork of the **Lambayeque** valley and region of the north coast of Peru. Sheet gold decorated with cutout and chasing/repoussé designs dates to the first millennium BC. Among the objects are crowns and other ornaments, usually found in caches. Other metals, such as silver and **copper**, were also worked on the north coast at the time in much larger numbers than in other neighboring regions. The **Moche** excelled in this **metallurgical** tradition, with the production of a variety of personal ornaments, **musical** instruments, tools, and **weapons**, and the use of several techniques including **lost-wax casting**. After the decline of Moche society around AD 700, the metallurgical activities continued with the Middle **Sican** groups, who used new alloys such as arsenical copper. *See also* BRONZE METALLURGY; CHONGOYAPE.

NORTHWESTERN LITHIC TRADITION. Term that applies to the **Las Vegas Tradition** of coastal Ecuador, dated to 8000–4500 BC.

NÚÑEZ ATENCIO, LAUTARO (1938–). Chilean archaeologist who has investigated the prehistory of northern Chile, particularly as regards early settlement and the origins of plant and animal domestication in the region. He published numerous articles and books, including *Desarrollo cultural prehispánico del norte de Chile* (1965); *Secuencia y cambio en los asentamientos humanos de la desembocadura del río Loa, en el norte de Chile* (1971); *La agricultura prehistórica en los Andes meridionales* (1974); *Geoglifos y tráfico de caravanas en el desierto chileno* (1976); *Movilidad giratoria, armonía social y desarrollo en los Andes meridionales: tráfico e inter-*

acción económica with Tom D. Dillehay (1978); *Paleoindio y arcaico en Chile: diversidad, secuencia y proceso* (1983); and *Ocupación paleoindio en Quereo: reconstrucción multidisciplinaria en el territorio semiárido de Chile* with J. Varela and R. Casamiquela (1983).

– Ñ –

ÑAMLAP. Mythical founder of the **Lambayeque** dynasties and of Lambayeque society in general, a cultural hero and civilizer similar to **Manco Capac** of the **Inka**. According to myths, Ñamlap and his wife arrived from the sea to the north coast of Peru and established the coastal dynasty.

ÑANDÚ (*RHEIDAE*). A rare flightless bird consisting of two species common to southern South America. *Rhea americana* ranges from central Argentina to eastern Brazil. This rhea lives in **pampas**, campos, cerrados, and open **chaco** woodland of South America and avoids open grassland. It inhabits areas with at least some tall vegetation. During the breeding season, it stays near rivers, lakes, or marshes. *Pterocnemia pennata* are found in two separate regions: the Chilean and Argentinean puna and the southern Patagonian steppes. This rhea lives exclusively on the open plains of South America in areas of open scrub, as in the **puna** of the Andean plateau and also in the areas of steppe, which extend over the eastern slope of the Andes and into the lowlands of Patagonia. It prefers to be near lakes, rivers, or swamps for breeding, even though its habitats are quite arid. It was **hunted** by many groups of Pampa and Patagonian peoples. Its skin is used for leather, and its meat and eggs are eaten.

ÑO CARLOS. One of the earliest **shell middens** (**conchero**) on the Venezuelan coast. It dates to between 4000 and 3000 BC. Ño Carlos is located inland, which suggests that at the moment of occupation, sea levels were higher and that the overall weather was warmer. The lithic industry is expedient with very few elaborate tools. Apart from shellfish, the inhabitants of Ño Carlos consumed a variety of maritime products. *See also* CARONÍ TRADITION.

– O –

OBSIDIAN. Volcanic rock of glassy texture with very sharp natural edges (similar to glass) that was exploited by native peoples of the Americas to make tools. In South America, several volcanoes of the Andean chain from southern Chile and Argentina to Colombia provided sources of obsidian. By analyzing trace elements (chemical elements that are present in parts per million), one can compare obsidian from natural sources and obsidian found in archaeological sites and thus determine the provenience. The most important sources include **Quispisisa** and **Chivay** (Peru), **Zapaleri** or Tripartito (Bolivia-Argentina border), **Ona** (northwest Argentina), **Laguna del Maule** (Central Chile), **El Pehuenche** (Central Argentina), **Yanaurco-Quiscatola** and **Mullumica** (Ecuador), and **Río Hondo** (southern Colombia). Obsidian was widely **traded** over long distances up to one thousand kilometers in the Andean region itself and to areas east of the Andes, particularly in Patagonia and central Argentina. *See also* CAÑADÓN SALAMANCA; CERRO HUENUL; CHUMBIVILCAS; CUEVA EPULLAN; ENGLEFIELD; JAMA-COAQUE STYLE; JAMPATILLA; LA ELVIRA; LUKURMATA; MACHUPICCHU; MIRRORS; PAMPA DEL ASADOR; QUEBRADA JAGUAY; SACANANA; SENO OTWAY; SORA SORA; TILIVICHE; TILOCALAR PHASE; TUMUKU.

OCA (*OXALIS TUBEROSA*). (Pronounced *oh*-kah.) One of the most important Andean domesticated tubers. It can be cultivated between 3,000 and 4,000 meters above sea level from northern Argentina and Chile to Venezuela. The preferred altitude falls between 3,500 and 3,800 meters above sea level. It is usually planted together with **ulluku**, **mashwa**, and **potatoes**. *See also* LA PALOMA; PUNA.

OCUCAJE. Paracas style in the Ica valley of the south coast of Peru. The style has been divided into a sequence of ten phases. Phases III and IV have **Chavín** elements, while the later phases exhibit **Pukara** and highland elements. *See also* OCULATE BEING.

OCULATE BEING. This was a major **deity** in the **Paracas** and **Ocucaje** cultures of the south coast of Peru. The figure variably took the form of a human, feline, or a combination of the two and is distinguished by very large round eyes. The figure usually carries **weapons** and/or **trophy heads**.

OLLANTAYTAMBO. Inka terraced site along the Urubamba River, Peru. Its monumental walls were built with stone brought from the **Kachiqata** quarry some five kilometers downstream and on the opposite side of the river. A ritual and **agricultural** site, it was the locus of an important battle with the Spanish.

OMEREQUE. A culture that developed in the southern and eastern valleys of Cochabamba, Bolivia, between AD 600 and 1000. Vast **irrigation** systems and terraces as well as houses with rectangular stone walls characterize this cultural tradition. Burials were often placed in **funerary urns** and in rock shelters associated with pictography. **Ceramics** are **polychrome** and diverse in style, consisting of globular or bell-shaped vases, jars, and "terrines."

OMO. Tiwanaku site in the Moquegua valley, southern Peru. The site of Omo has a semisubterranean temple and a Tiwanaku Monolith, the only examples found to date outside of the Titicaca basin, suggesting that it was an important center of Tiwanaku expansion.

ONA. 1. An important **obsidian** quarry exploited in northwestern Argentina. The quarry is located in the Salar de Antofalla (Catamarca) and was exploited at least since the Early **Formative** (600 BC) and into **Inka** times. Sites containing Ona obsidian are situated in the valleys and highlands of Salta and Catamarca. 2. Ona (Selk'nam) is also the name of an indigenous group of Tierra del Fuego (southernmost Argentina-Chile) that hunted **guanaco**.

ONGAMIRA. Large preceramic rock shelter located at 1,150 meters above sea level in the Sierra Chica hills of Cordoba, central Argentina. Four occupations were found here, the oldest one dating to 4600 BC. No stone projectile points were identified in the two oldest occupations and most of the stone tools were made with local quartz. The most recent occupations were associated with **ceramic** fragments. In the oldest levels, the most abundant faunal remains consist of deer. In later occupations, there is a greater variety of food resources, including terrestrial shellfish.

OREJONES. Spanish name given in the sixteenth century to native Andean elites on the basis of their large circular ear ornaments (ear spools). Facial ornaments like these and the **tembetá** were common in many regions of South America as markers of privileged social status.

OSOIDE TRADITION. Ceramic manufacturing groups who lived in the western savannas of Venezuela from around 900 BC to AD 1200. They were relatively isolated groups. Their ceramics are very elaborate; among them are characteristic human **figurines**, most of them representing females. The Early Osoide Tradition is characterized by small villages close to rivers and the cultivation of **maize** and **manioc**. **Hunting** with the use of **bolas** and fishing were also important. In the Late Osoide Tradition, villages are larger and have houses on platforms. Causeways allow the villages to communicate among themselves and with areas of intensive **agriculture**. An example of this type of site is **Gaván**.

– P –

PACATNAMU. Walled urban site in the Jequetepeque Valley, north coast of Peru. It overlooks the Pacific Ocean and the Jequetepeque River and dates to **Moche**, **Lambayeque**, and **Chimú** times (AD 200–1370). The center of the city occupies one square kilometer and consists of walls, roads, and more than fifty **adobe mounds**, some of them with summit constructions. Elaborate elite compounds were built adjacent to these mounds. Several large cemeteries were also identified both inside and outside the city walls. Pacatnamu is thought to have served as an important **pilgrimage** center on the north coast. The site is also surrounded by **agricultural** fields.

PACHACAMAC (PACHAKAMAQ). Ceremonial and **pilgrimage** center located in the central coast of Peru. It was one of the most sacred sites in ancient Peru and was associated with the **Ichma** culture. Constructions were made in **adobe** over the course of many centuries. A sector of the **Inka** site probably served as the residence of *acllakuna* (young **women** recluded to weave fine cloths and produce **chicha** for the royal family). Pachacamac was sacked by Pedro Pizarro at the time of the Spanish conquest. *See also* CHAVÍN DE HUANTAR.

PACOPAMPA. Large site in the Chamaya basin of northern Peru situated at 2,400 meters above sea level. Corporate **architecture** dates to the Initial Period and Early Horizon (2000–200 BC) and covers ten hectares. There is a series of terraced platforms at this site that probably functioned as stages for large-scale public rituals. Pacopampa is one of the northernmost ceremonial centers in present-day Peru. *See also* NORTH PERUVIAN HIGHLANDS FORMATIVE PERIOD.

PADRE LAS CASAS. Mapuche site near Temuco, southern Chile. **Funerary urns** were placed inside canoes at this site. Variations in burial placement and offerings suggests status differences.

PAIJÁN. Paiján (8500–7000 BC) is by far the best-known and most archaeologically detectable Archaic culture on the northern coast of Peru, and many Paiján sites (more than 150 have been identified in the **Cupisnique** drainage alone) have been recorded between Zaña in the north and **Moche** in the south. This cultural-lithic category is famed for its finely pressured stemmed long point (very different from other contemporaneous points of North America), quarries, and small, seasonal campsites, often found on hills or near streams within canyons. Most lithic artifacts are of local raw materials. More permanent settlements (focused on particular activities, such as lithic procurement) have also been investigated in the **Moche** Valley. Paiján appears to have been a technologically and economically diversified adaptation to the environments of the coast and lower Andean foothills, emerging after the extinction of **megafaunal** species. Scholars argue that the characteristic points were designed to spear large fish and that many Paiján sites on the shoreline may have been submerged when ocean levels rose. Moreover, the discovery of milling stones and unifaces exhibiting "sheen" within Paiján sites indicates intense exploitation of wild plants. Migrating animals were hunted primarily in the spring and autumn near strategic passes of the shrubby foothills; in the winter and summer months, the dissolution of larger **hunting** parties coincided with seasonal movements by smaller bands to the coastal grasslands to exploit more varied resources.

In the Cupisnique quebrada, both abstract and figurative petroglyphs (**rock art**) have been tentatively dated to the Paiján Period. A Paiján burial was dated to 8200 BC, a date slightly earlier than the burials at the **Lauricocha** Cave. The distribution of Paiján material culture mirrors the later distribution of preceramic monumental **architecture**, suggesting the possible ancestry of this archaic tradition to coastal civilization. *See also* CHIVATEROS; QUIRIHUAC ROCK SHELTER.

PAJATÉN. Late Intermediate Period site in the eastern Andes (Chachapoyas province) of northern Peru located near **Abiseo** and **Los Pinchudos**. Like other sites of the region, Pajatén is characterized by high round stone platforms with exterior decoration (human and animal figures).

PALEOINDÍGENA TRADITION. These were the earliest settlers of the middle Uruguay River (northeastern Argentina, western Uruguay, and southern Brazil). Their sites date to the Late Pleistocene-Early Holocene transition. This tradition consists of two principal phases: Ibicuí (to the north), 10,700 BC, and Uruguay (to the south) dated to 9500–6500 BC. Stone tools are bifacial (projectile points) and unifacial.

PALERMO. Largest Sillumocco (Upper **Formative**) and **Tiwanaku**-Period settlement in the Juli-Pomata area, Titicaca basin, Peru. The corporate **architecture** of the site dates to the Upper Formative, and it was later rebuilt. A semisubterranean court that measures fifteen by fifteen meters was also used in Tiwanaku times.

PALLESTRINI, LUCIANA. Brazilian archaeologist who worked in Brazil and Paraguay. She obtained her doctorate in 1970 from the University of Paris with *Fouilles dans trois sites brésiliens du haute Paranapanema, méthode et résultats*. Pallestrini is one of the founding members of the Sociedade de Arqueología Brasileira (Brazilian Archaeological Society). She published *Sitio Arqueológico Fonseca*,

Arqueología Pré-História Brasileira with José Luis de Morais (1982); *Arqueología: Métodos y Técnicas em Superfícies Amplias* with José Antonio Gomez Perasso (1984); and *Sambaquí da Beirada a luz da metodologia por superficies amplas: Saquarema, Rio de Janeiro* with Lina Maria Kneip (1990).

PALLI AIKE. Cave located close to the Strait of Magellan, southern Chile. Along with **Fell Cave**, it is one of the earliest sites excavated in South America's southernmost region. Palli Aike was dated to 6600 BC. The characteristic stone tool is the **fishtail point**. *See also* PAMPA DEL ASADOR.

PAMBAMARCA. Vast complex of **Inka** stone fortresses located in the northern highlands of Ecuador. All are situated between 2,900 and 4,100 meters above sea level, with the vast majority over 3,600 meters above sea level. *See also* FORTIFICATIONS.

PAMPA DE LAS LLAMAS (PAMPA DE LOS INCAS). Pampa de los Incas represents the premier **Moche** ceremonial and administrative center in the Santa valley, north coast of Peru. It is located in the lower valley and covers an area of more than two square kilometers. The site is dominated by a network of characteristic **adobe** platforms and walls. As was common in other Moche ceremonial agglomerations, **ceramic** production workshops were located here. They appear to have specialized in specific and restricted types, suggesting the presence of a central administration dictating the conditions of production. *See also* SECHÍN ALTO.

PAMPA DEL ASADOR. Important **obsidian** quarry in north-central Santa Cruz, southern Argentina. Obsidian from this source was transported over long distances in the Patagonian region, from the Andes to the Atlantic coast. This black obsidian was exploited at least since 7700 BC at the nearby site of Cerro Casa de Piedra 7. Pampa del Asador obsidian was used in **Palli Aike**'s Period II (8000–6500 BC), reached Tierra del Fuego more than six hundred kilometers to the south, and was found in Peninsula Valdez more than eight hundred kilometers to the northeast.

PAMPA GRANDE. Large **Moche** V site in the **Lambayeque** valley on the north coast of Peru that covers six square kilometers. The Moche V Period extends from AD 600 to 800. In the central zone of the site there are two large **pyramids**, including the most imposing construction of Huaca Fortaleza (or Huaca 1), nearly 250 by 150 meters on the side and 50 meters tall. This **huaca** is made of **adobe** and appears to have served as the main temple and elite residence of the site. Numerous compounds—rectangular enclosures with rooms in the interior—characterize Pampa Grande. Inhabitants of Pampa Grande had access to a wide variety of food resources, including **agriculture** (**maize**, beans, squash, avocado, peanut, **algarroba**, guava, lúcuma, and chili pepper), **domesticated animals** (dog, **guinea pig**, **Muscovy duck** and **llama**), marine resources (fish, shellfish, mammals, and birds), and terrestrial wild animals (deer, fox, *vizcacha*, opossum, and lizards).

The urban center of Pampa Grande in the Lambayeque valley is the impressive counterpart of **Galindo** (both dating to the Late Moche Period) in the Moche Valley, and it has been the subject of extensive archaeological analysis in recent decades. The city is characterized by a dense conglomeration of differentiated ceremonial constructions, residences, craft facilities, and administrative architecture. The enormous Huaca Fortaleza and elaborate precincts point to urban planning and a highly specialized administrative apparatus. At its height, an estimated 10,000–15,000 people inhabited the city.

The scale and complexity of monumental architecture at Pampa Grande has led archaeologists to assume that it served as the preeminent capital of the Late Moche Period, and it was undoubtedly one of the largest urban settlements to ever develop in the ancient Andes. Although greater continuity characterized the establishment of Pampa Grande, such as the construction of Huaca Fortaleza and the propagation of certain Moche iconographic themes, this city demonstrates significant deviation from urban settlement in the preceding Middle Period. Adoption of expedient construction methods, the integration of ceremonial architecture in large walled compounds, and evidence of strict social division are novel developments that find parallels at Galindo. For instance, the southern piedmont of the site is thought to have housed a large population of subjugated **Gallinazo** farmers.

The city can be divided into fourteen sectors comprised of monumental **architecture**, forty compounds, workshops, and a mass of contiguous room blocks similar to the small, agglutinated rooms at **Chan Chan**. Pampa Grande is dominated by an enormous compound ("The Great Compound") 600 by 400 meters in area that enclosed Huaca Fortaleza and specialized storage and administrative facilities. The huaca itself is one of the largest erected on the north coast, measuring 270 by 180 meters and 38 meters tall, and it was constructed with a core infrastructure of adobe chambers filled with sand and rubble. This chamber-and-fill technique, possibly adopted from the central coast, permitted much more rapid construction of the edifice than did earlier bricklaying. Only two building episodes have been detected (in contrast to the eight stages of **Huaca del Sol**), and it is evident that the principal monument was expediently built and actively used for a relatively short period.

Huaca Fortaleza, located on the highest point of the pampa, consists of a three-tiered pyramid accessed by a gradually ascending ramp 290 meters long. Three checkpoints along the ramp suggest that access to the huaca was strictly controlled. Excavations revealed that the pyramid was the setting of elaborate ritual activity and possibly elite residence.

The Great Compound and the pyramid of Compound B (considerably smaller than Huaca Fortaleza but an impressive temple nonetheless) were surrounded by smaller precincts associated with raised **mounds** and workshops. Research has shown that the civic ceremonial center of Pampa Grande was an important manufacturing center. Laborers appear to have inhabited peripheral sectors of the city and to have worked in the well-planned shops of the nonresidential center. Workshops or procurement structures dedicated to the production of textiles, ***Spondylus*** shell ornaments, **ceramics**, and **metallurgy** usually clustered according to **trade** in the central sectors of the city. They are often associated with "hierarchical terraced complexes" with ramps, which are believed to have been involved in the supervision of craft production. The large volume of specialized storage space in the numerous compounds indicates that elite-directed redistribution of agricultural surpluses and craft goods underwrote the political economy of the Pampa Grande state.

Pampa Grande could have been a city-state, and the depth and extent of its territorial hegemony remains a subject of debate. It seems likely that this paramount city exercised considerable influence in the Lambayeque region and in Zaña to the south. Similarities in ceramic industries also indicate contact with the inhabitants of Jequetepeque. Significantly, Pampa Grande (AD 600–750), like Galindo (AD 550–650/700), was relatively short-lived and was destroyed in a conflagration thought to have resulted from internal social discord and political revolt.

PAMPA KOANI. *See* KOANI PAMPA.

PANAQA (PANAKA). Royal **ayllu** of the **Inka** state in the **Cuzco** region, Peru. Panaqas included all descendants of a former Inka who lived in large palaces in the city of Cuzco and maintained the estate and **mummy** bundle of the deceased Inka king. Panaqa members followed many traditions to preserve the deeds of the former ruler. These included taking care of his mummy bundle and the use of quipus and paintings as devices to record important deeds of the life of their ancestors. In certain celebrations, the members of the panaqa brought the mummy to the main square of Cuzco. Panaqa members included numerous servants, called *yana* (plural *yanakuna* or *yanacona*). *See also* CEQUE SYSTEM; MACHU PICCHU; YUCAY.

PAÑAMARCA. Moche civic-ceremonial center in the Nepeña Valley, north coast of Peru. Pañamarca is the most impressive monumental complex of the Moche Tradition in this area, and consists of a five-tiered platform **mound** surrounded by ample plazas. Its summit, reached from below by a steep side ramp, was constructed with chambers containing important burials and **adobe** wall friezes. The murals include a procession of eight warriors and a famous depiction of the **sacrifice ceremony**. The majority of Moche domestic settlements clustered around this important ceremonial center.

PANTANAL TRADITION. Sites with characteristic **ceramics** of the same name and consisting of **mounds** in the area of the Gran Pantanal, southwestern Brazil, near the border of Brazil, Bolivia, and Paraguay. The tradition is defined by two phases (Pantanal and Jacadigo) identified at isolated sites in the Gran Pantanal region.

PANZALEO. Ceramic style from the north-central highlands of Ecuador dating to the Early Period of **Regional Development** (500 BC–AD 600). The ceramics depict individuals chewing **coca** leaves, individuals with masks, and individuals holding **trophy heads**. This ceramic style is also found in the upper Amazon basin of Ecuador.

PARACAS. Art style and culture from southern Peru. Paracas sites are distributed in **Chincha**, Pisco, the Paracas Peninsula, and Ica. They date to the Early Horizon (800 BC–AD 1). The Paracas art style is closely linked to the figure of the **Oculate Being** and has been divided into ten phases (**Ocucaje** 1 to 10). A large cemetery on the **Cerro Colorado** hill (Paracas Necropolis) contained numerous **mummy** bundles with very fine textiles and offerings. *See also* TOPARÁ.

PARANAÍBA PHASE. Late Pleistocene-Early Holocene group of sites in the Serranópolis region of Goias, central Brazil. Sites are located in rock shelters and caves as well as open-air sites. The dates range from 9000 to 6500 BC. Stone tools are mostly unifacial (endscrapers and sidescrapers) and were manufactured with local raw materials. Ground and polished tools are also characteristic of this phase, as well as bone tools. **Hunting** was very important in Paranaíba culture: deer, tatú, large and small rodents, carnivores, reptiles, and birds. Fish were also important in their diet. There are no remains of **megafauna**. Occupation levels consist of broad deposits of charcoal, bones, and tools. *See also* TRADITION.

PASO OTERO 5. Late Pleistocene-early Holocene site located along the banks of the Quequén Grande River in the province of Buenos Aires, Argentina. This site dates to around 8200 BC. **Megafauna** remains (undetermined species of the genus *Equus*, *Megatherium*, *Toxodon*, and *Hemiauchenia*) were associated with the material culture of the site. A fragment of what could be a **fishtail projectile point** was found among a great quantity of burned and unburned bone fragments.

PASTORALISM. In pre-Columbian South America, pastoralism is equated with the **domestication** of **camelids** (**llama** and **alpaca**) in the Andes. Camelid herds were important for many groups living in the higher altitudes of the central and southern Andes during the last 7,000 years. *See also* WANKARANI.

PAYPASO. Late Pleistocene open-air site in Artigas, northwest Uruguay. It has been dated to between 7890 BC and AD 1. Stone tools of the earliest occupation include stemmed triangular projectile points, similar to those of contemporaneous sites of the Uruguay phase of southern Brazil.

PEDRA PINTADA CAVE. A cave located in the lower Amazon in Brazil. The earlier occupation, designated Monte Alegre, dated to around 9200 BC. The name in Portuguese means "painted stone" and refers to the **rock art**, which includes geometric, animal, and human figures (hands of adults and children). **Hunting** scenes and animals giving birth are also depicted. As fragments of pigments were found in the deepest layers, it can be assumed that at least part of the rock art dates to around 9200 BC. People living in Pedra Pintada subsisted on a diverse diet: there is a wide variety of faunal remains, including fish, reptiles, birds, rodents, and mammals associated with the archaeological deposits. Plant remains include palm fruits, nuts, and leguminous plants, and the stone tools include triangular projectile points made of quartz. The second occupation, named Paituna, dates to 2,000 years later and is associated with **ceramics** that were manufactured between 5500 and 3000 BC and could thus be the earliest in the Americas. They were fabricated with sand or shell temper and consisted largely of simple bowls, some of which exhibit **incised and punctated** decoration on or below the rims. Ceramics and subsistence were similar to the site of **Taperinha**. Numerous disk beads of shell were also found at this site, as well as stone points made of chalcedony.

PEINE. Small **Inka tampu** located along the Inka road in the southeastern shores of the Salar de Atacama, northern Chile.

PEÑA ROJA. Early preceramic site in the upper Caquetá River, southeastern Colombia, at 170 meters above sea level. The earliest occupation dates between 7200 and 7100 BC. Most artifacts were manufactured from small **chert** cobbles, locally found. Bifacial artifacts and fine retouch are conspicuously absent at this site. Most artifacts appear to have been expedient and *ad hoc*. A heavy reliance on plants is suggested by the botanical remains recovered from Peña Roja.

PIEDRA MUSEO. Group of rock shelters in the central plateau of Santa Cruz, southern Argentina, associated with Late Pleistocene occupations. Rock shelter AEP-1 yielded the earliest date of occupation of southernmost Patagonia: 10,890 BC. **Fishtail projectile points** were found at the end of the oldest occupation (8500 BC).

PIKILLACTA. One of the largest grid-shaped **Wari** monumental complexes, located in the **Cuzco** valley, southern Peru. It occupies an area of approximately two square kilometers. Large rectangular compounds are imposed over the irregular topography. The site has few internal roads (avenues, streets, or gateways), suggesting that there was limited access to its subdivisions. These were residential, ceremonial, and administrative units. *See also* TURQUOISE.

PILGRIMAGE. Important aspect of some South American **religions**. In the central Andes, **Chavín de Huantar**, **Pachacamac**, and the **Island of the Sun** in Lake Titicaca were important pilgrimage centers. *See also* LA PLATA ISLAND; PACATNAMU.

PIMAPIRU (PIRURU). Located in the upper Marañón valley of central-northern Peru and distinguished by two small preceramic temples that date to 3000–2500 BC. They predate the **Kotosh Religious Tradition** temples.

PIPE. Many South American groups used pipes, usually made of **ceramics**, for the ritual inhalation of tobacco or **hallucinogenic substances**. In Brazil, the term **cachimbo** is used. Ceramic pipes are common in **Formative** (Early Period) cultures of northwest Argentina such as **Ciénaga**, **Condorhuasi**, and **Tafí**, and in Colombia, pipes are present in **Calima** sites. In Brazil, cachimbos are part of archaeological assemblages in Tapajós. *See also* SAPUCAÍ.

PIRCA. Wall made with cobbles or fieldstones with or without mortar. It is a common **architectural** form in Andean coastal and interior valleys as well as in the highlands, but it is not universal. **Adobe** was also widely used. *See also* EL ALFARCITO; EL INDÍGENO; HUANUCO PAMPA; LA PAYA; LLULLAILLACO; MOLLO CULTURE; QUILMES; RANCHILLOS; TASTIL; TILCARA.

PIRINCAY. Site in the Paute valley near the modern city of Cuenca, southern Ecuadorian highlands. The Paute valley constituted a major **trade** route between the valleys and highlands of southern Ecuador. Eggshell **ceramics** and exotic materials (shell and crystal) were recovered from the site. Thirty-seven radiocarbon dates have been obtained from Pirincay. In the Late **Formative Period**, from 1400 to 1200 BC, the site of Pirincay became a permanent village and the first ceramics were manufactured there. Pirincay is also known for its rock crystal bead industry, and quartz hammerstones were the main tools used to manufacture the beads. These beads were highly valued by coastal people. Pirincay was abandoned in the first century AD.

PISAQ. Inka site along the Urubamba River, situated near the city of **Cuzco**. Pisaq exhibits some of the most elaborate Inka stonework and numerous **agricultural** terraces.

PITRÉN PHASE OR COMPLEX. Archaeological sites that correspond to the Early **Mapuche** culture of southern Chile. The Mapuche lived in the region extending from the Bio River to Lake Llanquihue. They also lived west of the Andes in the Neuquén province of southern Argentina. Pitrén is equivalent to the **Formative period** of other regions. The sites of this complex include Vergel I, Tirúa, Pucón VI, and Huimpil, with dates of circa AD 660. The inhabitants of these sites were **hunters** and gatherers. *See also* MALACHITE.

PLANÁLTICA TRADITION. This tradition includes a number of sites with **ceramics** that are distributed in the southern Brazilian plateau (*planalto*) and the Atlantic coast. The Planáltica Tradition includes four subtraditions: Taquara (AD 170–1700), **Itararé** (AD 500–1500), Casa de Pedra (around AD 900–1100) (Brazil), and Eldoradense in northeastern Argentina. Taquara sites have semisubterranean houses, particularly in the higher—and colder—parts of the planalto, where there are pine forests (*Araucaria angustifolia*). Small ceramic vessels decorated with incisions or basketry molds are characteristic of this subtradition. The lithic artifacts of the Planáltica Tradition are similar to those of the **Humaitá Tradition**.

PLATENSE TRADITION. *See* VIEIRA TRADITION.

PLATINUM. Rare metal used by craftspeople of several groups in Ecuador and Colombia, including **La Tolita** and **Muisca**. *See also* METALLURGY.

POLITICAL ORGANIZATION. Indigenous societies of South America were organized under different forms of political organization based on how power was concentrated in specific individuals or groups of people. **Agriculturally**-based communities of central and northern South America usually formed small political units, what traditionally have been called **señoríos**. The position of the *señores* or *principales* was sometimes hereditary, while in other societies their power was very limited. They were involved in directing communal labor activities, solving disputes, redistributing goods, organizing religious ceremonies, and other public activities. In the central Andes, larger political units were formed under the aegis of divine kings, such as the **Chimú** and the **Inka**, which can be considered large states or empires. **Hunters** and gatherers of **Chaco**, Pampa, Patagonia, and other regions of South America were organized in autonomous groups called bands. *See also* SEÑORÍO; MANCO CAPAC.

POLYCHROME HORIZON. This **ceramic** style horizon is associated with the emergence of complex societies in the Amazon basin. Its origins can be dated to around AD 1. One of the earliest examples is the **Marajoara**, situated in the mouth of the Amazon. Widespread use of **funerary urns** and ancestor cults constitute an overarching practice of cultures belonging to this tradition. *See also* THÉMIRE.

PONCE SANGINÉS, CARLOS (1925–2005). Bolivian archaeologist whose research concentrated on the urban site of **Tiwanaku**, where he excavated since the late 1950s. He pioneered in the study of sourcing lithic materials (sandstone, andesite, **obsidian**, and **basalt**) in the Lake Titicaca basin. Among his published articles and books are *Cerámica Tiwanacota* (1957); *Descripción Sumaria del Templete Semisubterraneo de Tiwanaku* (1969); *La ciudad de Tiwanaku* (1969); *Las culturas Wankarani y Chiripa, y su relación con Tiwanaku* (1970); *Acerca de la Procedencia del Material Lítico de los Monumentos de Tiwanaku. Examen Arqueológico* with G. *Mogrovejo Terrazas* (1970); *Pumapunku* (1971); *Tiwanaku: Espacio, Tiempo y*

Cultura. Ensayo de síntesis arqueológica (1972, a second edition in 1981); *La Cerámica de la Época I de Tiwanaku* (1976); *Panorama de la arqueología boliviana* (1980); *Exploraciones arqueológicas subacuáticas en el lago Titikaka. Informe científico* with J. Reinhard, M. Portugal, E. Pareja, and L. Ticlla (1992); and *Tiwanaku: 200 años de investigaciones arqueológicas* (1995). In 1957, he organized in La Paz the first national archaeology round table (Mesa Redonda de Arqueología Boliviana). One of the **monoliths** located in **Tiwanaku**'s **Kalasasaya** temple takes his name ("Monolito Ponce").

PONSOMBY. Site located in southernmost Chile. Its Level B dates to 1700 BC and contained large lanceolate points similar to those of **Lancha Packewaia**'s ancient component (2000 BC).

PORTRAIT VESSELS. *See* HUACO (WACO) RETRATO.

POTATO (*SOLANUM TUBEROSUM*). Important crop domesticated in the Andean highlands, probably in the Titicaca basin, where there are at present some 300 varieties of different shapes, colors, textures, and flavors. Potatoes are transformed into **chuño** by exposing them to several nights of freezing temperatures. *See also* PUNA.

POTRERO DE PAYOGASTA. Large **Inka** garrison surrounded by several walls in Salta, northwest Argentina. The constructions are very elaborate and built with many quarried stones; walls often reach two meters high or more, especially the ramparts that form part of the forty-meter-long **kallanka**. The central square contains an **ushnu**. The site was also a center of **metallurgical** production. Most **ceramics** are Inka in style. Potrero is one of Argentina's national historic monuments.

POTTERY. *See* CERAMICS.

PRESENTATION SCENE. *See* SACRIFICE SCENE.

PUEBLITO. Large **Tairona** site in northern Colombia with numerous stone structures and stone-paved roads covering several hectares. It has been partly restored and is located in a national park. It is not far from **Ciudad Perdida**.

PUÉMAPE. Large site of the Middle **Cupisnique** and **Salinar** cultures of the northern coast of Peru. The site was abandoned at the end of Cupisnique and was expanded by the Salinar. It occupies twenty hectares, with numerous residences, cemeteries, temples, and other constructions.

PUERTO HORMIGA. One of the earliest **ceramic** sites in South America. Puerto Hormiga dates to the Archaic Period, between 4000–3000 BC, and is located near the Caribbean coast immediately south of the city of Cartagena, on the lower Magdalena River, Colombia. Puerto Hormiga is located one hundred kilometers northwest of **San Jacinto 1**, another early ceramic site. It consists of a ring-shaped **shell midden** formed of oyster shells and fish bones. Globular bowls are typical of this early period, and the clay temper is of plant fiber. The **pottery** is decorated with incisions and punctations, with some human or animal heads modeled on the rims. *See also* MALAMBO CULTURE; TECOMATE.

PUKARA (PUCARA). 1. Site on a hill or mountain top, usually surrounded by walls, in Peru, Bolivia, northern Chile, and northwest Argentina. They usually date to the Late Intermediate Period (1000–1400 AD), the period characterized by the fragmentation of preexisting larger polities. 2. Urban site and ceremonial center located in the northern Titicaca basin, Peru. Several platforms with temples and **sunken courts** represent the most prominent **architecture** of the site. Pukara dates to the **Formative Period**, and it was occupied from 200 BC to AD 200. The residential area extends over four square kilometers at the foot of the hill. Characteristic **ceramics**—**polychrome**, modeled, and **incised**—and other material elements with Pukara iconography were found in the Titicaca basin, in the **Cuzco** area, and in sites of the northern Chilean coast, suggesting that Pukara was the first Titicaca-basin polity to establish colonies in these areas. Pukara was an important center of the **Yaya-Mama Religious Tradition**. *See also* OCUCAJE; QALUYU.

PUKARA DE ANDALGALÁ. Important **fortified Inka** site in the southeastern frontier of the empire (Catamarca, Argentina). It is surrounded by narrow doors and high stone walls that measure three kilometers in length and sometimes up to four meters high.

PUKARA JULI. A primary regional center in the Late Intermediate (**Altiplano**) Period, Titicaca basin, Peru. There are five defensive walls that surround the site: they are massive, reaching approximately 2 meters high and 1.5 meters wide. A high density of throwing stones was recovered from the site, and excavations in one sector uncovered numerous storage vessels, probably to support sustained sieges. *See also* FORTIFICATIONS.

PUKIO. A sunken garden found in pre-Columbian sites along the desert coast of Peru. The soil was excavated to reach the water table and the most elaborate examples were built by **Nasca** groups.

PUMA (*FELIS CONCOLOR*). Large feline that lives in many regions of western and southern South America. The puma was an important element in the **religion** of many indigenous cultures. Pumas were represented in **ceramics**, textiles, **metallurgy**, bone, and other media.

PUMPU. Important **Inka** site in the north shores of Lake Junín, central Peru. Pumpu is located along the main Inka highland road. In its center is a large trapezoidal plaza with a central **ushnu** that covers seventeen hectares. Several hundred **qolcas**, some **kallankas**, dwellings, and the remains of a bridge over the Mantaro River also form a large part of the site.

PUNA. High plateau formed between the two cordilleras in the central and southern Andes. The average altitude of the puna is between 3,500 and 4,000 meters above sea level. The puna was the center of domestication of **camelids** and highland tubers (**potato**, **oca**, **ulluku**, **mashwa**, and so on) and an area of dense population in pre-Columbian times. Rainfall, which is concentrated between December and March, decreases from north to south. In the northern and central puna, lakes are present including Lake Titicaca, the locus of dense population in pre-Columbian times. The southern puna (southern Bolivia, northern Chile, and northwest Argentina) is extremely dry. *See also* SALT.

PUQUI STYLE. Ceramic style that characterizes the settlements of the Middle Period (AD 600–1000) of the southern highlands of Bolivia, particularly around the salares. This style was in use by **llama** caravaners who lived around the Coipasa and Uyuni salares of Potosí and Oruro. Users of Puqui ceramics probably connected the inhabitants of the **Tiwanaku** heartland area with villages from the southern **altiplano**. The typical ceramic forms are **keros** and bowls with red bands painted on a light orange slip; they present stylistic similarities with Tiwanaku wares.

PURIPICA-1. Archaic site located some kilometers north of the Salar de Atacama, northern Chile, at approximately 2,300 meters above sea level. The site was dated to 2800–2000 BC. Thirty to forty circular domestic structures dominate this site. The inhabitants of Puripica-1 were **hunters**, and their most common projectile point was the leaf-shaped type (**Ayampitín-Lauricocha** type).

PYRAMID. Architectural structures made of **adobe** and/or stone that were constructed in many regions of Andean South America. Some pyramids reached colossal dimensions and thus are among the most spectacular constructions of pre-Columbian America. They represent an enormous organization of labor and planned engineering. Some served as temples and mausoleums, such as **Sipán** in **Lambayeque**, Peru, which contained burials of powerful elites. The largest pyramids were located in Peru's coastal region and are locally known as **huacas**. Pyramids were likely simulacra of Andean mountain peaks, which were considered supernatural beings (*apus*) in the Andes. These monuments were considered the center of the cosmos and part of a connection or *axis mundi* between the upper and lower worlds. In **Tiwanaku**, the two pyramids of the site contained a **sunken court** on the top and a series of underground canals that moved water collected during the rainy season from the top to the base, paralleling the movement of water along mountain slopes. Many pyramids were **looted** and severely destroyed during and after the Spanish conquest. *See also* ASPERO; CABALLO MUERTO; HUACA DE LA LUNA;

HUACA DE LOS REYES; HUACA DEL SOL; PAMPA GRANDE; TALAMBO; TÚCUME.

– Q –

QALUYU. Formative culture and site in the northern Titicaca basin, Peru, that dates to 1300–500 BC. Qaluyu people constructed **raised fields** and canals along the flatlands that surround the lake shores, which underwrote an expansion in the economic basis of the society. Qaluyu was succeeded by **Pukara**.

QEYA. Late **Formative** Phase from the Titicaca basin (Bolivia and southern Peru) that dates to around AD 300–500. Its characteristic painted **ceramics** include **keros** and tripod vessels.

QOLCA (COLCA). Quechua name for stone warehouses, which are usually circular in shape and found in groups on the outskirts of an **Inka** site. **Huánuco Pampa** provides excellent examples of multiple and well preserved qolcas. The Inka stored local tribute in foodstuffs, cloth, weapons, and other materials in these masonry depositories as described in sixteenth-century Spanish documents and confirmed by archaeological investigations. Qolcas are rather good indicators of state planning and were also used by pre-Inka polities. Guaman Poma de Ayala illustrates qolcas with quipucamayocs, the accounting officers of the Inka empire who used quipus (knotted threads) to record stored items. *See also* CHOQE K'IRAW; HATUN XAUXA; NEVADO DEL ACONQUIJA; RAQCHI; SAMAIPATA; TAMBO COLORADO.

QUEBRADA DE LAS PIRCAS. Preceramic site in an upper valley of the north coast of Peru which dates to the Middle Preceramic (6200–5500 BC). It is one of the earliest sites in the Andes associated with domesticated plants, mainly squash, **quinoa**, **manioc**, *ciruela de fraile*, and peanut. It is probable that peanut and manioc were introduced from the areas east of the Andes and quinoa from the highlands.

QUEBRADA EL MEMBRILLO. Late Pleistocene site in north-central Chile, located near **Quereo**. The association of stone tools with

megafauna (*Mylodon* sp., *Paleolama*, and horse), suggests two **hunting** and butchering events that took place at the end of the Pleistocene (11,500 BC).

QUEBRADA JAGUAY. Late Pleistocene site in the department of Arequipa, southern Peru. The earliest occupations date from 9000 to 8000 BC. Settlers of camps at Quebrada Jaguay fished and collected sea mollusks. They lived most of the year close to the coast and probably moved into the high mountains during part of the year, as suggested by the presence of **obsidian**.

QUEBRADA SECA 3. Early Holocene site in the Puna of Catamarca, northwest Argentina. The earliest occupations have been dated to 8000–7000 BC.

QUECHUA (KICHUA). 1. Also known as Runa Simi, Quechua is the most widely spoken indigenous language of South America. Quechua has several dialects, and is spoken nowadays by approximately ten million people living in the valleys of Ecuador, Peru, Bolivia, parts of northern Argentina and Chile, and the southernmost part of Colombia. It was the main language used in the **Inka** empire; now it is one of the official languages of Bolivia and Peru. Quechua was also spoken in Colonial times as a *lingua franca* to convert indigenous people to Christianity, and thus it was spread into regions where Quechua was not spoken before, such as Santiago del Estero (Argentina). **Coca**, condor, pampa, **puna**, and **vicuña** are examples of Quechua words. 2. Ecological zone of the Andes located between 1,500 and 3,500 meters above sea level, characterized by a temperate year-round climate and a great variety of domesticated crops, including **maize**, beans, and squash. This valley region is where Quechua speakers traditionally live. *See also* HANAN; HURIN; INTIHUASI; QOLCA; RUMIQOLCA; TAMPU; TINCULLPA.

QUEREO. Late Pleistocene **hunting** site in central Chile, situated by the seaside resort of Los Vilos. Two radiocarbon dates of 9600 and 9400 BC were obtained for the earliest level of occupation (Quereo I). People who lived at this site hunted horse and extinct **camelid**.

However, no projectile points have been recovered from the site. The second-oldest level, Quereo II, has yielded similar dates and **megafauna** remains, mainly mastodon, horse, and paleolama, among others. Maritime resources are scarce at Quereo, which is unsurprising given that the site functioned first and foremost as a hunting-butchering site and not a campsite. *See also* QUEBRADA EL MEMBRILLO.

QUERIMITA (KERIMITA OR KEREMITA). Important **basalt** quarry located on the southwestern shores of Lake Poopó (Oruro, Bolivia). Basalt was mined from several galleries (mine shafts) and artifacts were manufactured *in situ*. Numerous piles of debris remain at various parts of the basaltic dome (flow). Basalt from Querimita is very fine-grained and thus was highly valued and transported over long distances throughout the **altiplano**. Tools made of material from this quarry were found as far north as **Tiwanaku**, **Khonko Wankane**, and **Lukurmata**, approximately three hundred kilometers to the northwest.

QUERO. *See* KERO.

QUIANI. Preceramic culture adapted to coastal maritime life situated along the north coast of Chile from Quiani to Taltal. The earliest settlements are large **shell mounds**, which date to approximately 5000 BC. The main part of the diet relied on fish, including deep-sea fish (which suggests that Quiani people fished far away from the coast); shellfish; sea mammals; turtles; and birds. **Guanaco** bones were also recovered from Quiani sites, along with domesticated plants including **maize** (first appeared around 4000 BC).

QUILLACINGA. *See* NARIÑO.

QUILMES. Large Late Period settlement located in the valley of **Santa María**, Tucumán, northwest Argentina, which dates to after AD 1000 and into the Colonial Period. Many of its **pirca** walls have been reconstructed. During the sixteenth and seventeenth centuries, Quilmes and its region became a center of resistance to Spanish domination. After several campaigns, the Quilmes were defeated and sent into exile. There is a site museum.

QUIMBAYA. Culture that developed in the Cauca River valley and central cordillera of Colombia from AD 200 to 1500. Quimbaya people cultivated **maize**, beans, and **potato**. **Coca** consumption has also been documented. **Salt** exploitation and gold **metallurgy** also constituted important activities of Quimbaya social groups. Quimbaya gold objects are usually found in **shaft and chamber tombs**, common in the Colombian highlands, and are among the finest in South America.

QUINCHA. This is a type of construction that uses perishable materials. The three main types of earthen construction in indigenous South America are **adobe**, **tapia**, and quincha. Quincha is particular to the central Pacific coast and regions where rain is absent (*see* **Angualasto**). Quincha construction is normally based on the erection of a wall panel held within a wood frame and using some type of cane as infill. This panel is covered on both sides with mud and then finished with a thin layer of plaster. Quincha is lighter than adobe, and two-story quincha buildings usually require adobe for the construction of the first floor. These buildings often survive severe earthquake activity. *See also* LLOLLEO.

QUINOA OR QUINUA (*CHENOPODIUM QUINUA*). (Pronounced *keen*-wa or *kee*-noo-ah.) Important Andean grain. Pseudocereal that was cultivated in the northern, central, and southern Andes from Colombia to central Chile and Argentina. In some regions, it was cultivated since Preceramic times, from approximately 3000 BC. Quinoa is very resistant to frost and can be cultivated as high as 4,500 meters above sea level. It is still an important staple in the central Andes. *See also* AGUA DE LA TINAJAI; ANSILTA; CASERONES; GRUTA DEL INDIO; NARIÑO; QUEBRADAS DE LAS PIRCAS; VILUCO.

QUIRIHUAC ROCK SHELTER. Paiján site in the **Moche** Valley, north coast of Peru. Two primary burials were excavated here (adult and child). The adult was dated to 7000 BC and the child to around 8000 BC. Radiocarbon dates from the rock shelter range from 10,800 to 6500 BC.

QUIRÍPA. Perforated shells used as an exchange item in Venezuela during pre-Columbian times. As early as 1535, European travelers report the use of shell beads as currency in Venezuela, and it is highly probable that quirípa was a product of late complex society ceremonial exchanges in the region, particularly in the Andean area of Venezuela. *See also* TRADE.

QUISPISISA. The most important **obsidian** source in Peru. It was exploited since the Late Pleistocene and into **Inka** times. Quispisisa obsidian has been found from **Marca Huamachuco** in the north to **Cerro Baúl**, **Tiwanaku,** and **Lukurmata** in the south. Its distribution has been documented in coastal, valley, and **altiplano** sites. The **Chavín** cult and the **Wari** state made extensive use of this type of obsidian and probably monopolized the source. The presence of Quispisisa obsidian in Tiwanaku sites suggests formalized exchange between the Wari and Tiwanaku states. *See also* HACHA.

– R –

RAIMONDI STELA. Stone carving found in **Chavín de Huantar**, Peru. The Raimondi stela corresponds to the Late **Chavín** art style. It consists of a granite slat two meters high and portrays a staff-bearing **deity** with an intricate headdress that covers more than half of the sculpture.

RAISED FIELDS. Agricultural feature utilized in many regions of lowland and highland South America. Synonymous indigenous terms for these fields include **sukakollos** or **wara wara**. Large portions of flatlands, encompassing several hundred or thousands of square kilometers in area, were transformed into vast agricultural areas. Other construction features such as canals, aqueducts, and causeways are associated with the raised fields. Most raised fields were abandoned at the time of the European conquest or shortly after, and very few references to their use were recorded during the Colonial Period. Only recently have ancient raised fields been reutilized, and they have produced high yields, suggesting that raised fields in pre-Columbian times provided food to sustain vast populations. *See also* KOANI PAMPA; MOXOS; QALUYU; TIWANAKU.

RANCHILLOS. One of the southernmost **Inka** sites, located in northern Mendoza, Argentina. Ranchillos is located at 1,950 meters above sea level, above the **agricultural** limits. Numerous **pirca** constructions, covering approximately three hectares and often built with trapezoidal doors and windows, constitute the bulk of the site's built environment. A **kallanka** is also present and an Inka road crosses the site.

RANCHO PELUDO. Archaic site in the interior of Venezuela in the Coro region of the basin of Lake Maracaibo. The discovery of clay griddles or **budares** indicate the importance of **agricultural** activities at this site. **Ceramic funerary urns** have also been recovered here. *See also* DABAJUROID.

RANCHO PELUDO STYLE. The earliest style of the **Dabajuro** cultural tradition. Rancho Peludo is a large site with several occupations that date from 1800 BC to AD 1500.

RAQCHI. Important **Inka** site located south of **Cuzco**. It is situated in an area of lava flows exploited by Inka masons for building material. The site covers eighty hectares and is surrounded by a wall. The most important building is the Temple of **Viracocha**, a **kallanka** that measures ninety-two by twenty-five meters. It was one of the largest roofed Inka buildings and represents one of the few Inka structures in the highlands constructed in part from **adobe**. In the southern sector of the site, there are remains of dozens of circular **qolcas**.

RAYED DEITY. One of the mythological beings that form the pantheon of the north coast of Peru. *See also* DEITIES; SACRIFICE CEREMONY OR SCENE.

REAL ALTO. Large **Valdivia** settlement in coastal Ecuador with origins around 3200 BC. The settlement grew in size and complexity through several hundred years. Paired structures situated across from each other on either side of a large plaza constituted the monumental core of the settlement during an early phase (Phase 2B). In the later Phase 3, these precincts were rebuilt to form platforms supporting public structures on their summits. One of the structures contained burials of twenty individuals, and the other served as a public space for communal feasting. This suggests that the Valdivia society was becoming hierarchical, and it was probably divided into moieties. The two **mounds** were expanded in several periods, including the renovation of the temple that crowned the mounds. *See also STROMBUS*.

RECUAY CULTURE. A culture that developed in the Callejón de Huaylas and the headwaters of the Santa River in the northern highlands of Peru during the Early Intermediate Period (AD 1 to AD 500). Most information on Recuay Culture derives from **looted tombs** and stone sculpture, although recent excavations of important Recuay sites have improved our understanding of this enigmatic culture. The **ceramics** are elaborate, exhibiting negative painting, positive painting, and three-dimensional modeling. The vessels portray scenes of daily life, military activities, and religious imagery, and supernatural figures are commonly depicted (serpents, two-headed animals, and dragonlike creatures). Recuay ceramics are also occasionally present in rich **Moche** tombs, suggesting that status goods were exchanged between Recuay and Moche elites. Sculpture represents human figures with crossed hands, phalluses, and stereotyped expressions. *See also* TRANSPORTATION.

REGIONAL DEVELOPMENT PERIOD. In northwest Argentina, this term designates the period from AD 1000 to 1400, while in Ecuador and Colombia it refers to the period from 200 BC to AD 500, or in some instances up to the Spanish conquest. This period is characterized by several small-scale independent political units (**señoríos**) and regional variation in **ceramic** styles. *See also* BAHÍA; LA PLATA ISLAND.

REICHEL-DOLMATOFF, GERARDO (1912–1994). Famous Austrian ethnographer and archaeologist who was born in Salzburg but in the 1940s traveled to Colombia, where he spent most of his life. His main work was in ethnography, but he laid the basis for archaeological research in Colombia. His published works include *Investigaciones arqueológicas en la Sierra Nevada de Santa Marta*, parts 1, 2, and 3 (1954) and part 4 with Alicia Reichel-Dolmatoff (1955); *Excavaciones en los conchales de la Costa de Barlovento* (1955); *Momil. Excavaciones arqueológicas en el Sinú* with Alicia Reichel-Dolmatoff (1956); *Reconocimiento arqueológico de la hoya del río Sinú* with Alicia Reichel-Dolmatoff (1957); *La mesa. Un complejo arqueológico de la Sierra Nevada de Santa Marta* with Alicia Reichel-Dolmatoff (1959); *Investigaciones arqueológicas en la Costa Pacífica de Colombia. I: El Sitio de Cupica* with Alicia Reichel (1961); *Excavaciones arqueológicas en Puerto Hormiga, departamento de Bolivar* (1965); *Colombia: Ancient Peoples and Places* (1965); and *Monsú, un sitio arqueológico* (1985). In 1964, Reichel-Dolmatoff founded the first department of anthropology in a Colombian university at Universidad de los Andes.

RELIGION. South American indigenous religions permeated everyday life in a variety of ways. The belief that everything in nature was animated by supernatural forces was universal to South American indigenous societies. Religious specialists were mediators between the people and supernatural forces. **Deities** were associated with the **agricultural** cycle or the cycle of nature in general, landscape, and **warfare**, among others, and were propitiated with different types of offerings that included natural (***Spondylus***, crystals, and so on) or human-made products (textiles, metal ornaments, and so on). Some deities were anthropomorphic, others were zoomorphic (**jaguar**-like). *See also* CAPACOCHA; CHACHAPUMA; CHORRERA; CHUCARIPUPATA; DEITIES; FANGED DEITY; HALLUCINOGENIC SUBSTANCES; HUACA; INTI; ILLAPA; JAGUAR; KALLANKA; KOTOSH RELIGIOUS TRADITION; LAMBAYEQUE; MACHU PICCHU; MAIZE; MAIZE GOD; NANCHOC; NORTH PERUVIAN HIGHLANDS FORMATIVE PERIOD; OCULATE BEING; PILGRIMAGE; PUMA; RAYED DEITY; SACRIFICE; SHAFT AND CHAMBER TOMB; SMILING GOD; SUNKEN COURT; TIWANAKU; TROPHY HEADS; U-SHAPED CENTERS; YAYAMAMA.

RIBEREÑOS PLÁSTICOS STYLE. Modeled **ceramic** from the low Paraná-Uruguay basin that dates to AD 500–1600. The ceramics have thick walls and are characterized by the modeling of bird heads and representations of mammals, reptiles, and mollusks. Many forms are similar to those of the **Sabanas Bajas Tradition**.

RÍO HONDO. Obsidian source located close to Popayán in the southern Colombian highlands. It is probably the northernmost obsidian source in South America. Obsidian from this source was found in highland sites up to two hundred kilometers to the north and was exploited since the Late Pleistocene or Early Holocene (8000 BC). The use of obsidian in the region declined with the transition from **hunting** and gathering to **agricultural** lifestyles.

ROCK ART. Throughout South America many indigenous groups utilized boulders, rock shelters, and caves to produce engraved and/or painted images of religious significance for them, many of which have been preserved to date. Drawings include geometric figures and naturalistic representations of animals, plants, and humans. Among the earliest forms of rock art are those of the Late Pleistocene-Early Holocene **hunters** of **Cueva de las Manos Pintadas**. *See also* CERRO COLORADO; CUEVA DEL CERRO GAVILÁN; CUEVA DEL HUENUL; CUEVA DEL SANTO; CUEVA PINTADA; CUEVA SUSUDE INAVA; EL CEIBO; GRADIN, CARLOS J.; GRUTA DEL INDIO; INCA CUEVA 4; ITAPARICA TRADITION; MOSTNY, GRETE; NIEMEYER, HANS WALTER; NORDESTE TRADITION; PAIJÁN; PEDRA PINTADA CAVE; SANTANA DO RIACHO; SCHOBINGER, JUAN; TOQUEPALA CAVES; TRANSPORTATION.

RONQUÍN. 1. Site with Formative and later occupations in the middle Orinoco, Venezuela. 2. **Ceramic** style of the Amazonian **Formative Period**, a phase of the **Saladoid** series. Broad-line incision, modeling, and carving are common. Some vessels are painted with red and white. Ronquín has several phases; one of the most important is Ronquín Sombra. *See also* COROZAL; LA GRUTA.

ROWE, JOHN HOWLAND (1918–2004). American archaeologist whose scholarly research focused on the **Inka** empire through analyses of archaeological and ethnohistoric materials. His works include *An Introduction to the Archaeology of Cuzco* (1944); *Inca Culture at* *the Time of the Spanish Conquest* (1946); *The Kingdom of Chimor* (1948); *Archaeological Explorations in Southern Peru, 1954–55* (1956); *Chavín Art, an Inquiry into its Form and Meaning* (1962); *Urban Settlements in Ancient Peru* (1963); *Form and Meaning in Chavín Art* (1967); and *Peruvian Archaeology: Selected Readings*, edited with Dorothy Menzel (1967). *See also* UHLE, MAX.

RUMIQOLCA. Inka quarry for construction stone located thirty-five kilometers southwest of **Cuzco**. Its name in **Quechua** means "rock warehouse"—*rumi* (stone), *qolca* (warehouse). The quarry is still in use today. Many fragments of blocks of different stages of masonry production illustrate the process of ancient quarrying. Workers used wood, stone, and/or **bronze** tools to extract blocks along natural fractures of the quarry.

RYDEN, STIG (1908–1965). Swedish archaeologist who worked in several regions of the Andes. He also conducted ethnographic research in the lowlands of Bolivia. He published *Archaeological Researches in the Department of La Candelaria* (Province of Salta, Argentina) with J. Kultkranz and W. Kaudern (1936) and *Contribution to the Archaeology of the Río Loa Region* (1944) from his research in northern Chile. His later works focused on Bolivia and included *Archaeological Researches in the Highlands of Bolivia* (1947); *Chullpa Pampa: A Pre Tiahuanacu Archaeological Site in the Cochabamba Region; A Preliminary Report* (1952); *The Erland Nordenskjold Archaeological Collection from the Mizque Valley, Bolivia* (1956); *Andean Excavations I—The Tiahuanaco Era East of Lake Titicaca* (1957); and *Andean Excavations II—Tupuraya and Cayhuasi: Two Tiahuanaco Sites* (1959), as well as *Complementary Notes on the Pre-Tiahuanacu Site of Chullpa Pampa, Cochabamba Area and Notes on One Tiahuanaco Site in La Paz* (1961).

– S –

SABANAS BAJAS TRADITION. This **ceramic** tradition includes the **Vieira**, Salto Grande, and Ibicueña subtraditions of the La Plata basin, located throughout the lowland savannas of northeastern

Argentina, western Uruguay, and southeastern Brazil. *See also* RIBEREÑOS PLÁSTICOS STYLE.

SACANANA. Obsidian source located in northern Chubut, Patagonia, Argentina. This black obsidian was used by groups living in a one hundred-kilometer radius of the source since approximately 200 BC.

SACRIFICE. Animal and human sacrifice was practiced by several South American pre-Columbian societies, such as the **Aguada**, **Moche**, **Nasca**, **Tiwanaku**, and **Inka**, in important ritual celebrations. Spaniard chroniclers describe the sacrifice of **llamas** in **Cuzco** and the ritual sacrifice of children, known as **capacocha**. The **Muisca** of Colombia buried children who were sacrificial victims under house floors. These children appear to have been brought from the lowlands. Among the indigenous people of Venezuela, ritual cannibalism was an important form of human sacrifice. *See also* DOS CABEZAS; HIGH-ALTITUDE SANCTUARIES; HUACA DE LA LUNA; HUACA EL BRUJO; LAMBAYEQUE; PAÑAMARCA; SAN JOSÉ DE MORO; SIPÁN; TROPHY HEADS.

SACRIFICE CEREMONY OR SCENE. This is also referred as the Presentation Theme. It is a representation of a standardized scene that appears in **Moche ceramics**. In this scene, prisoners are sacrificed and their blood is offered to the **fanged** or **rayed deity**. Evidence that these sacrifices took place were found in several Moche sites including **San José de Moro**. *See also* SIPÁN.

SACSAYWAMAN. Inka fortress and site of ritual celebrations located in the outskirts of the city of **Cuzco**. Its massive zigzagging walls with very elaborate stonework represent the epitome of Inka **architectural** genius. A large open space or plaza that served to stage major public gatherings (military or other), as it does nowadays for the Inti Raymi celebrations (winter solstice), fronts the main series of walls.

SALADOID. Ceramic tradition from the Orinoco region, a part of the **Saladoid-Barrancoid Tradition**. The type site for this complex is Saladero in the lower Orinoco River, Venezuela. Saladoid ceramics are characterized by a reddish-ochre paste tempered with fine sand and commonly decorated with broad-line **incised** curvilinear figures and white-on-red paintings. Saladoid ceramics are fairly frequent along the middle Orinoco and its tributaries. Saladoid is found in deep underground deposits in open-air habitational sites and on the floor in ceremonial/funerary rock shelters and caves. It is commonly believed that Saladoid represents **Arawak**-speaking populations expanding from the northwest Amazon toward the middle Orinoco and from there toward the Antilles. Three Saladoid phases were identified: **La Gruta**, **Ronquín**, and **Ronquín Sombra**. Although there has been some controversy regarding the chronological span of these phases and their relationships with other series in the Orinoco basin, the last part of this sequence exhibits Barrancoid influences.

The Saladoid series has been considered the earliest ceramic tradition in the area. It has also been interpreted as signaling the introduction of **agriculture** in the middle Orinoco. Because Saladoid ceramic assemblages include some of the earliest pottery manioc griddles or **budares**, it is often assumed that this ceramic assemblage identifies the first populations whose economy was based predominantly on **manioc** production. Although frequently associated with ceremonial sites in the middle Orinoco, very little else is known about these early semi-sedentary agriculturalist societies. Saladoid groups also cultivated **maize**, as can be inferred by the presence of **manos and metates**. Saladoid groups migrated to the Guyana coast and from there to the Lesser Antilles. *See also* CEDEÑOID; COROZAL; CUEVA DEL CERRO GAVILÁN; CUEVA DEL SANTO; CUEVA SUSUDE INAVA; TIMEHRI PETROGLYPH TYPE.

SALADOID-BARRANCOID TRADITION. Some scholars have observed strong continuities between the **Saladoid** and **Barrancoid** traditions, with the Barrancoid as an outcome of Saladoid. *See also* ZONE HATCHURED HORIZON.

SALANGO ISLAND. Located off the coast of Ecuador, this site served as an important source of ***Spondylus*** during the Early Ceramic periods.

SALINAR. Early Intermediate Period culture of the north coast of Peru. It developed in the first centuries BC. Its largest settlement was

Cerro Arena. The Salinar Phase is considered to be relatively short, "transitional," and transformative, although its precise temporal parameters remain unclear. It has even been proposed that Salinar and **Gallinazo** represent divergent artistic styles practiced by contemporaneous north coast populations. Despite such uncertainties, analysis of settlement and **architecture** (transcending studies of corporate ceramic styles) indicates the existence of two distinct sociopolitical and temporal phases preceding the **Moche**, which are designated Salinar and Gallinazo in the Moche Valley region. Salinar ceramics are an outgrowth of **Cupisnique** traditions and belong to the white-on-red horizon. Salinar vessels exhibit variety in form, quality, and decoration according to region and even according to settlement. Decorative attributes were geometric or figurative and were burnished, **incised**, slip-painted (bichrome), or molded. **Double-spouted vessels** (spout-and-bridge bottle) were common and mold-made **ceramics** depicted various animals (felines, monkeys, owls, and so on) and stylized humans in standard poses or engaging in activities such as sexual intercourse. Shards exhibiting negative painting techniques, a common Gallinazo practice, were also recovered from Salinar contexts at **Puémape** in Jequetepeque. Moche pottery incorporated many of these elements and it ultimately evolved from the Salinar ceramic tradition (along with Gallinazo). Other Salinar material diacritics are thought to include stone architecture, including megalithic compounds, platform **mounds**, stone **tombs**, and ground stone blades.

The archaeological record indicates that Salinar settlements were **fortified**, located in defensible positions (usually steep hills), and concentrated in the middle and upper portions of coastal valleys (especially in Chicama, Moche, Virú, Santa, and Nepeña). In contrast to the Late Cupisnique Period, the more open, lower plains were virtually abandoned south of Jequetepeque. Indeed, endemic **warfare**, insecurity, and sectarianism evidently characterized Salinar sociopolitical dynamics. Scholars have argued that social unrest and involuted cycles of raiding encouraged social aggregation and the development of early urban centers, exemplified by Cerro Arena in the south Moche Valley. The origins of the state during this period have also been inferred on the basis of settlement hierarchies and the presence of fortified sites on **transportation** routes and near canal intakes. Demographic pressures and competition over scarce resources (mainly between discrete valleys) are believed to have led to specialized militaristic and managerial organizations characteristic of state institutions. *See also* CHANKILLO; PUÉMAPE.

SALINAS DE CHAO. The preceramic center of Salinas de Chao is located in the Chao valley on the north coast of Peru. It consists of an eight-hectare site with rectangular platforms that exhibit a diversity of **architectural** styles. The main temples at Salinas de Chao were designed as integrated units of broad ascending terraces, which lead to summit constructions via ramps, inset stairways, and projecting stairways. Summit friezes and **sunken stone circular courts**, characteristic of the preceramic era, are also present at this site.

SALT. Salt was a valuable resource exploited in South America and was **traded** over long distances since ancient times. It was extracted from sea water (either by natural evaporation or by boiling), from dried salt lakes (*salares* or *salinas*), and by mining. For example, in Colombia, salt was extracted from the salt mines of Zipaquirá, Nemocón and **Tierradentro**, and it was also boiled in large **ceramic** vessels known as *gachas*. Similar practices occurred among the Tierra de los Indios groups of the Quíbor valley of Venezuela. In the southern Andes, salt was exploited from the saltpans of the dry **puna** and transported by **llama** caravans to the valleys and lowlands. *See also* MARKETS; MUISCA; QUIMBAYA; TUMACO.

SAMAIPATA. Carved rock outcrop of great dimensions located in Santa Cruz, Bolivia. It covers approximately 10,000 square meters and is oriented on an east-west axis. Geometric and human/animal figures represent the main figurative designs of the rock carving. Channels carved in the rock suggest that liquids, either **chicha** and/or blood, were drained in ritual libations at this site. Occupations around the rock correspond to the Middle Period as well as to the **Inka**. The Inka portion of the settlement (one of the easternmost Inka sites in the Andes) includes residential compounds, a **kallanka**, and several **qolcas**. Samaipata is a **World Heritage Site of UNESCO**.

SAMBAQUÍ. From the Tupí words *tamba* (shellfish) and *ki* (piled up, accumulated). Term used in Brazil to refer to **shell middens** produced by the accumulation of shell and other remains by human action. The largest **mound** measured 400 by 100 meters in the base and 30 meters high; on average they are 50–70 meters in diameter and approximately 10 meters high. These sambaquí are found mostly in the central and southern coast of Brazil, south of the mouth of the Amazon. The earliest, which date to around 6000 BC, are located in the region of São Paulo, while more recent examples date to AD 1000 (although the majority date to between 3000 and 1000 BC). In Spanish-speaking countries, the term used is **conchero** (*concha* means shell).

Paleonutritional studies have indicated that sambaquí inhabitants ate more fish than shellfish. In some cases, houses on Sambaquís were circular, with postholes and hearths. There could be forty houses in a sambaquí. Cemeteries were found outside of the residential area, usually toward the sea. Numerous grinding tools (**manos and metates**) have been collected from sambaquís. Plant remains, such as palm fruits, are also abundant. Skeletons in some sambaquís have teeth with a high incidence of cavities. This high incidence suggests that sambaquí dwellers consumed large amounts of seeds and vegetable products. Two of the archaeological sites in Brazil that are protected by the Instituto do Patrimônio Histórico e Artístico Nacional (IPHAN) are sambaquís: the Sambaquí do Pindaí (São Luís, Maranhão) and the Sambaquí da Barra do Rio Itapitangui (Cananéia, São Paulo). *See also* HURT, WESLEY R.; LITORAL (LITORALEÑA) TRADITION; LUND, WILHELM PETER; MINA PHASE; TAPERINHA.

SAN AGUSTÍN. Culture and main site of the southern portion of the upper basin of the Magdalena River in the Andean region of Colombia. A main feature of this culture is elaborately carved stone sculpture, mostly of human figures with animal traits (felines, birds, and so on). They were usually placed around funerary **mounds**. Stone sculptures appear in several sites of the region, although the majority have been **looted** from their original provenience. The earliest complex polities of the San Agustín culture, often considered **chiefdoms**, emerged around 600 BC in San Agustín's early period. In the Intermediate Period (AD 100–1000), more stratified polities arose. San Agustín is a **World Heritage Site of UNESCO**.

SAN FRANCISCO CULTURE. One of the oldest **ceramics** (and material culture complex) in northern Argentina, which dates to 620 BC. San Francisco ceramics are found in eastern Andean valleys in Salta and Jujuy, northern Argentina). Adults were buried in large **funerary urns** with offerings including beads and metal artifacts (tin **bronze** and gold-silver-**copper** alloys) depicting **camelid** imagery. San Francisco ceramics exhibit tropical lowland elements, such as corrugation, modeled decoration, thick rims, cord and corncob impression, finger-impressed techniques, and **figurines**. *See also* TILOCALAR PHASE.

SAN ISIDRO. 1. Early preceramic site located some fifty kilometers north of Popayán on the upper Cauca River, Colombia, at 1,690 meters above sea level. The oldest occupation dates to between 8000 and 7500 BC. Bifacial and unifacial flaked tools as well as grinding tools were recovered here. Scholars found in San Isidro probable evidence of arrowroot (*Maranta arundinacea*), a plant that was domesticated in Panama by 7000 BC. Botanical remains suggest a heavy reliance on edible plants. 2. Late **Valdivia** ceremonial site located in the province of Manabí, northern Ecuador. San Isidro was contemporaneous to **La Emerenciana** and **San Lorenzo del Mate**. The three sites are similar in size.

SAN JACINTO 1. Early **ceramics** at this site in the savanna of Bolívar in northern Colombia, situated at 220 meters above sea level, have been dated to between 4000 and 3300 BC. San Jacinto 1 is located one hundred kilometers approximately southeast of the site of **Puerto Hormiga**. There are numerous fire pits and many **manos and metates**, which suggest that plants were processed at the site. Most of the botanical remains are of grass seeds. *See also* TECOMATE.

SAN JOSÉ DE MORO (PRIESTESS OF SAN JOSÉ). A large site in the Jequetepeque Valley, north coast of Peru, San José de Moro was occupied during the Early Intermediate (AD 200–700) and Middle Horizon (AD 700–1000). The site has two sectors: in the south, there are several **mounds** and elite residences. In the northern part of the site, **Moche** and **Lambayeque** cemeteries predominate. The elaborate **tombs** at San José de Moro are among the most spectacular discoveries associated with the Late Moche Period on the north coast. This site also contains boot-shaped burials that date to the Middle Moche Period. The Late Period burials confirm that elites continued to define and legitimize their authority through enactment of public rites associated with the **sacrifice ceremony**. San José de Moro appears to have secured a strategic position on important communication and **transportation** routes and was surrounded by prime **agricultural** land. The site clearly served as a preeminent ceremonial and political center, and it probably represented one of the most powerful settlements in the Jequetepeque region.

The site occupies an area of ten hectares and consists of a series of **adobe** brick platforms, subsidiary mounds, and associated plazas surrounded by poorly preserved domestic architecture. The eight principal **huacas** (of fourteen recorded distinct mounds) have been devastatingly eroded and **looted** to the point that their original form is indiscernible. The amorphous mounds appear to have been pyramidal in shape and stand approximately eight meters tall. Looting reveals that the platforms were associated with high-quality Late Moche and foreign **ceramics**. Inspection of looters' tunnels and stratigraphic excavation confirms that large-scale labor mobilization was involved in the construction of the adobe edifices. Many of the principal mounds served as important residential areas as well as funerary and ceremonial space. Deep stratigraphy (eight meters or more) distinguished by superimposed use floors and fill layers were common in several of the excavated mounds. The discovery of intrusive burials indicates that the function of several platforms was later reoriented to mortuary ritual.

Communities from within and outside the valley could have congregated at San José de Moro to participate in coordinated **religious** festivities which entailed the large-scale production and consumption of **chicha**, based on the discovery of a series of semi-subterranean adobe-lined chambers that were filled with the tools and ceramics needed to manufacture and ferment **maize** beer. Tombs were clustered in lines and circles and were associated with above ground plazas delineated by adobe bricks. Feasting rites engaging living celebrants and deceased ancestors probably occurred in these spaces.

Elite chamber tombs, a number of which were excavated to the east of Huaca La Capilla, characterize the Late Period at San José de Moro. Boot-shaped sepulchers also continued to be used and were associated with high quantities of utilitarian ware, unlike the burials of the preceding Middle Period. The rectangular tombs were walled with plastered adobe bricks and varied in depth according to the status of the interred individual. Niches commonly adorned the upper portions of the east, south, and west walls of the tombs. A north antechamber and a roof supported by wooden beams were also common features of tomb construction. The configuration of the tombs is highly reminiscent of stylized burial chambers depicted in the famous Burial Theme of Phase V ceramics, an iconographic narrative produced perhaps exclusively in the Pacasmayo Region (and most likely at San José). The most elaborate tombs were abundantly furnished with ceramics, **copper** objects, **bronze** masks, headdresses, ***Spondylus*** shell, precious stone adornments, ceramic architectural models, and offerings of **llama** remains (especially skulls). Human **sacrificial** victims also appear to have accompanied several of the high-status interments.

The most elaborate tomb was associated with the burial of an elite priestess, identified as one of the protagonists in the sacrifice ceremony. This tomb was placed in a large plaza fronting Huaca La Capilla. She was interred with over one hundred fine ceramics, **turquoise** and lapis lazuli jewels, ceremonial **tumi** knives, shell, and other fine objects. Metal masks, headdresses, and sandals, which closely resemble the ceremonial gear and accouterment of the so-called Priestess of the Presentation Theme, were also recovered from the tomb. This figure represents the principal female divinity of the Moche Pantheon and is a dominant personage in other Moche iconographic narratives. In fact, the peculiar headdress of the interred female lord, manufactured of copper and silver and consisting of two sweeping trapezoidal plumes, is identical to the headdress of the great female divinity depicted in Moche iconography. Moreover, a characteristic ceramic goblet, painted with running anthropomorphic shields and clubs holding cups, was buried with the high-status female. Significantly, the priestess is shown presenting an identical chalice of blood to the principal **fanged deity** at the presumed climax of the sacrifice ceremony. Moreover, the tomb of a second and younger priestess was discovered in 1992 in the same plaza as the first tomb. The characteristic headdress, a copper chalice, and a massive copper funerary mask were among the many offerings of this equally extravagant burial. *See also* DEITIES; RELIGION.

SAN LORENZO DEL MATE. Late **Valdivia** ceremonial center in the province of Guayas, southern coast of Ecuador. San Lorenzo del Mate was contemporaneous and similar in hierarchy to **La Emerenciana** and **San Isidro**.

SAN PEDRO DE ATACAMA. Colonial town on the northern shores of the Salar de Atacama situated at 2,400 meters above sea level in northern Chile. The area of San Pedro was inhabited by people who are known archaeologically as the San Pedro Complex, dating from around 600 BC to AD 1000. After AD 1000, the people living in San Pedro de Atacama are referred to as the Atacamas, a term used at the time of the Spanish conquest. Most of the knowledge about San Pedro comes from **tombs**. San Pedro tombs are covered by burial **mounds** and have an **algarroba** log as a marker. Burials are accompanied by animals (dogs and **llamas**), **snuff trays**, decorated gourds, and sometimes human skulls, as well as **copper** and gold ornaments. The **ceramic** types of San Pedro I and II have a long continuity and are characterized by polished blackware and polished redware. Several cemeteries were found in the area, including Sequitor, Coyo Oriental, and Larache. In these tombs, many items of wood, textile, ceramic, metal, and other materials of local and **Tiwanaku** styles indicate that there was a close association between these two groups. Many prestige items with Tiwanaku iconography were found, including gold **keros**, snuff trays, textiles, and ceramics. Larache is one of Chile's national monuments. *See also* TULOR; ZAPALERI-CALDERA VILAMA.

SANOJA OBEDIENTE, MARIO (1938–). Venezuelan archaeologist who wrote numerous articles and books on archaeology, ethnography, and Venezuelan history. Among them are *La Fase Zancudo: Investigaciones Arqueológicas en el Lago de Maracaibo* (1969), *Las Culturas Formativas del Oriente de Venezuela. La Tradición Barrancas del Bajo Orinoco* (1979), *Los Hombres de la Yuca y el Maíz*

(1997), *Early Modes of Life of the Indigenous Populations of Northeastern Venezuela* with Iraida Vargas-Arenas (1998), and *Orígenes de Venezuela. Regiones Geohistóricas Aborígenes hasta 1500 d.c.* with Iraida Vargas-Arena (1999).

SANTA MARÍA. Culture of the Late Period of the valleys of northwest Argentina (AD 1000–1400). Many sites, referred to as **pukaras**, are located on hilltops. In lower areas there are dense settlements, often with large cemeteries containing **funerary urns**. Santa María people were **agriculturalists**; built terraces, canals, and other features; and were also **camelid** herders. **Bronze metallurgy** was very advanced, as indicated by the discovery of bronze plaques (*placas metálicas*). Santa María sites located along river valleys or in piedmonts were later occupied by the **Inka**, such as Fuerte Quemado. *See also* QUILMES.

SANTANA DO RIACHO. Early Holocene cave site in Minas Gerais, Brazil, which dates to between 8000 and 6000 BC. More than forty burials were found here situated around a large stone. The corpses were wrapped in nets and covered with red pigment. Some of the burials have missing bones, which suggests that they were intentionally removed. The individuals were physically similar to those found in the **Lagoa Santa** region. **Hunting** of small animals was complemented by a significant quantity of wild vegetable products. **Rock art** (paintings) adorn the cave wall, but it is uncertain to what period they correspond.

SANTAREM. Ceramic style, culture, and large site from the lower Amazon basin, Brazil, that was occupied from AD 1000–1500. The ceramic style defines a component of the **Incised and Punctate Horizon** that spread in Amazonia and contiguous regions from AD 500 to 1500. The first Europeans who visited the area in the sixteenth century described the Tapajós **chiefdom** (people using Santarem-style ceramics) as one of the largest and strongest polities of the Amazon. The site of Santarem occupied approximately five square kilometers and is characterized by **mounds** and large **middens** (**terras pretas**), suggesting that it was the capital of a large chiefdom. Some of the smaller Santarem sites were connected by elevated earth roads. The subsistence of the Santarem people was based on **maize** and **manioc** cultivation as well as **hunting**, fishing, and food gathering. Ceramics often represented human figures (elite members).

SAPUCAÍ. One of the **ceramic**-producing cultures of Minas Gerais, central Brazil. The Sapucaí lived in this region of hills with lush vegetation from AD 900 until 1700. Their settlements consisted of large villages with one to thirty dwellings or **malocas** surrounding a central open area for ceremonies. Their main crop was **maize**. Among the ceramic vessels, the larger ones were used as **funerary urns** or to store liquids. Cooking vessels are rarely decorated. **Spindle whorls** suggest the use of **cotton** or other fibers to make textiles. Ceramic **pipes** (**cachimbos**) were common in Sapucaí sites and the polished stone tool industry was comprised of ground axes, used to clear the forest, and anchor-shaped polished axes (*machados semilunares*). The Sapucaí and **Aratú** probably were ancestors of the historic Gé groups of central Brazil.

SCHMITZ, PEDRO IGNACIO (1929–). Brazilian archaeologist from Rio Grande do Sul who focused his investigations on the south and center of the country. He published more than one hundred articles in journals and several books, including *Sitios de Pesca Lacustre em Río Grande, RS, Brasil* (1976); *Caçadores e Coletores da Pré-História do Brasil* (1984); and *Arqueología nos Cerrados do Brasil Central: Sudoeste da Bahía e Leste de Goiás* (1996), as coauthor. Among his articles are "Prehistoric Hunters and Gatherers of Brazil" (1987) and "O povoamento pleistocênico do Brasil" (1990). Schmitz is one of the founding members of the Sociedade de Arqueología Brasileira (Brazilian Archaeological Society).

SCHOBINGER, JUAN (1928–). Swiss-born Argentinean archaeologist who worked at the Universidad Nacional de Cuyo (Mendoza). His interests include the early settlers of the Americas, **high-altitude sites**, and **rock art**. He published books on local research and on wider topics, such as the prehistory of South America and of the Americas. Among his published works are *La "Momia" del Cerro El Toro. Investigaciones arqueológicas en la Cordillera de la Provincia de San Juan* (1966); *Prehistoria de Suramérica* (1969); *Prehistoria* *de Sudamérica. Culturas precerámicas* (1988); *Sacrifices of the High Andes* (1991); *Shamanismo Sudamericano*, an edited volume (1997); *The Ancient Americans: A Reference Guide to the Art, Culture and History of Pre-Columbian North and South America*, 2 volumes (2000); and the compiled volume *El santuario incaico del Cerro Aconcagua* (2001).

SECHÍN ALTO. Large **Cupisnique** site in the Casma Valley, north coast of Peru. Sechín Alto was contemporaneous with **Moxeke-Pampa de las Llamas**. A massive **mound** measuring 300 by 250 meters and 44 meters high, it was built with quarried stone and was one of the largest of its kind in the Americas at the time. The mound was built on top of an earlier **adobe** construction that dated to 1500 BC or earlier.

SENO OTWAY. Name given to an **obsidian** type, the exact source of which is unknown. Seno Otway obsidian is found in sites around the Seno Otway (Otway fjord) of Tierra del Fuego. Scholars speculate that the source could be located in that region.

SEÑORÍO. Spanish term used for stratified societies governed directly or indirectly through a series of hierarchically related lords. Also known as chiefdoms, señoríos were the most common **political organization** form in South America at the time of the Iberian conquest. Cacique, a term that originated in the Caribbean, was used by the Spaniards to refer to the leader/s of a señorío. *See also* CHINCHA; CHUCUITO; HUARPA; INTERMEDIATE AREA; JAMACOAQUE STYLE; SAN AGUSTÍN; SANTAREM; SINU.

SERPENTINITE. Green stone similar to **jadeite**, used to manufacture ornaments by several South American groups, such as the **Tairona** and Andean groups of Venezuela. The so-called "batwing pendants" or "winged pendants" are among the objects manufactured with serpentinite. These pectorals, thought to represent bats, are very common in the Andean region of Venezuela and could have served several purposes, including funerary offerings, as many of them were found in **tombs** since the first century AD. Serpentinite workshops of these batwing pendants were found at two archaeological sites in the

Venezuelan Andes, one dating to AD 650 and the other to AD 1100, but the source of serpentinite for these workshops is unknown. The vast cemetery of Las Locas in the Quíbor valley of Venezuela contained winged pectorals made of serpentinite and **amber** beads, among other valuable goods. *See also* JEWELRY.

SHAFT AND CHAMBER TOMB. Type of **tomb** common in the northern, central, and southern Andes. The shaft can be circular, oval, or rectangular, with either one or more chambers. There is a large variation in form, number of individuals buried, and accompanying objects that have been preserved (**ceramic** vessels, metal ornaments, and so on). Tombs were an important part of ancestor worship: for maintaining the continuous interrelation between the living and the dead, and for the removal of the corpses or **mummies** for specific ritual occasions. *See also* LOMA NEGRA; QUIMBAYA.

SHELL MIDDEN OR SHELL MOUND. *See* CONCHERO; SAMBAQUÍ.

SHILLACOTO. One of the earliest **religious** centers on the Huallaga River, in the vicinity of Huánuco city, central-southern highland Peru. Shillacoto is five kilometers from the site of **Kotosh**. The four occupations of the site include Higueras, Kotosh, Wairajirca, and **Mito**, which all predate the **Chavín** Horizon. The Early Mito Phase was characterized by a very large square-based temple with a hearth in the center and two other monumental constructions. The few **ceramics** that appear in the context of the Mito temple are of the elaborate Wairajirca style, the first ceramics in the region. Magnificent stone **tombs** characterize the Wairajirca and Kotosh periods. These tombs suggest that there was some social stratification in this site, probably connected to religious offices.

SHINCAL. An important **Inka** provincial center in Catamarca, northwest Argentina. The colonial town of Londres, one of the first Spanish settlements in the region, was founded close to Shincal. The site occupies twenty-three hectares and has numerous Inka features, such as **kallankas** around the main plaza, an **ushnu**, a road, and an aqueduct. Shincal is one of Argentina's national historic monuments.

SICAN. *See* LAMBAYEQUE.

SINÚ. The inhabitants of the Gulf of Urabá and the San Jorge River of northern Colombia at the time of the Spanish conquest, who were linked politically to the documented Sinú **señorío**. They were famous metalsmiths who manufactured small cast gold and **tumbaga** ornaments in many styles characteristic of central Colombia. These objects were exchanged throughout the **Intermediate Area** (Colombia and Central America) under the control of chiefs. *See also* "EAGLE" PECTORALS.

SIPALIWINI. A **hunter**-gatherer type site and group of sites that represent the oldest human settlements in Suriname. Sipaliwini groups date to approximately 10,000–5000 BC. These hunters and gatherers lived in small camps in a savanna region of south Suriname, and the main prey was deer. They manufactured stone tools with local raw materials such as quartz and rhyolite.

SIPÁN. Site with **adobe pyramids** on the north coast of Peru where important elite members (Lords of Sipán) were buried The Sipán Complex, consisting of the massive Huaca Rajada, two smaller pyramids (including the principal burial **mound**), and twenty-five smaller mounds, appears to have been the seat of a formidable polity that likely controlled much of the lower **Lambayeque** drainage during the Middle **Moche** Period (AD 250–500). The three superimposed **tombs** excavated in the 1980s represent the most extraordinary and luxurious tombs ever documented in the ancient Andes. The Sipán lords were interred with **sacrificed** humans and **llamas**, precious stone and shell pectorals, and prodigal quantities of masterfully crafted gold masks, ornaments, rattles, **weapons**, and other utensils as well as simpler molded **ceramics**. The burial assemblages, ornaments, and headdresses confidently identified the figures as protagonists of the **sacrifice ceremony** depicted in Moche iconography.

The lords and priests of Sipán directed the principal elite cult which defined and instantiated Moche politico-**religious** ideology. The Sipán burials, replete with symbols of ritual homicide, dualistic ordering, and predatory power, attest to the divine role of the Lambayeque warrior-priests who interceded with the supernatural to guarantee the perpetuation of socio-cosmic order and, by extension, terrestrial political privileges. It is certainly no exaggeration to say that the interred elite of Sipán formed part of a noble class that can be described as royalty. They undoubtedly secured the following or submission of a large segment of the Lambayeque population and effectively channeled surplus production for the construction of monuments, the manufacture of highly specialized **metallurgy**, and the finance of elaborately staged ceremonies.

SLASH-AND-BURN AGRICULTURE. *See* SWIDDEN.

SMILING GOD. Name given to the representation of a feline-like creature in the Lanzón of the Old Temple of **Chavín de Huantar**. Has both male and female elements, thus probably representing an androgynous god of fertility.

SNUFF TRAY (OR TABLETS). A small flat tray made of wood, stone, bone, or metal, used to hold **hallucinogenic** snuffs inhaled with a tube. Snuff trays are common in **tombs** of **Tiwanaku** sites, in the Late Period Jujuy **puna** sites of northwest Argentina, and in the grasslands between Colombia and Venezuela. In Venezuela, they were made of wood for the consumption of *yopo* (*Anadenanthera* sp.). They usually have decorations, either **incised** or modeled. *See also* SAN PEDRO DE ATACAMA.

SODALITE. Light bluish stone (sodium aluminum silicate chloride) used in ornamentation by numerous Andean and sub-Andean **agriculturalist** groups since approximately 2000 BC. It was also probably used as a pigment in stucco, in **adobe** walls such as those of **Tiwanaku**'s Palace of Multicolored Rooms. One of its main sources is the **Cerro Sapo** quarry (Cochabamba, Bolivia). Other sources are located in the Azogues-Cuenca in the southern highlands of Ecuador. Sodalite, like other blue-colored stones such as **turquoise** and lapis lazuli, was widely **traded** and transported over long distances along the Andes and to the eastern valleys and lowlands. *See also* CONCHU PATA.

SORA SORA. Obsidian quarry located in the vicinity of the present-day town of Turco (Oruro, Bolivia). It was the first obsidian quarry to be discovered in Bolivia. Another such quarry, Cerro Zapaleri-Vilama, was exploited mostly by groups living in present-day northern Argentina and northern Chile. Sora Sora's opaque black materials were transported to the urban center of **Tiwanaku**. Obsidian from this source has only been identified here, but future trace element studies could point to a more extensive distribution. *See also* TRADE.

SPINDLE WHORLS. Usually circular artifacts (in **Aguada** they are also oval or rectangular) usually made of **ceramic** shards or stone with a central hole, used as weights in spindles. In regions where textiles are not preserved, spindle whorls are good archaeological indicators of textile production. The Spanish term for spindle whorl is *tortero*, and the Portuguese term is *tortual*. *See also* LAS ANIMAS CULTURE; MANTEÑO CULTURE; SAPUCAÍ.

***SPONDYLUS* (*MULLU* IN THE CENTRAL AND NORTH ANDES).** Marine shell found in the warm waters of the Pacific Ocean from the Ecuadorian coast to the Gulf of California. Two important fishing sites for *Spondylus* were **Isla de Puna** and **Salango Island** in Ecuador. Many Andean people imparted great value and ritual significance to *Spondylus* shell, especially as offerings related to fertility. It was obtained through long-distance **trade** since the preceramic period until the sixteenth century AD. Among the earliest findings are the ceremonial centers of **Real Alto**'s **Valdivia** III levels (2700 BC) and **Aspero** (2500 BC). The southernmost finding of *Spondylus* is from the **Inka** sanctuary of **Aconcagua** (central Argentina-Chile), located some 3,500 kilometers from its source. Along with **obsidian** and **turquoise**, it was one of the elements of long-distance **trade** in the Andean region. Its exchange increased in the central Andes since the Early Horizon. *Spondylus* is represented in several media, including **ceramics**, stone, bone, textile, and metals. A figure carved in relief in the patio of the New Temple of **Chavín de Huantar** wields a *Spondylus* shell in its left hand. *Spondylus* was recovered in ritual contexts in several **Wari** sites. In Inka times, the *mullu chasqui camayoc* (person in charge of transporting **mullu**) supervised the distribution of mullu to the sanctuaries of the empire. *See also* LLULLAILLACO; MANTEÑO CULTURE; PAMPA GRANDE; RELIGION; SAN JOSÉ DE MORO.

STAFF GOD. Main **religious** figure in **Tiwanaku** and **Wari** corporate art. Equivalents have also been identified as early as the **Chavín** Period. The Staff God is represented in stone sculpture, **ceramics**, textiles, metal, and other media. It is a standing individual looking frontward and holding elements in both hands, usually **weapons** (axes, arrows) or staffs, such as in the case of the **Bennett Monolith**. *See also* DEITIES.

STAFF GODDESS. Female **deity** represented in **Chavín** art of the south coast of Peru. The figure has staffs in both hands.

STIRRUP BOTTLE. This vessel form, characterized by a looped arc attached to a conical **ceramic** vessel and topped by a narrow spout, represents one of the most recognizable and long-lasting ceramic types of ancient Ecuador and Peru. Stirrup jars were first produced by the **Machalilla** (2000–1000 BC) and **Chorrera** (1000–500 BC) cultures of coastal Ecuador, but their production later shifted to the north Peruvian coast and highlands. This vessel form continued to be produced by **Cupisnique**, **Chavín**, **Moche**, **Lambayeque**, **Chimú**, and Chimú-**Inka** cultural groups, and its ritual and funerary importance lasted for more than three millennia. *See also* CHONGOYAPE.

***STROMBUS PERUVIANUS* AND *S. GALEATUS*.** Large shell distributed from the coast of Peru to western Mexico (*peruvianus*) and Ecuador to the Gulf of California (*galeatus*), which many South American groups used as a **musical** instrument. This ritual Andean trumpet is called *pututu* in the central Andes and *quipa* in Ecuador. These shells were found in **Valdivia** II and III **tombs** and in the base of the ceremonial **mound** of **Real Alto**. *See also* CHONGOYAPE.

SUEVA I. Late Pleistocene-Early Holocene site in the savannas of Bogotá, Colombia. Sueva is close to and contemporaneous with **Tequendama**, **Tibitó**, and **El Abra**. The earliest occupation dates to 8900 BC. Early evidence of **guinea pig** has been documented at this site. Most of the animals **hunted** by Sueva I inhabitants were deer. Stone tools were unifacial flakes, and there are no projectile points.

SUKAKOLLO. **Aymara** term for **raised fields**. Sukakollos were built along the shores of Lake Titicaca during the **Formative** and **Tiwanaku** Period, in the **Koani Pampa**, in the Juli-Pomata area, and in other flat areas. Sukakollos increased the productivity of this area, allowing the support of a large population density. The water of the canals protected the crops from frosts. The **Quechua** term is **wara wara**.

SUNKEN COURT. The sunken court is an important element in Andean **religious architecture** and consists of a sunken plaza, usually circular or square in shape and accessed by steps. It may have served as a metaphorical axis mundi connecting the terrestrial with the subterranean and supernatural realms. Sunken courts are located in ceremonial centers of the coast and highlands of Peru and the Bolivian **altiplano**, and were built from the Initial Period until the Middle Horizon (AD 600–1000). In large sites of the Titicaca basin, sunken courts are part of the **Yaya-Mama Religious Tradition**. In **Tiwanaku**, for example, sunken courts are found on the two **pyramids** (Akapana and Puma Punku) and in front of the **Kalasasaya** temple. That sunken court is known as the semisubterranean temple. *See also* PUKARA.

SUPLICANTE. Stone sculptures from the early **ceramic** period of northwest Argentina, dating to 500 BC to 300 AD, and associated with **Ciénaga** and **Condorhuasi** styles and the **Alamito** culture. Most suplicantes were found in the Andalgalá and **Ambato** regions of Catamarca, very few located in archaeological excavations. The sculptures were carved from andesite, diorite, dacite, diabase, and so on, and their heights range from thirty to forty centimeters. They are thought to represent ancestors of descent groups or lineages.

SWIDDEN. Also known as slash-and-burn **agriculture** or horticulture, this is a form of agriculture practiced in tropical and subtropical forest areas of South America. The first step is to cut the smaller bushes, let them dry, and set them on fire. After the ashes cool, **maize**, squash, beans, **manioc**, and/or other crops are planted. In these environments, most of the nutrients are stored in the plants instead of in the soils themselves. Nutrients pass from the ashes to the soil during the rainy season. Plots can be cultivated for a limited number of years; after that they are abandoned and new plots are opened.

– T –

TABATINGA. Archaic site in Guyana. The stone tools consist mostly of flake endscrapers, while projectile points are absent.

TABUCHILA PHASE. In northern Manabí (Ecuador), Tabuchila is the most complex regional manifestation of **Chorrera** culture investigated in Ecuador. Sites of the Tabuchila Phase are characterized by ceremonial **mounds**, **maize agriculture** involving both intensive floodplain farming and some upland **swiddening**, elaborate **ceramic** production (including mold-made **figurines**), and high-status burial. All of these elements point to the emergence of a complex society centered around the **San Isidro** ceremonial center.

TACALZHAPA. Formative ceramic style from the region of Cuenca distributed in the highlands of Ecuador. Tacalzhapa I dates to 500–100 BC. **Keros** constituted an important form of this ceramic complex.

TADDEI, ANTONIO (1908–1995). Self-trained Uruguayan archaeologist who researched the early settlers of the country, particularly along the Negro and Uruguay rivers. After his death, the Archeological Museum of Canelones (Uruguay) was named "Prof. Antonio Taddei."

TAFÍ. Early Period **ceramic** culture of northwestern Argentina. The type-site is Tafí del Valle, characterized by numerous groups of circular dwellings with cobble basements and menhirs or **monoliths**. Among its crafts are stone masks and mortars with feline shapes, probably used to grind **hallucinogenic** materials.

TAGUA-TAGUA. Late Pleistocene site located on the shore of an ancient lagoon in central-southern Chile and dated to 9300 and 9100

BC. This site was known since the nineteenth century as a paleontological site for its **megafauna**: mastodon and horse were identified here. Bones recovered from the site also exhibit artificial cut marks. Tagua-Tagua was abandoned around 9100 BC. There is a more recent occupation that dates to 4000 BC.

TAIMA-TAIMA. Late Pleistocene site near Cobo, western Venezuela, located in the vicinity of the **El Jobo** site. The site dates to around 12,000–11,000 BC. **Megafauna** remains were found associated with archaeological signatures of human activity at Taima-Taima. Fragments of leaf-shaped El Jobo points were found in association with a mastodon.

TAIRONA. Late Period (AD 1000 to Spanish Conquest) culture of the Sierra Nevada de Santa Marta and the Caribbean coast in the department of Magdalena of Colombia. As with the **Muisca**, these were **Chibcha** speakers and practiced gold **metallurgy**. Tairona culture is characterized by **irrigation agriculture** and complex, stratified **political organization**. *See also* JADEITE; SERPENTINITE.

TALAMBO. Talambo and the adjacent site of Huacho to the northeast are located in the Jequetepeque Valley of the north coast of Peru. Talambo lies twelve kilometers upriver from **Farfán** and is a massive settlement, one of the largest prehistoric cities in the valley (around three square kilometers), occupying much of the slopes of the cerro and adjacent pampa. A large Late **Moche** sector is located in a northeast portion of the site (though **Chimú** remains were documented here as well), while the largest area of the settlement dates to the Late Intermediate Period. In fact, Early Horizon **ceramics** were also identified here in smaller numbers, indicating a long history of occupation at the site. The pampa west of the Cerro Talambo is dominated by three large **pyramids**, one of which is located at the north end of an **adobe** compound delineated by massive walls. The pyramids were probably first constructed in the Transitional (**Lambayeque**) Period (AD 600–800) or earlier, but they were clearly maintained (and possibly remodeled) after the Chimú conquest. The freestanding pyramidal platforms were built of adobe brick, while the smaller pyramid within the compound was constructed of earth and stone. The monumental enclosure, which contains various subsidiary walls and constructions, is dominated by a large, open space. The form and technical properties of the precinct indicate that it was built sometime during the Chimú era and it is similar to **architecture** at **Chan Chan**.

Numerous quadrilateral enclosures and smaller trapezoidal or rectangular structures built of stone are also spread across the pampa and cerro hills of Talambo. The larger and more elaborate of these constructions are thought to have served in an administrative or possibly ritual capacity, while smaller precincts may simply have had a domestic function. Moreover, the slopes of Cerro Talambo east of the monumental pyramids were systematically transformed by human engineering, and the rocky hillside was terraced, walled, and surfaced with rectilinear architectural units exhibiting varying internal partitions and chambers. The domestic terraces and room blocks were built predominately of earth and stone, although adobe brick was occasionally used. Talambo secured a critical location at the lower valley neck, and all major prehistoric canal intakes of the north bank (as well as their modern counterparts) pass through the narrow section of the valley dominated by the site. In fact, the ancient maximum elevation canal of the Talambo system was constructed north of the main cluster of pyramids. Clearly, Talambo played an important role in the regulation of lower valley **irrigation** systems as well as in the control of movement and exchange up-valley.

TAMBERIA DEL INCA. Inka settlement in Chilecito, La Rioja, northwest Argentina. Constructions were made of **adobe** and the most prominent features are an **ushnu**, a **kallanka**, and a wall that surrounds the central area of the site. An Inka road crosses the site. Tambería del Inca is one of Argentina's national historic monuments.

TAMBO COLORADO. Inka site in the Pisco Valley of Peru. It has one of the best-preserved **adobe** Inka structures, some of which are painted red (for that reason the name "red tambo"). Tambo Colorado also has pre-Inka constructions. Apart from adobe, walls are of **tapia** and stone mixed with clay. The site is distinguished by an **ushnu**, **qolcas**, and a large trapezoidal plaza.

TAMBO VIEJO. Nasca settlement in the Acarí valley, characterized by several thousand rooms located between two walled areas that cover less than four hectares. The site was inhabited in **Inka** and Colonial times. The Inka built an **ushnu**, and the site was strategically located along the coastal road.

TAMPU. Architectural infrastructure consisting of a group of rooms and corrals located along **Inka** roads where travelers stopped to rest overnight. Several place names in the Andes include the **Quechua** word *tampu* (or its Spanish version *tambo*). *See also* CATARPE.

TAMPUMACHAY. Inka site in the Urubamba Valley located on a mountainside and characterized by several water fountains. Tampumachay is situated near **Cuzco**.

TANKA TANKA. Very prominent massif with massive **fortification** walls, several meters high and two meters wide, located in the western Titicaca basin, Peru. They are the most impressive constructions in terms of size during the Late Intermediate Period in the **altiplano** (AD 1000–1400). The site covers some fifty hectares.

TAPERINHA. A **shell mound** that dates to 5000 BC located close to the **Pedra Pintada Cave** in the Santarem region of the Lower Amazon. It stands 6.5 meters high and 5 hectares wide at its base. Some of the earliest **ceramics** in South America were found at this site. A small portion of the vessels had curvilinear incisions around the rim. Subsistence at the site focused on aquatic resources.

TAPIA. One of the main construction techniques utilized by South American indigenous groups. Clay is mixed with gravel and this matrix is poured in wood or cane molds and left to dry. Tapia, together with **adobe** and **quincha**, was used in many regions of South America. *See also* CAÑONCILLO; CHANCAY; GALLINAZO; LOMA NEGRA; TAMBO COLORADO.

TARWI (*LUPINUS MUTABILIS*). (Pronounced tar-*wee*.) An annual legume, tarwi is grown from Bolivia to Colombia in mid-altitude regions, from 800 to 3,000 meters above sea level. Tarwi, also locally known as *chocho*, has seeds rich in protein and oil similar to soybeans. As its seeds are bitter, they have to be soaked in water for several hours before eating. *See also* YURAJ MOLINO.

TASTIL (SANTA ROSA DE TASTIL). Large Late Period (AD 1000–1400) settlement on the Las Cuevas River, Salta, northwest Argentina. This town once contained more than 1,000 stone-walled (**pirca**) rooms and is one of the largest settlements in northwest Argentina. The **Inka** road that unites the highlands with the low-altitude valleys crosses through this site. Tastil is one of Argentina's national historic monuments.

TAWANTINSUYU. Quechua name of the **Inka** empire. This name comes from the terms *tawa* (four) and *suyu* (parts). The Inka empire was the largest political unit in pre-Columbian America, encompassing central Argentina and Chile in the south to southern Colombia in the north. The two largest sections of the empire were the Chinchaysuyu to the northwest and Collasuyu to the southeast. The smaller suyus were Cuntisuyu to the southwest and Antisuyu to the northeast. The four suyus originated and converged in the city of **Cuzco**, which was the center and origin of the empire, and were united by the Inka road system.

TECOMATE. Nahuatl term used in Colombia to describe globular **ceramic** vessels with rounded bases lacking necks. Tecomates predominate in the earliest ceramic assemblages—Early **Formative**—on the Colombian Caribbean coast (4000–3000 BC), such as in **San Jacinto** 1 and 2 and in **Puerto Hormiga**.

TELARMACHAY. Caves in the highlands (**puna**) of Junín, central Peru, situated at 4,420 meters above sea level and characterized by preceramic and **Formative** occupations beginning around 10,000 BC. Early evidence of **camelid domestication** has been documented at this site. These sites were occupied part of the year in a cycle of migration from lower altitudes to the puna. The caves had hearths and specialized activity areas for butchery, cooking, stone tool manufacture, and hide preparation. Stone and bone tools were also abundant and include scrapers and numerous bifacial projectile points.

TELLO, JULIO CESAR (1880–1947). Tello is considered the father of Peruvian archaeology. He discovered and studied the site of **Chavín de Huántar** and **Chavín** civilization, and proposed that Chavín was the first civilization in Peru. He published *Wirakocha* (1923); *Antiguo Perú* (1929); *Chavín, cultura matriz de la civilización andina* (1930); *Origen y desarrollo de la civilización andina* (1942); and *Discovery of the Chavín Culture in Peru* (1943). After his death, his text *Arqueología del valle de Casma* (1956) was published, and in 1960 there was a reprint of his 1930 book. A lithic sculpture of Chavín was given his name: the Tello Obelisk.

TEMBETÁ. **Guaraní** term for lip plug or labret made of stone, shell, metal, or **ceramic**, common in many South American cultures both in the lowlands and highlands during different time periods (**Tiwanaku**, **El Molle**, **Viluco**, **Tairona**, **Manteño**, **Ansilta**, and Guaraní, among others). Tembetás are of different sizes, usually only a few centimeters long, although longer examples have been documented (ten to fifteen centimeters). Apart from the tembetás themselves, there are pictorial representations of individuals wearing them (Tiwanaku). *See also* OREJONES.

TEQUENDAMA. Late Pleistocene-Early Holocene site in the sabana of Bogotá, Colombia. The earliest occupation, Tequendama I, was dated to 8900 BC. The inhabitants **hunted** modern fauna; most of the remains are of deer. There are very few stone tools in these early levels, but they include a bifacial projectile point and cutting tools made with stones brought from other regions (valleys and highlands). Tequendama is close to the contemporaneous sites of **El Abra** and **Tibitó**.

TERRA PRETA. Portuguese term for soils of anthropic origin (the Spanish term is *tierras negras*). In the tropical forests, prehistoric settlements (villages) were made with perishable wood and other plant materials, but can be identified through soil discoloration produced by the accumulation of organic materials (bones, plant remains, and so on). The considerable depth of many of these terras pretas suggests that villages remained in the same place for many decades (in some cases even a century or more), and thus were more permanent than suspected. *See also* INCISED AND PUNCTATE HORIZON; MARCELINA KUÉ; SANTAREM.

THÉMIRE. Cultural complex of the coast of Guyane that is dated to AD 1300–1650. Some Thémire sites are related to **Arauquinoid**, while others can be included in the **Polychrome** Tradition of the Amazon basin. Thémire is one of the easternmost and most recent branches of the Arauquinoid Tradition. Some Thémire sites are associated to drained fields, where **manioc**, **maize**, ñame, and/or sweet potato were cultivated. Thémire **ceramics** are characterized by painting and incision. Ceramic polishers are abundant, suggesting that ceramics were locally made. Numerous stone flakes suggest that **budares** were used. *See also* MONT GRAND MATOURY.

TIBITÓ. Late Pleistocene site in the Sabana de Bogotá, Colombia. Tibitó is a small campsite where bones of extinct horse and mastodon were found associated with bone and stone tools and human osteological remains. Tibitó has a date of 9740 BC. Unifacially retouched **chert** tools have been recovered from this site. Tibitó is close to the contemporaneous **El Abra** and **Tequendama**. *See also* CUMBE CAVE.

TIERRADENTRO. Culture and site in the highlands of Colombia situated along the upper Cauca River. It developed from around AD 1 to 1500. Its subsistence was based on **maize agriculture**, **hunting** of small animals, and fishing. The stone sculptures are similar to those of **San Agustín**. Other important Tierradentro crafts are gold objects. Painted underground chambers are characteristic burial sites of the Tierradentro culture. Burials were secondary, sometimes cremated, and placed in **funerary urns**. The site of Tierradentro is listed in the **World Heritage Sites of UNESCO**.

TIERROID CULTURES. These cultures are named after the site of Tierra de los Indios located in western Venezuela and dating to after AD 1350. Tierroid sites contain low platform **mounds**. They manufactured **polychrome pottery**, similar to the earlier **Tocuyanoid** and to the Herra style in Panama.

TILCARA (PUCARÁ DE TILCARA). Large settlement in the Quebrada de Humahuaca (Jujuy, Argentina). Tilcara dates to the Late Period (AD 1000–1400). The **Inka** road that united the highlands with the low valleys passes by the site. As with most sites in the region, Tilcara contains **pirca** walls, some of which were restored in the 1930s when Tilcara became an important tourist site.

TILIVICHE. Preceramic (Archaic) site in the north coast of Chile, where there is early evidence of adaptation to maritime resources dating to 7700 BC. The inhabitants of Tiliviche were also **hunters** and manufactured leaf-shaped stone projectile points (**Lauricocha-Ayampitín**). Some of the points were made of **obsidian**, which suggests that these groups migrated to the highlands under certain circumstances or exchanged local products with highland people. Tiliviche is in the vicinity of the site of **Las Conchas**.

TILOCALAR PHASE. The site of **Tulan**-54 in the Salar de Atacama, northern Chile, dates to 1200–300 BC and provides evidence of early sedentary villages of **pastoralist** groups (Early **Formative**) in the area. People used **copper** and gold objects at Tulan-54. Imported **ceramics** of the **San Francisco** *corrugada* tradition from the eastern Andean valleys and eastern lowlands have been identified at this site. Local and exotic lithic raw materials, including **obsidian**, have further been recovered from Tulan-54.

TIMEHRI PETROGLYPH TYPE. The type site is Timehri Island, Guyana. Timehri designs are similar to and thus can be affiliated with **Saladoid ceramics** in the Caribbean area.

TINCULLPA. Quechua term used for circular metallic plaques from Ecuador and Peru. Usually they have two hanging holes, which suggest that they were used as body ornaments. The tincullpa date to the Late Period (AD 1000–1400). Some were made of gold and others of silver. They have felinic iconography. During the Colonial Period, they were used in rituals associated with lightning. Their shape and iconography is similar to the *placas metálicas* of northwest Argentina.

TITIMANI. Yaya-Mama Tradition site of the Middle **Formative**, located on the eastern shores of Lake Titicaca, Peru, near the modern town of Escoma.

TIWANAKU (ALSO SPELLED TIAHUANACO OR TIAHUANACU). Urban site and capital of the Tiwanaku state. The city of Tiwanaku is located near the southern shores of Lake Titicaca (Bolivia) at 3,800 meters above sea level, thus representing the highest pre-Columbian city in the Americas. Originally a ceremonial center, after AD 600 the site expanded to form a true city with numerous neighborhoods enclosed by walls and covering approximately six square kilometers. Most of the domestic **architecture** was made with **adobe**. Elite domestic architecture was constructed with a masonry foundation, with the upper sections built with adobe. The ceremonial center includes the two pyramidal structures, the Akapana, a seven-level **pyramid**, and the Puma Punku. The **Kalasasaya**, a large enclosure, also formed part of the monumental core. Putuni and Kerikala, which served as elite residences, were located adjacent to the Kalasasaya. Three concentric moats divided the city. Most of the ceremonial and elite structures were located in the area surrounded by the first moat.

Tiwanaku's economic basis was intensive **agriculture** with the use of **sukakollos** and **camelid** husbandry. After AD 700, the Tiwanaku polity expanded outside of the Titicaca basin. Tiwanaku established colonies in the Moquegua valley and had indirect influence over smaller political units in the Bolivian **altiplano**, the northern Chilean coast, and the **San Pedro de Atacama** desert, as well as in northwestern Argentina. Material items with Tiwanaku iconography, such as the **Staff God** and others, were found in this vast region. Tiwanaku was important in Andean mythology: some myths of origin present the city as the center of creation of humankind. Tiwanaku is one of the **World Heritage Sites of UNESCO**.

Tiwanaku was a ritual center embodying Andean notions of dualism or bipartition of society. Two halves or moieties could be associated with the two main pyramids: the Akapana to the north and the Pumapunku to the south. Akapana and its associated complex of public architecture was deliberately surrounded by a moat to establish this complex as a ringed sacred island, the cosmogenic center of the city and the state. The Akapana is an elaborate mountain shrine designed to collect water and thread it from one structural terrace to the next as a powerful icon of fertility and agricultural abundance. Puma Punku is similarly configured for the southern moiety.

Tiwanaku secured and maintained power over other Titicaca-basin polities through **huaca** capture. The sunken semisubterranean temple associated with the Akapana Complex was a site for display of captured icons. It is full of sculptures in non-Tiwanaku styles, representing huacas that are geographically, temporally, stylistically, and ethnically foreign to Tiwanaku; these are placed in a subordinate position to the great, centrally located **Bennett Monolith**, which encoded the primary tenets of Tiwanaku state ideology and cosmology. Similarly, the proposed headless **mummy** bundles from the Akapana, along with the lavish display of **trophy heads** on the staffs of condor- and **puma**-masked dancers on ritual drinking cups and on monumental sculpture, are seen as another representation of decapitating and coopting other polities through removal of their ruling elites in order to incorporate the conquered group into the broader body of Tiwanaku society.

The Palace of the Multicolored Rooms, part of the Putuni Complex of palaces with **polychrome** colored walls, suggests that the Tiwanaku elite constructed symbols emblematic of their mystical union with the divine in their dwellings. The palace structure is intertwined with rituals of consecration that are seen as transforming the quarters into profoundly sacred space.

In an area to the east of the civic-ceremonial core, a series of cardinally aligned compound structures were exposed. While these structures displayed a diversity of features, the ubiquity of metal and lapidary items was interpreted to define the occupants as retainers associated with the presumed palaces, with higher status than the inhabitants of peripheral areas and rural commoners. The eastern periphery of the site included a district called Chiji Jawira with a large **ceramic** workshop suggesting that specialized craft neighborhoods existed within the city. *See also* CHIRIBAYA; CHIRIPA; CHIVAY; CHUCARIPUPATA; ISLAND OF THE MOON; ISLAND OF THE SUN; KALLAMARKA; KHONKO WANKANE; KOANI PAMPA; LUKURMATA; OMO; PALERMO; PUQUI STYLE; QUERIMITA; QUISPISISA; SAN PEDRO DE ATACAMA; SODALITE; ZAPALERI-CALDERA VILAMA.

TOCUYANOID. Ceramic style that belongs to the **First Painted Horizon** in northwestern Venezuela, dated to 400 BC to AD 500. The settlements associated with this style consist of small villages. Pottery was painted with red and black on white. One of the diagnostic elements of Tocuyanoid sites are characteristic **ceramic** human **figurines**. *See also* TIERROID CULTURES.

TOLA. Artificial dwelling or ceremonial **mound**, such as those of **La Tolita**, from the coast, highlands, and Amazon basin of Ecuador and southern Colombia. They are usually found in groups and represent the most important pre-Hispanic **architectural** feature of the region. The northernmost tola, known as Morro de Tulcán, is located in Popayán, Colombia. *See also* BAHÍA; LOS ESTEROS; TUMACO.

TOLDENSE. Stone tool industry from the Early Holocene of Patagonia. It was first defined at the site of **Los Toldos**. It is characterized by finely manufactured bifacial projectile points.

TOLOMBÓN. Large Late Period/**Inka**/Colonial settlement in Salta, northwestern Argentina. Tolombón is located in the Calchaquí Valley and includes a lower residential section and a higher defensive portion or **pukara**. When the Spaniards arrived, Juan de Calchaquí united the local groups and resisted the Spanish invasion from that site. It is one of Argentina's national historic monuments.

TOMBS. Indigenous peoples of South America generally buried their dead in and around their homes. In many cases, the individual was accompanied by ornaments, tools, **ceramic** vessels, food, and other items of daily use, which indicate the belief in life after death. Many rites took place during long periods of time after the death of the individual. Bodies were placed in different positions; flexed bodies were very common in many groups. In some cases, burials are primary, if the individual was placed there shortly after death and never removed. Secondary burials are when the body is removed and the bones are rearranged and reburied. Differences in tomb offerings might suggest social stratification and other forms of group identity. *See also* CAPACOCHA; "EAGLE" PECTORALS; FUNERARY URNS; SHAFT AND CHAMBER TOMB.

TOMEBAMBA (ALSO TUMIPAMPA). Inka site in Cuenca in the highlands of Ecuador. According to Inka traditions, Tomebamba was founded by Inka Tupac Yupanqui around AD 1465 or 1470 in the rich territory of the Cañari. It was a center of military operations in the area from which the Inka expanded to the Ecuadorian coast and later to northern Ecuador. Tomebamba was designed following the plan of **Cuzco**, with **Hanan** and **Hurin** sections, palaces, and temples. It is said that the Inka Wayna Capac was born there. In AD 1557, the Spaniards settled the city of Cuenca on the ruins of Tomebamba. It is now a **World Heritage Site of UNESCO**. *See also* EMERALDS.

TOPARÁ. Early Intermediate Period (AD 200–600) culture of the southern coast of Peru. Topará **ceramics** were found in the Cañete, **Chincha**, and Pisco valleys, at **Paracas**, and at Arena Blanca/Cabeza Larga.

TOQUEPALA CAVES. Located in the upper Moquegua valley of southern Peru, these caves contain **rock art** and a long occupational sequence that extends back to 7500 BC. These sites were probably occupied during the rainy season, which lasts from November through March. A variety of projectile-point types have been recovered from these caves.

TRADE. Indigenous groups began trading goods when they settled in South America. **Obsidian** was obtained from mountainous sources of southern Peru and brought to coastal areas already in the Late Pleistocene. There was also trade in precious and semiprecious gems such as **amber**, **emeralds**, **jadeite**, **malachite**, **sodalite**, **turquoise**, and also ***Spondylus***. Other products were **ceramics** and **salt**. Trade routes followed the main rivers in eastern South America, such as the Amazon, the Orinoco, the Paraná, and the Uruguay, and along mountain passes in the Andes. Trade also took place along maritime routes along the Pacific coast and connecting South and Central America. Trade goods were transported along a well-organized road system that covered vast portions of South America. Some of these routes were taken by the early Iberian conquerors. *See also* CHINCHA; LAMBAYEQUE; LOMA NEGRA; MARKETS; MANTEÑO; MINDALÁ; PIRINCAY; TRANSPORTATION.

TRANSPORTATION. South American people relied on **camelid**, seafaring, and pedestrian modes of transportation. Transportation by water (sea coast and inland rivers) was made possible through the use of canoes and rafts, illustrated in **Moche ceramics** and **Muisca metallurgy**. Remains of pre-Columbian rafts made with hides of sea mammals were found in late coastal sites of northern Chile. Wooden rafts in the same area were dated to AD 760. Rafts are represented in several **rock art** sites of the southern highlands of Peru. For inland transport, roads existed in several regions of the highlands and lowlands. European explorers in the sixteenth century used and described these roads, particularly the **Inka** road network. This network was formed by two main north-south segments, one following the coast, the other along the highlands, interconnected by transversal lines. In the Andes, the **llama** and **alpaca** were and are used as pack animals, illustrated in Moche and **Recuay** ceramics. Llamas can carry up to 40 kilograms of weight. *See also* SALINAR; SAN JOSÉ DE MORO; TRADE; YOTOCO.

TRES ARROYOS. Early Holocene cave site in Tierra del Fuego, Chile, situated near the **Marazzi** rock shelter. It is the earliest human settlement in the southernmost part of South America, dated to 9800–8200 BC. One bifacial fragment and several unifacially retouched tools were associated with extinct fauna (horse, **ground sloth**, and fox) as well as **guanaco**. Sea lion and sea shellfish remains, suggesting an adaptation to both maritime and terrestrial environments, were also recovered from this site (twenty kilometers to the east).

TRES DE MAYO CAVE. Large cave with two occupations located in Misiones, northeastern Argentina. The earliest occupation corresponds to the **Humaitá** Tradition, the most recent one to the Eldoradense (early **ceramic** period). Several burials were excavated here although radiometric analysis has not been conducted.

TROPHY HEAD. Important iconographic element in the **religious** paraphernalia of several South American indigenous groups. In many South American cultures, heads of mostly young men were separated from the rest of the body (at the moment of death or after or as a cause of death), and used in ritual activities. Sometimes a hole was made on the upper part of the skull in order to introduce a rope for its display. Trophy heads, sometimes in groups or caches, were found in **Nasca** sites and others such as **El Alfarcito**. Images of trophy heads are present in **ceramics** (**Tiwanaku**, Nasca, **Moche**, **Alto Ramirez**, **Belén**, **Jama-Coaque**, and **La Tolita**, among many others), in textiles, metals, and bone, and there are Colonial documents that describe them. *See also* ASIA; CUPISNIQUE; LORD OF THE SEA; OCULATE BEING; PANZALEO; SACRIFICE.

TÚCUME (ALSO KNOWN AS EL PURGATORIO). Large urban site with monumental **architecture** located in the north coast of Peru. The site covers 150 hectares. It was the center of **Lambayeque** society after the collapse of **Batán Grande** around AD 1100. Túcume was occupied by the expanding **Chimú** state in approximately AD 1350. The site contains a vast number of imposing **adobe** constructions that surround Cerro La Raya, which was constructed around a coastal hill and a **huaca** (**waca**) 146 meters tall. Around AD 1470, Túcume was conquered by the **Inka**, who established their center at Huaca Larga, an adobe construction twenty meters high. *See also* MANCHÁN.

TULÁN. Name of a *quebrada* (ravine) close to Salar de Atacama, northern Chile, where there are a series of preceramic sites with evidence of early **camelid domestication**. The sites are located between 2,000 and 3,000 meters above sea level.

TULOR. Sites in the **San Pedro de Atacama** area of northern Chile. Tulor Algarrobo and Tulor Ayllo or Tulor Pueblo 1 are two of the main settlements. The latter is an earthen village similar to **Guatacondo** with circular houses. It has dates of AD 500. Tulor is one of Chile's national monuments.

TUMACO. Culture that developed in the southern coast of Colombia and northern coast of Ecuador (where it is called Esmeraldas and Manabí) from 400 BC to AD 1. The ceremonial centers of Tumaco sites are characterized by the presence of tolas. The subsistence of Tumaco people was based on **agriculture**, fishing, and **salt** exploitation. The presence of **manos and metates** and **budares** suggest that **maize** and **manioc** were cultivated. Tumaco **ceramics** are characterized by **double-spout vessels** or *alcazarras* and modeled vessels portraying houses; **musical** instruments; human figures, some of which are performing sexual activities; and animals (**jaguars**, reptiles, owls, monkeys, fish, and marine birds).

TUMBAGA. A gold and **copper** alloy that was used in pre-Columbian Colombia and Peru, appearing in various cultures including the **Moche**, the **Lambayeque**, and the **Chimú**. In **Batán Grande**, **mummy** bundles of elite members had tumbaga funerary masks. *See also* LOMA NEGRA; MUISCA; SINÚ; TUMI.

TUMBES. Port where the Spanish conquistador Francisco Pizarro first landed in Peru in AD 1532 and began to move south by land with a small army toward **Cuzco**. The site is located close to the border between Peru and Ecuador.

TUMI. Ceremonial knife used in the Andes, usually made of **bronze**, **tumbaga**, or gold and associated with the Peruvian north coast polities. The blade has a semicircular shape. *See also* DOS CABEZAS; SAN JOSÉ DE MORO.

TUMIPAMPA. *See* TOMEBAMBA.

TUMUKU. Obsidian type from the southern highlands of Peru. Its source has not yet been located. It was used since the preceramic period in the department of Puno.

TUNEL 1. Site located along the Beagle Channel, Tierra del Fuego, southern Argentina. The earliest occupation dates to 5000 BC and consisted of a small group of **guanaco hunters**. Later occupants of the site were groups which exploited maritime resources.

TUPIGUARANÍ. Ceramic tradition and culture found along the rivers of the Plata basin and Brazilian coast. The Tupiguaraní Tradition originated in the southern Amazon basin around AD 500. Tupiguaraní settlements were formed by one or more **malocas** or communal houses. The Tupiguaraní Tradition is divided in three subtraditions according to the prevalent exterior decoration of ceramics. The earliest subtradition is the Corrugated, followed by the **Polychrome**, and the last is the Brushed subtradition. The southernmost Tupiguaraní settlements are located in the lower Paraná delta and were dated to the Late Prehistoric Period. In Colonial times, Tupiguaraní living in the Brazilian coast spoke Tupí, and the Tupiguaraní from the Plata basin spoke **Guaraní**.

TUPURAYA. Ceramic style and culture from the Mizque region, Cochabamba, Bolivia. It dates from AD 200 or 400 to 700 and consists of **fortified** villages with rectangular houses. **Keros** constituted important forms and ceramic designs were characterized by geometric motifs in red and black on a white or cream-colored base. **Waco retratos**, anthropomorphic vessels, and tripod vessels are all lacking in the Tupuraya repertoire.

TURQUOISE. Bluish stone (a hydrated **copper** aluminum phosphate) used for beads and other ornaments. It was procured throughout the central and southern Andes from northern Chile and unknown sources since the second millennium BC. One of the earliest finds is from a **tomb** in **Lauricocha** (8000 BC). Turquoise was used in numerous types of ornaments including necklace beads, **figurines**, and mosaics. **Angualasto** ceremonial shields from San Juan at the Museo de Luján and Museo Arqueológico de San Juan (Argentina) contain approximately 3,800 turquoise beads each. Forty turquoise human figurines were recovered in a cache at the **Wari** site of **Pikillacta**. They probably represent community (**ayllu**) leaders or mythical heads of lineages. *See also* JEWELRY; LAMBAYEQUE; SAN JOSÉ DE MORO; TRADE.

TUTISHCAINYO. Early **ceramic** site on the Ucayali River near the modern city of Pucallpa on the eastern slopes of the Peruvian Andes. The earliest dates obtained for this site are 2000 BC. **Agriculture** was based on **manioc** cultivation and probably **maize**. *See also* ZONE HATCHURED HORIZON.

– U –

UHLE, MAX (1856–1944). German archaeologist. He is called the father of Peruvian archaeology and he traveled and conducted excavations in several countries of South America beginning in 1892. He also published numerous articles and books. Among them are *Die Ruinenstaette von Tiahuanaco im Hochlande des alten Peru* (1892) with Alphons Stubel; *Pachacámac: Report of the William Pepper Peruvian Expedition of 1896* (1903); *Las relaciones prehistóricas entre el Perú y la Argentina* (1912); *Los Aborígenes de Arica* (1917); and *Estudios esmeraldeños* (1927). **John H. Rowe** published some of Uhle's manuscripts under the title *Max Uhle, 1856–1944: a Memoir of the Father of Peruvian Archaeology* (1954). Many of Uhle's collections are at the Phoebe A. Hearst Museum of Anthropology of the University of California at Berkeley.

ULLUKU (*ULLUCUS TUBEROSUS*). (Pronounced oo-*yoo*-koh.) Locally known as *papa lisa*. One of the most important domesticated Andean tubers, ulluku is cultivated in the upper valleys and **altiplano** between 3,500 and 3,800 meters above sea level from Bolivia to Colombia. The tubers are brightly colored and are rich in carbohydrates. Ulluku is very resistant to pests. *See also* OCA; PUNA.

UMBÚ TRADITION. Preceramic tradition extending over large portions of the states of Paraná, Santa Catarina, and Rio Grande do Sul, Brazil, particularly along the valleys of the Uruguay, Jacuí, Caí, and Dos Sinos rivers. It has a broad temporal range, divided into three phases, lasting from 9500 BC to AD 1600. Most sites are in the open air, but some shelters were also occupied. In these rock shelters, remains of several animal species such as deer, tapir, peccary, armadillo, coati, lizard, tortoises, birds, river mollusks, and fish were found. Plant remains in Umbú sites include palm and pine nuts (*Araucaria*). The characteristic stone tool is a stemmed triangular projectile point. Other characteristic elements of the Umbú Tradition are **incised** plaques. Ground tools include **bolas**, **manos and metates**, and axes. Most sites of the Umbú Tradition date to after

2500 BC, a time when grasslands and savannahs expanded due to climatic changes. *See also* INDIA MUERTA.

UNA TRADITION. Sites of the Una Tradition are located in Goiás, central Brazil, and date to after AD 1000. In most Una Tradition sites, there is an earlier occupation of the **Paranaíba Phase**. Subsistence was based on the cultivation of **maize**, gourd, and **cotton**. Among its lithic tools are large axes, either retouched, ground, or polished. **Ceramics** are small, utilitarian, and usually dark-colored.

URU TRADITION. A **ceramic** tradition of Matto Grosso, central Brazil that is related to the **Aratú Tradition**. The first circular villages associated with this tradition emerged in the region in AD 600. By AD 800 they became the most common type of settlement in eastern Brazil. These villages were often five hundred meters in diameter consisting of several rows of houses situated around an open space or plaza. Village inhabitants cultivated **maize**. After AD 850, the Uru groups coexisted with **Tupiguaraní** settlements in the area.

U-SHAPED CENTERS. Ceremonial sites of the north and central coast of Peru designed with **mounds** enclosing a central plaza on three sides, thus forming a U-shape. The U is always parallel to the river course and is usually open in the direction of the river facing the east or northeast. This pattern of orientation could suggest that the U-shaped spaces were related to the development of **irrigation agriculture** and fertility rites. These constructions are among the earliest planned centers of South America, and of the Americas in general, and the earliest can be dated to 2700 BC. *See also* CABALLO MUERTO; CARDAL; GARAGAY; LA FLORIDA; LIMONCARRO; RELIGION.

USHNU. A feature of **Inka architecture**. Ushnus are platforms with elaborate drains that were usually located in the center of an open area or plaza. Several Inka sites in different parts of the empire (highlands, coast, north, and south) contained ushnus: **Chena**, **Choqe K'iraw**, **Huánuco Pampa**, **Pachacamac**, **Pumpu**, **Tambo Viejo**, **Nevado del**

Aconquija, **Potrero de Payogasta**, **Shincal**, **Tambería del Inca**, and **Tambo Colorado**.

– V –

VALDIVIA. One of the earliest **ceramic** traditions and cultures of South America, found in coastal Ecuador. Valdivia chronology is subdivided into eleven phases: the earliest (1a) was dated to 4400–3800 BC, and the most recent one (8b) was dated from 1600 to 1450 BC. Valdivia settlements are villages with a central open space or plaza. Houses were usually elliptic in shape and had storage pits. The site of **Real Alto** was an important Valdivia center with ceremonial **mounds**. Subsistence was based on horticulture of **maize**, squash, and beans. **Hunting** and fishing complemented the Valdivia diet. Among the Valdivia ceramic artifacts are human **figurines**, most of which are female. These figurines could have been part of fertility cults or shamanic elements for medicine, divination, and/or magic. *See also* EMERENCIANA; MACHALILLA; SAN ISIDRO; SAN LORENZO DEL MATE; *STROMBUS*.

VALENCIOID (VALENCIA) CULTURE. This culture developed during the Late Period (after AD 900) around Lake Valencia along the Caribbean coast of Venezuela. Earth **mounds** with **funerary urns** distinguish sites of this cultural tradition. **Ceramics** are unpainted but modeled, showing human faces with "coffee bean"-shaped eyes. Female **figurines** have prominent buttocks. Valencia is also characterized by very elaborate polished stone celts and batwing pendants.

VALLOID. Ceramic series in the Orinoco basin, Venezuela (AD 900–1500). This ceramic series, identified from a number of archaeological sites in the middle Orinoco, is not a mere variant of **Arauquinoid**. Although they share a number of attributes, Valloid exhibits enough distinctive elements to divide it from the former so as to represent a quite different ceramic tradition. Valloid ceramics are characterized by a yellowish paste tempered with large grains of sand or ground rocks. Decoration consists of distinctive **incised-**

punctated dots of clay applied in rows, chains, or bands following angular or diamond-shaped geometric patterns. These chains of small raised dots of clay applied to the surface form bands that subdivide the surface of the pottery into different sectors. **Figurines** are also frequent, often representing animal forms. Dating from between AD 900–1500, Valloid pottery is very well represented throughout the middle Orinoco, particularly in the hinterland between the Maniapure and the Parguaza rivers, where it is systematically found in combination with Late Arauquinoid materials.

As with most ceramic traditions of the Orinoco, there has been a tendency to treat these ceramics as representing distinctive ethnic or linguistic groups cohabiting the area and to interpret the combined occurrence of these ceramics as evidence of a multicomponent ethnic complex. Furthermore, Valloid pottery has been stylistically associated with the Corobal Phase of the upper Ventuari River. This apparent relationship has contributed to the hypothesis that Valloid ceramic may be associated with western Carib-speaking populations, probably ancestors of the Mapoyo and the Pareca, populations that entered into contact with the Europeans in the eighteenth century. The area traditionally inhabited by these groups, between the Parguaza and the Suapure rivers, was occupied by a people using ceramics that have been defined stylistically as the Valloid series (AD 1000–1530). Despite the existence of linguistic correlations between the Mapoyo and other Carib languages of the middle Orinoco Region (such as the Panare or Eñepa), the Mapoyo language is not a mere dialectal variation. The Mapoyo and the Panare, for example, have been separated for at least 2,000 to 3,000 years. *See also* CUEVA DEL CERRO GAVILÁN; CUEVA DEL SANTO.

VELARDE (MOUND VELARDE). Mound located in the Llanos de **Moxos** in the lowlands of Bolivia. Its dimensions are forty-five by twenty-five meters and it is five meters high. It is characterized by two occupations. The later occupation is characterized by **funerary urns**, painted tripod bowls, and other **ceramic** vessels, while the oldest occupation is distinguished by rounded and globular bowls. **Hunting** of deer, paca, opossum, and alligator was common to both occupations, and mollusks also constituted an important dimension of the diet throughout the two occupations.

VENTILLA. Largest urban center of the **Nasca culture** in the southern coast of Peru, dating to AD 1 to 400. Ventilla occupied approximately two hundred hectares and consisted of habitation terraces, walled compounds, and **mounds**. Ventilla may have served as one of the two capitals of the Nasca polity, with the much larger and more elaborate ceremonial center of **Cahuachi** as the religious capital and Ventilla as the urban capital. Both centers were united by a linear **geoglyph**.

VICUÑA. A wild **camelid**. Its habitat is restricted to the high Andean plateau of Peru, Bolivia, northern Chile, and northwest Argentina. During **Inka** times, inhabitants of the high Andes practiced the **chaco** or the **hunting** of vicuña. This activity was restricted by the state, and it took place at specific times of the year to provide fine wool for the members of the elite. Vicuña has the finest wool of all camelids and it remains highly valued.

VICÚS (ALSO CALLED SECHURA VICÚS). Culture of the north coast of Peru, found north of the Piura valley between AD 1 and 700. Vicús **ceramics** are very elaborate, with sculptural style and negative painting.

VIEIRA TRADITION. Ceramic tradition that appeared in **Umbú** sites of southern Brazil. *See also* SABANAS BAJAS TRADITION.

VILCA. Quechua term (*willka* in **Aymara**) for a **hallucinogenic substance** consumed in pre-Columbian South America. This substance was extracted from seeds of a Leguminosae tree called *vilca*, *cebil*, *angico prieto*, or *curupay-atá (Anadenanthera colubrina)*, at least since 2130 BC according to findings in **Inca Cueva 4**. Vilca was used as **snuff** powder, in enemas, or smoked. The term also applies to a very powerful person with superhuman powers.

VILUCO. Late Period site type and culture (AD 1200–1700) from Mendoza, central Argentina. Viluco is the name given to the ancestors of the Huarpe, who inhabited the valleys of northern and central Mendoza at the time of the Spanish conquest. Viluco society was characterized by a subsistence based on **irrigation agriculture** of **maize**, **quinoa**, beans, and squash; **cotton**; **llama pastoralism**; **hunt-**

ing of **guanaco**, **ñandú**, and smaller animals (hares and partridges); and gathering of **algarroba** and **chañar** fruits. Their main tools were triangular unstemmed projectile points and **bolas**. The Viluco people produced tools and ornaments of **copper** and **bronze** (pins, *topu*, punches, and tweezers). Many individuals practiced **cranial deformation** (mainly tabular erect, but also some cases of tabular oblique). Among their characteristic **ceramic** vessels are **keros**.

VIÑA DEL CERRO. **Inka** site in the Copiapó valley, north-central Chile (Norte Chico). Scholars consider Viña del Cerro an important center for the processing of **copper** in Chile. An **ushnu** is one of the important elements of Inka **architecture** in Viña del Cerro. Viña del Cerro is one of Chile's national monuments.

VINITÚ PHASE. Preceramic **hunter** and gatherer culture that lived in open areas with limited forests in the upper Paraná and Uruguay basin (northeastern Argentina and southern Brazil) around 6000–5000 BC. Projectile points and a great variety of scrapers have been found at Vinitú sites.

VIRACOCHA (WIRACOCHA). Andean creator **god**. It was a very important figure in the Andean pantheon. Its importance may have been augmented through **Inka** patronage. *See also* RAQCHI.

VIRACOCHAPAMPA. **Wari** administrative center located near **Marca Huamachuco** (also known as Huamachuco) in the northernmost fringes of the Wari state. Viracochapampa has a trapezoidal site-plan with great enclosing walls, rectangular buildings around patios, and limited patterns of access. Large halls or galleries are characterized by niches with walls that are six meters high. It is believed to represent one of the earliest Wari provincial centers, but was apparently never completed.

VISCACHANI. Open-air quarry site in the highlands of Bolivia. Many large leaf-shaped projectile points were found there, and thus the term Viscachani is applied to those points found in other parts of Bolivia. These points are similar to the **Lauricocha** and **Ayampitín** types.

VOLCAN CHAITÉN. Obsidian source located in southern Chile on the mainland across from the Chiloé Island. This gray translucid obsidian was used by people living at sites of the Pacific coast up to four hundred kilometers to the north and south of the source since 5500 BC.

– W –

WACA. *See* HUACA.

WACO (HUACO) RETRATO. *See* PORTRAIT VESSELS.

WAGNER, ERIKA. Venezuelan archaeologist. She obtained a PhD from Yale University. Wagner has been working at the Instituto Venezolano de Investigaciones Científicas (IVIC, Venezuelan Institute of Scientific Research) since 1965. Among her many publications are *The Prehistory and Ethnohistory of the Carache Area in Western Venezuela* (1967); *La Protohistoria e Historia Inicial de Boconó, Estado Trujillo* (1972); *Prehispanic Workshop of Serpentinite Artifacts, Venezuelan Andes and Possible Raw Material Source* with C. Schubert (1972); *Relaciones prehispánicas de Venezuela* (1984, editor); and *The Future of the Past in Latin America* (1987).

WANKARANI. First **agricultural** settlements (**mounds**) in the central highland or **altiplano** region of Bolivia. Settlements were formed by several circular **adobe** houses with thatched roofs (ranging from 15 to 780 per site). Most Wankarani sites are located around the Desaguadero River or to the northeast of Lake Poopó. Wankarani people were agriculturalists and **pastoralists**. Some of the earliest **copper metallurgy** in South America, dated to between 1200 and 800 BC, derives from these sites. Another important element in Wankarani society are the stone sculptures in the shape of **camelid** heads. Some Wankarani villages were also found in the lower valleys in Cochabamba, suggesting that these were colonists sent to warmer areas to cultivate **maize** and other crops. *See also* LA BARCA.

WARA WARA. Quechua term for **raised field**. *See* SUKAKOLLO.

WARFARE. Warfare was practiced by many South American indigenous groups, with the earliest evidence dating to around 5000 BC. Warfare activities were often closely associated with other social practices, such as **religion** and games. Evidence of warfare include **fortifications**, **weapons**, iconography (in **ceramics**, bone, textiles, **metallurgy**, **rock art**, and so on), as well as skeletal remains. The Iberian conquerors describe warfare that took place between groups, including **Inka** militarism. *See also* BOLA; CERRO SECHÍN; HUACA EL BRUJO; JAMA-CORQUE STYLE; NASCA CULTURE; PUKARA; WEAPONS.

WARI (ALSO SPELLED HUARI). Urban site and capital of the Wari state during the Middle Horizon (AD 600–1000). Wari is located at 2,800 meters above sea level in the Huarpa River basin in the vicinity of the modern Peruvian city of Ayacucho. It was the center of a road system that connected to other sites such as the planned settlements of **Azangaro**, **Pikillacta**, and Jingamoto. The site of Wari occupied around six square kilometers and was inhabited by an estimated population of 70,000 people. By AD 600, Wari became a ceremonial and residential center, with several enclosures surrounding ceremonial structures of masonry blocks. Among the important buildings of Wari are the temple complexes of Vegachayoq Moqo and the semisubterranean temple of Moraduchayoq. Wari population and size expanded until around AD 800. Most of the residential areas were built with quarried stone set in mud mortar. Several of these residential units were grouped in compounds surrounded by narrow streets and some dwellings had a lower and upper floor. *See also* HACHA; HUARPA; LAMBAYEQUE; QUISPISISA; *SPONDYLUS*; TURQUOISE; VIRACOCHAPAMPA.

WATTLE AND DAUB. A method of constructing walls by sewing a base of branches and other vegetal material inside a wooden frame and daubing mud to it. It was and is a very common method of building houses and other structures in many parts of South America. *See also* ARCHITECTURE.

WATUNGASTA (ALSO SPELLED BATUNGASTA). Late Intermediate Period and **Inka** site in Catamarca, northwest Argentina.

A **kallanka** and **qolcas** are Inka **architectural** features at Watungasta.

WAYWAKA. Site in the Andahuaylas valley in the central highlands of Peru. In the Muyu Moqo sector of the site was a stone bowl dating to 1500 BC with metalworking tools and thin gold foil, which is one of the earliest evidences of gold metalworking in the Andes.

WEAPONS. South American indigenous groups used a variety of weapons for different types of violent encounters: bows and arrows, darts, spears, lances, slings, clubs, maces, and so on of wood, stone, bone, and metal. Weapons are represented in **ceramics**, textile, bone, and metal. Weapons such as bows and arrows and clubs were found in **tombs**, particularly in the dry coast of Peru and Chile. In some cases, weapons were found *in situ* in well-preserved corpses in the Peruvian coast. Some authors trace the evidence of weapons and organized **warfare** to the Late Preceramic, as suggested by defensive walls and piles of sling stones. *See also* DOS CABEZAS; NORTHERN PERUVIAN COASTAL METALLURGICAL TRADITION; OCULATE BEING; STAFF GOD.

WICHQANA. Initial Period site in the central highlands of Peru that dates to between 1500 and 700 BC. This site has a **U-shaped** ceremonial structure where skulls of decapitated **women** were found.

WILLEY, GORDON R. (1913–2002). Renowned American archaeologist who worked in Central and South America and made innovative contributions to settlement pattern analysis and archaeological theory. Willey conducted most of his fieldwork in Central America and the north coast of Peru. Among his works are *Prehistoric Settlement Patterns in the Virú Valley, Peru* (1953); *An Introduction to American Archaeology vol. 2 South America* (1971); *Some Continuing Problems in New World Culture History* (1985); and *New World Archaeology and Culture History: Collected Essays and Articles* (1990). An edited volume in his honor was published in 1983: *Prehistoric Settlement Patterns. Essays in Honor of Gordon R. Willey* (E. Z. Vogt and R. M. Leventhal, eds.).

WILLIAMS, DENIS (1923–1998). Pioneer of the archaeology of Guyana. Williams founded the Walter Roth Museum of Anthropology in Georgetown, Guyana, in 1977. Among his published works are two books in which he summarized Guyanese archaeology: *Ancient Guyana* (1985) and *Prehistoric Guiana* (2003), and numerous articles including "Petroglyphs in the Prehistory of Northern Amazonia and the Antilles" (1985), "El Arcaico en el noroeste de Guyana y los comienzos de la horticultura" (1992), "Pages in Guyanese Prehistory" (1995), and "Prehistoric Cultures of the Iwokrama Rainforest" (1996).

WOMEN. Women had important roles in South American indigenous societies, as ancient iconographic motifs and other archaeological evidence suggest. In the **religious** sphere, **goddesses** and priestesses connected the generation and regeneration of human life with the movement of the cosmos. In all pre-Columbian societies, the division of labor was based on gender and age, and social classes if they existed. In societies where tribute or taxation was imposed on the household, women contributed to the payments, be they in goods or labor. The **Inka** constructed the gender category of *aclla*. These were young women who were selected in different regions of the empire and were confined to live in special edifices called *acllawasi* (*wasi* means house in **Quechua**). There these young women dedicated most of their time to weaving fine cloths, called *cumbi*, for the use of *kurakas* (local elite) and other powerful individuals of the empire, including members of royal lineages. Guaman Poma de Ayala illustrates activities associated with the stages of life both of women and men. He suggests that adult women's main roles were weaving and taking care of children and **domesticated** animals. *See also* MANO AND METATE; PACHACAMAC; SAN JOSÉ DE MORO; STAFF GODDESS.

WORLD HERITAGE SITES OF UNESCO. The United Nations Organization for Education, Science, and Culture has identified cultural and natural monuments that have outstanding historical or cultural value and supports their protection for future generations. Twelve pre-Columbian archaeological sites (or groups of sites) in South

America have been included in the list of World Heritage Sites: **Chan Chan** (1986), **Chavín** (1985), **Cuzco** (1983), **Cueva de las Manos Pintadas** (1999), **Machu Picchu** (1983), **Nazsca** and Pampa de Jumana Lines (1994), Rio **Abiseo** National Park (1990)—mixed, primarily for its natural conditions, **Samaipata** (1998), Serra da Capivara National Park (1991)—several rock shelters with Pleistocene occupations in northeastern Brazil, National Archaeological Park of **Tierradentro** (1995), **San Agustín** Archaeological Park (1995), and **Tiwanaku** (2000).

WUST, IRMHILD. Brazilian archaeologist. She received a doctorate from the University of São Paulo and conducted research in sedentary villages of central Brazil. Among her publications are *The Eastern Bororo from an Archaeological Perspective* (1994), *Novas perspectivas para o estudo dos ceramistas précoloniais do Centro-oeste Brasileiro: a análise espacial do sitio Guará 1 (GO-NI-100)* with H. B. Carvalho (1996), and *The Ring Villages of Central Brazil: A Challenge for Amazonian Archaeology* with Cristiana Barreto (1999).

– X –

XAUXA. *See* HATUN XAUXA.

– Y –

YAMPARÁ. Ceramic style from the valleys of Chuquisaca and Cochabamba, Bolivia. This style was dated to AD 1000–1400. Among its characteristic forms are globular vessels and bowls, some with human shape. The vessels are painted with geometric and zoomorphic designs. Yampará textiles have been preserved; some of the motifs are animals such as frogs, bats, and birds.

YANAURCO-QUISCATOLA. Important **obsidian** source in the northern highlands of Ecuador. Yanaurco-Quiscatola was exploited at least since the Early Holocene and obsidian from this source was found in the highlands (**Chobshi Cave**, **Cotocollao**, and **El Inga**) and coast (La Carolina) of Ecuador. The majority of stone tools of sites in the vicinity of the source are of obsidian. **Mullumica**, the other important Ecuadorian obsidian source, is located close to Yanaurco-Quiscatola.

YAYA-MAMA. Religious tradition from the **Formative Period** of the Titicaca basin (Peru-Bolivia), dating from 600 BC to AD 1. The name derives from the **Quechua** *yaya* (father) and *mama* (mother). The ceremonial and civic centers of the Yaya-Mama Tradition are characterized by **sunken** temples, storage areas, carved **monoliths** (the original stela that gave the name to the tradition is at the site of Taraco, Peru), and a complex iconography. Two of the largest sites are **Pukara** in the north basin and **Chiripa** in the south basin. Other sites are **Chisi** and **Titimani**.

YERBA MATE (*ILEX PARAGUAYENSIS*). Tree native to the upper Paraná and Uruguay basin, the leaves of which were used by the indigenous people of the region, the **Guaraní**, for infusion in ritual ceremonies. Leaves were crushed and dried over fire. Even though the Spaniards made efforts to eliminate the use of yerba mate, it became one of the most popular beverages in eastern and southern South America, as it is to this day.

YOTOCO. Ceramic-producing culture in the **Calima** region in the western Cordillera, southern Colombia. Yotoco developed from the first century AD to AD 1200 as a derivative of the previous Ilama culture. Gold-working was highly developed among the Yotoco. Another important feature of Yotoco culture was roads that interconnected several villages.

YUCAY. Inka resort in the Urubamba Valley, southern Peru. According to historical accounts, Yucay belonged to the **panaqa** of Inka Wayna Kapak, who was one of the last Inka. Wayna Kapak, also spelled as Huayna Capac, spent part of his time in his royal estate in Yucay and the rest in his palace in **Cuzco**.

YURAJ MOLINO. Formative village site in Cochabamba, Bolivia, dating to between 1300 and 900 BC. The site is characterized by three activity areas: a cemetery, a **ceramic** workshop area, and a **metallurgical** area. Evidence of **domesticated camelids**, **hunting** of deer, and cultivation of **maize** and **tarwi** characterizes this village. The ceramics exhibit decorations similar to those of eastern lowland areas, and include some ceramic human **figurines**, which are rare in the region. Among exotic elements are **obsidian**, **turquoise**, and ceramics from lowland sites. *See also* CONCHU PATA.

– Z –

ZANJON SECO. Group of sites along the Quequén Grande valley in the southern province of Buenos Aires, Argentina. Four open-air sites with early **ceramics** dating to 1000 BC occupied by **hunters** and gatherers define the Zanjón Seco Complex. These are among the earliest ceramics of the region.

ZAPALERI-CALDERA VILAMA. Obsidian quarry located on the border between Bolivia, Argentina, and Chile. This quarry was exploited since 1000 BC and its products were distributed throughout Jujuy (northern Argentina), the **San Pedro de Atacama** oasis (northern Chile), and **Tiwanaku** (Bolivia). The presence of Zapaleri obsidian in Tiwanaku suggests exchanges between southern **altiplano** polities and Tiwanaku around AD 600–1000.

ZAQUE. At the time of the Spanish conquest in AD 1537, the zaque was the highest lord of the northern **Chibcha** in the Colombian highlands, in what is today the city of Tunja. *See also* ZIPA.

ZIPA. Highest lord of the southern **Chibcha** in the Colombian highlands, in what is today the city of Bogotá. Similar to the **zaque**.

ZONED HATCHURED HORIZON. Early **ceramic** style found in northern South America. Together with the **Saladoid-Barrancoid Horizon**, the Zoned Hatchured Horizon forms the basis of the **Formative Period** in the region. The time period extends approximately from 2000 BC to AD 1. As in other regions of South America, the term "formative" usually refers to the earliest sedentary villages. Ceramic decorations are mostly geometric and zoomorphic with modeled parts and red and/or white paint. There is a great variation in styles, spatial distribution, and time periods, and thus not all representatives of these horizons can be considered to be contemporaneous. Some representatives of the Zoned Hatchured Horizon are the **Tutishcainyo** Phase in the Upper Amazon and the **Ananatuba Phase** of the island of Marajo, located at the mouth of the Amazon. Sedentary villages with a mixture of cultivation of root crops, gathering of wild plants, **hunting**, and fishing constituted the subsistence basis of these groups. *See also* LA GRUTA.

ZOOLITHS. Animal-shaped portable polished stone sculptures from southern Brazil and Uruguay. They were manufactured in different shapes, including mammals, birds, fish, and turtles. Zooliths are usually flat and have a concave surface that could have served to grind either pigments or **hallucinogenic substances**. In Brazil, they are associated with the **Sambaquí**, where they probably came from **tombs**. *See also* HUMAITÁ.

ZUCCHI, ALBERTA (1938–). Italian-born Venezuelan archaeologist. She received her degrees from the Universidad Central de Venezuela. Zucchi conducted research in the Venezuelan llanos and in the Orinoco basin. In the past decade, Zucchi has extended her work to historical archaeology. Zucchi published numerous articles, including "Campos Elevados e Historia Cultural Prehispánica en los Llanos Occidentales de Venezuela" with William M. Denevan (1979),"Evidencias arqueológicas sobre grupos de posible lengua Caribe" (1985), "Los Cedeñoides: un nuevo grupo prehispánico del Orinoco medio" with Kay Tarble (1984), and "The Ceramic Sequence and New TL and C14 Dates for the Aguerito Site of the Middle Orinoco, Venezuela" with K. Tarble and J. E. Vaz (1984).

Appendix 1

Museums

NORTH AMERICA

United States of America

American Museum of Natural History
Central Park West and 79th Street
New York, NY 10024
www.amnh.org

Dumbarton Oaks
Pre-Columbian Museum
1703 32nd Street NW
Washington, DC 20007
www.doaks.org

Field Museum of Chicago
1400 South Lake Shore Drive
Chicago, IL 60605
www.fieldmuseum.org

Peabody Museum of Archaeology and Ethnology
Harvard University
11 Divinity Avenue
Cambridge, MA 02138
www.peabody.harvard.edu

Peabody Museum of Natural History
Yale University
New Haven, CT 06520
www.peabody.yale.edu

SOUTH AMERICA

Argentina

Instituto de Arqueología y Museo
San Martín 1545
4000 San Miguel de Tucumán
Tucumán
www.unt.edu.ar/fcsnat/arqueo/dependencias.htm

Museo de Antropología
Universidad Nacional de Córdoba
Avda. Hipólito Irigoyen 174
5000 Córdoba
www.unc.edu.ar

Museo de Antropología y Arqueología de Alta Montaña (MAAM)
Mitre 71
Salta
www.antropologico.gov.ar

Museo Arqueológico Adán Quiroga
Sarmiento 450
4700 San Fernando del Valle de Catamarca
Catamarca

Museo Arqueológico Dr. Eduardo Casanova
Belgrano 445
4624 Tilcara
Jujuy
www.tilcarajujuy.com.ar

Museo de Ciencias Naturales
Universidad Nacional de La Plata
Paseo del Bosque
1900 La Plata
www.fcnym.unlp.edu.ar

Museo Etnográfico Juan Bautista Ambrosetti
Universidad de Buenos Aires
Moreno 350
1091 Capital Federal
www.uba.ar/extension/m_etnografico.html

Bolivia

Instituto de Investigaciones Antropológicas y Museo Arqueológico
Geraldine Byrne de Caballero
Universidad Mayor de San Simón
Cochabamba
www.umss.edu.bo

Museo Nacional de Arqueología/Instituto Nacional de Arqueología
Calle Tiwanaku
La Paz
www.bolivian.com/arqueologia

Museo Regional Arqueológico de Tiwanaku (Museo Convencional and Museo Lítico Monumental)
Tiwanaku
www.bolivianet.com/tiwanacu/

Brazil

Fundação Museu do Homem Americano
São Raimundo Nonato
Piauí
www.fumdham.org.br

Museu Antropológico da UFG
Universidade Federal de Goiás
Av. Universitária 1166
Goiânia
Goiás
www.museu.ufg.br

Museu de Arqueología e Etnología
Av. Prof. Almeida Prado, 1466
Cidade Universitaria
05508-900 São Paulo
www.mae.usp.br

Museu de Arqueología e Etnologíia (MAE)
Universidade Federal da Bahia
Terreiro de Jesus
Centro Historico de Salvador
Bahia
www.ufba.br/instituicoes/ufa/mae

Museu de Arqueología de Xingó
Universidade Federal de Sergipe
www.museuxingo.com.br

Museu Dom Bosco
Museu Salesiano de Historia Natural
Rua Barão de Rio Grande, 1843
Campo Grande
Matto Grosso do Sul
www.museum.ucdb.br

Museu de Historia Natural
Quinta da Boa Vista
São Cristovão
20940-640 Rio de Janeiro, RJ
www.museunacional.ufrj.br

Museu Paranaense
Rua Kellers, 289
Alto São Francisco
80410-100 Curitiba
Paraná
www.pr.gov.br/museupr

Museu Paraense Emilio Goeldi
Av. Perimetral, 1901 Terra Firme

66077 Belem
Pará
www.museu-goeldi.br

Chile

Museo Arqueológico R. P. Gustavo Le Paige
Universidad Católica del Norte
San Pedro de Atacama
www.ucn.cl/Museos_Cultura/museoarqueologico.htm

Museo Arqueológico de La Serena
Cienfuegos and Cordovez
La Serena

Museo Arqueológico de Santiago
José Victorino Lastarria 307
Plaza Mulato Gil de Castro
Santiago
www.mavi.cl/arqueologico/index.htm

Museo Chileno de Arte Precolombino
Bandera 361
Santiago
www.precolombino.cl

Museo Nacional de Historia Natural
Quinta Normal
Santiago
www.mnhn.cl

Colombia

Museo Arqueológico de San Agustín
San Agustín
www.icanh.gov.co/secciones/museos/parques.htm

Museo Arqueológico de Tierradentro
Tierradentro
www.icanh.gov.co/secciones/museos/parques.htm

Museo Nacional de Colombia
Bogotá
www.icanh.gov.co/secciones/museos/nacional_permanente.htm

Museo del Oro
Banco de la República
Cra. 6 esquina calle 16
Parque Santander
Bogotá
www.banrep.gov.co/museo/esphome.htm

Ecuador

Museo Antropológico del Banco Central
Avenida de las Américas 1100
Guayaquil
www.bce.fin.ec/contenido.php?CNT=ARB0000393

Guyana

Walter Roth Museum of Anthropology
61 Main Str.
Georgetown
www.sdnp.org/wrma

Guyane

Musées des Cultures Guyanaises
78 Rue Mme Payé
97300 Cayenne
www.mcg973.org

Paraguay

Instituto Museo Arqueológico y Etnográfico Guido Boggiani e
Instituto Paraguayo de Prehistoria

Coronel Bogado 888
San Lorenzo
P.O. Box 20288
Asunción
www.seltz.com.py/html/arte_indigena.html

Museo Andrés Barbero
Avda. España 217
Asunción
www.museobarbero.org.py

Peru

Museo de Arqueología y Antropología
Universidad Mayor de San Marcos
Avda. Nicolás de Piérola 1222
Parque Universitario
Cercado de Lima
Lima
www.museoarqueologiasanmarcos.perucultural.org.pe

Museo de Arqueología, Antropología, e Historia
Universidad Nacional de Trujillo
Trujillo
www/unitru.edu.pe/arq/museount.html

Suriname

Stichting Surinams Museum
Fort Zeelandia
Paramaribo
www.museumsuriname.nl

Uruguay

Museo Nacional de Historia Natural y Antropología
Montevideo
www.mec.gub.uy/natura/

Venezuela

Museo Arqueológico
Mérida

Museo de Ciencias (ex Museo Nacional)
Plaza de Los Museos
Parque Los Caobos
Caracas
www.museo-de-ciencias.org.ve

EUROPE

Austria

Museum für Völkerkunde
A-1010 Wien—Neue Burg
Vienna
www.ethno-museum.ac.at/en/museum.html

Belgium

Musées Royaux d'Art et d'Histoire de Bruxelles
Brussells
www.kmkg-mrah.be

Denmark

Department of Ethnography
National Museum of Denmark
Copenhagen
www.natmus.dk/sw1413.asp

France

Musée de l'Homme
Palais de Chaillot
17 place du Trocadero

75116 Paris
www.mnhn.fr/mnhn/sites/mushom.html

Musée du Quai Branly
Hôtel industriel Le Berlier
37 Quai-Branly
75007 Paris
www.quaibranly.fr

Musée Thomas Dobrée de la ville de Nantes
18 rue Voltaire
Nantes
www.nantes.fr/airie/services/responsabilites/dgc/musees/dobre

Great Britain

British Museum
Great Russell Street
London WC1B 3DG
www.british-museum.ac.uk

Manchester Museum
250 Oxford Road
Manchester M13
www.museum.man.ac.uk

The Royal Scottish Museum
Chambers Street
Edinburgh EH1 1JF
Scotland
www.nms.ac.uk/royal/

University Museum of Archaeology and Anthropology
Downing Street (between Pembroke College and Emmanuel College)
Cambridge CB2 3DZ
www.museum-server.archanth.cam.ac.uk

Germany

Museum für Völkerkunde
Johannisplatz 5-11
04103 Leipzig
www.mvl-grassimuseum.de

Museum für Völkerkunde der Staatlichen Museen zu Berlin
Lansstraße 8
14195 Berlin-Dahlem
www.smb.spk-berlin.de/mv

Niedersächsischen Landesmuseum
Willy-Brandt-Allee 5
D-30169 Hannover
www.nlmh.de/d/data/index.php

Italy

Museo Civico del Castello
Piazza Castello 3
20121 Milan
www.milanocastello.it

Spain

Museo de América
Avenida de los Reyes Católicos, 6
28040 Madrid
www.geocities.com/museo_de_america

Museo Antonio Ballesteros
Facultad de Geografía e Historia
Universidad Complutense
Ciudad Universitaria
28040 Madrid
www.ucm.es/info/america2/

Museo Etnològic
Parque de Montjuich
Barcelona
www.museuetnologic.bcn.es

Museo Nacional de Antropología
Alfonso XII, 68
28014 Madrid
www.mnantropologia.mcu.es

Sweden

Ethnographic Museum
Djurgårdsbrunnsvägen 34
Box 27140
102 52 Stockholm
www.etnografiska.se

ASIA

Japan

Kurita Museum
1542 Komaba-cho, Ashikaga-shi
Tochigi
www.kurita.or.jp

Morishita Art Museum
241-10 Hinase, Oaza, Hinase-cho, Waka-gun
Okayama
www.marsol.co.jp/museum.html

National Museum of Ethnology
10-1 Senri Expo Park, Suita
Osaka 565-8511
www.minpaku.ac.jp/english/

Appendix 2

Research Institutions

NORTH AMERICA

United States

Center for the Study of the First Americans
Department of Anthropology
Texas A&M University
210 Anthropology Building
4352 TAMU
College Station, TX 77843-4352
www.centerfirstamericans.com

Cornell University
Department of Anthropology
261 McGraw Hall
Ithaca, NY 14853
www.cornell.edu

Institute of Andean Studies
P.O. Box 9307
Berkeley, CA 94709
www.instituteofandeanstudies.org

University of California, Berkeley
Department of Anthropology
232 Kroeber Hall
Berkeley, CA 94720
www.berkeley.edu

University of California, Los Angeles
Department of Anthropology
Los Angeles, CA 90095
www.ucla.edu

University of Chicago
Department of Anthropology
1156 East 58th Street
Chicago, IL 60637
www.uchicago.edu

University of Illinois at Chicago
Department of Anthropology
Behavioral Science Building
1007 W. Harrison St.
Chicago, IL 60607
www.uic.edu

University of Illinois at Urbana-Champaign
Department of Anthropology
109 Davenport Hall
607 S. Mathews Ave.
Urbana, IL 61801
www.uiuc.edu

University of Pittsburgh
Department of Anthropology
3302 WWPH
Pittsburgh, PA 15260
www.pitt.edu

Stanford University
Department of Anthropological Sciences
Main Quad, Building 50
450 Serra Mall
Stanford, CA 94305
www.stanford.edu/dept/anthsci

Yale University
Department of Anthropology
P.O. Box 208277
New Haven, CT 06520
www.yale.edu

SOUTH AMERICA

Argentina

Universidad Nacional de Buenos Aires
Ciudad Autónoma de Buenos Aires
www.uba.ar

Universidad Nacional de La Plata
La Plata
www.fcnym.unlp.edu.ar

Universidad Nacional del Centro de la Provincia de Buenos Aires
Olavarría
www.soc.unicen.edu.ar

Universidad Nacional de Córdoba
Córdoba
www.ffyh.unc.edu.ar

Universidad Nacional de Tucumán
San Miguel de Tucumán
www.csnat.unt.edu.ar

Universidad Nacional de Catamarca
San Fernando del Valle de Catamarca
www.arqueologia.unca.edu.ar

Universidad Nacional de Jujuy
San Salvador de Jujuy
www.fhycs.unju.edu.ar/antropologia.htm

Universidad Nacional de Rosario
Rosario
www.fhumyar.unr.edu.ar

Bolivia

Universidad Mayor de San Andrés
La Paz
www.umsanet.edu.bo

Instituto de Investigaciones Antropológicas
Universidad Mayor de San Simón
Cochabamba
www.umss.edu.bo

Instituto Nacional de Arqueología
La Paz
www.bolivian.com/arqueologia

Brazil

Universidade de São Paulo
São Paulo
www.ffich.usp.br/da

Universidade Federal de Minas Gerais
Belo Horizonte
www.fafich.ufmg.edu.br/soa

Universidade Federal do Rio de Janeiro
Rio de Janeiro
www.ufrj.edu.br

Pontificia Universidade Católica do Rio Grande do Sul
Porto Alegre
www.pucrs.br/pghistoria/

Chile

Universidad de Chile
Santiago
www.rehue.csociales.uchile.cl/antropologia

Universidad Boliviariana
Iquique
www.ubolivariana.com

Colombia

Universidad de Los Andes
Bogotá
www.uniandes.edu.co

Ecuador

ESPOL (Escuela de Educación Politécnica del Litoral)
Guayaquil
www.espol.edu.ec

Peru

Universidad Nacional Mayor de San Marcos
Lima
www.unmsm.edu.pe

Universidad Nacional de San Antonio Abad
Cuzco
www.unsaac.edu.pe

Universidad Nacional de Trujillo
Trujillo
www.unitru.edu.pe

Universidad Nacional de San Agustín
Arequipa
www.unsa.edu.pe

Uruguay

Universidad de la República
Montevideo
www.rau.edu.uy/universidad/carreras/fhcet.htm#antro

Venezuela

Universidad Central de Venezuela
Caracas
www.faces.ucv.ve/antropologia

Appendix 3

Series and Journals

American Anthropologist. Journal of the American Anthropological Association. Arlington, Va.

American Antiquity. Journal of the Society of American Archaeology. Washington, D.C.

Anales de Arqueología y Etnología. Universidad Nacional de Cuyo. Mendoza, Argentina.

Anales del Instituto de Patagonia. Punta Arenas, Chile.

Andean Past. Cornell University. Ithaca, N.Y.

Antropológica. Fundación La Salle, Instituto Caribe de Antropología y Sociología. Caracas, Venezuela.

Archaeology and Anthropology. Journal of the Walter Roth Museum of Anthropology. Georgetown, Guyana.

Arqueología. Universidade Federal do Paraná. Curitiba, Paraná, Brazil.

Arqueología Contemporánea. Universidad de Buenos Aires. Buenos Aires, Argentina.

Arqueología del Area Intermedia. Instituto Colombiano de Antropología e Historia. Bogotá, Colombia.

Arquivos do Museu de Historia Natural. Belo Horizonte, Brazil.

Boletín de Arqueología. Santafé de Bogotá, Colombia.

Boletín de Arqueología. Pontificia Universidad Católica del Perú. Lima, Peru.

Boletín del Museo del Oro. Bogotá, Colombia.

Boletín de la Sociedad Chilena de Arqueología. Santiago, Chile.

Bulletin de l' Institut Français d'Études Andines. Lima, Peru.

Cahiers d'Archéologie d' Amérique du Sud. Centre national de la recherche scientifique (CNRS). Paris, France.

Chungará. Departamento de Antropología, Universidad de Tarapacá. Arica, Chile.

Comunicaciones Antropológicas. Museo Nacional de Historia Natural y Antropología. Montevideo, Uruguay.

Clio. Série Arqueológica, Universidade Federal do Pernambuco. Recife, Brazil.
Cuadernos del INAPL. Instituto Nacional de Antropología y Pensamiento Latinoamericano. Buenos Aires, Argentina.
Cuadernos de Investigación. Museo Arqueológico. Universidad Mayor de San Simón. Cochabamba, Bolivia.
Current Research in the Pleistocene. Center for the Study of the First Americans, Oregon State University. Corvallis, Ore.
Dédalo. Museu de Arte e Arqueología, Universidade de São Paulo. São Paulo, Brazil (ended in 1990).
Estudios Atacameños. Universidad del Norte. San Pedro de Atacama, Chile.
Estudos Iberoamericanos. Pontificia Universidade Católica do Rio Grande do Sul. Porto Alegre, Rio Grande do Sul, Brazil.
Etnía. Olavarría, Buenos Aires, Argentina.
Gaceta Arqueológica Andina. Instituto Andino de Estudios Arqueológicos. Lima, Peru.
GENS. Boletín de la Sociedad Venezolana de Arqueólogos.
Journal of Field Archaeology. Boston, Mass.
Journal de la Société des Américanistes. Paris, France.
Journal of World Archaeology. Plenum Press. New York, N.Y.
L'Anthropologie. Paris, France.
Latin American Antiquity. Journal of the Society of American Archaeology. Washington, D.C.
Maguaré. Revista del Departamento de Antropología, Universidad Nacional de Colombia, Bogotá. Bogotá, Colombia.
Mammoth Trumpet. Center for the Study of the First Americans, Texas A&M University. College Station, Tex.
Mededelingen Surinaams Museum. Paramaribo, Suriname.
Memoirs in Latin American Archaeology. University of Pittsburgh. Pittsburgh, Pa.
Miscelánea Antropológica Ecuatoriana. Boletín de los Museos del Banco Central del Ecuador.
Mundo de Antes. Instituto de Arqueología y Museo. Universidad Nacional de Tucumán. Tucamán, Argentina.
Ñawpa Pacha. Institute of Andean Studies. Berkeley, Calif.
Palimpsesto. Revista de Arqueología. Capital Federal, Argentina.
Pesquisas. Antropolgía. Instituto Anchietano de Pesquisas. São Leopoldo, Rio Grande do Sul, Brazil.

Publicaciones de Arqueología. Centro de Investigaciones, Facultad de Filosifía y Humanidades, Universidad Nacional de Córdoba. Córdoba, Argentina.

Publicaçoes Avulsas Museu Paraense Emílio Goeldi. P.R.O.N.A.P.A. Belém, Pará, Brazil.

Pumapunku. Revista del Centro de Investigaciones Antropológicas Tiwanaku. La Paz, Bolivia.

Relaciones de la Sociedad Argentina de Antropología. Buenos Aires, Argentina.

Revista de Antropología y Arqueología. Universidad de los Andes, Facultad de Ciencias Sociales, Departamento de Antropología. Bogotá, Colombia.

Revista de Arqueología. Museu Paraense Emílio Goeldi. Belém, Brazil.

Revista de Arqueología Americana (*Journal of American Archaeology*, *Revue d'Archéologie Américaine*). Instituto Panamericano de Geografía e Historia. Washington, D.C.

Revista Canindé. Museu de Arqueología de Xingó, Universidade Federal de Sergipé. Sergipé, Brazil.

Revista do CEPA. Centro de Ensino e Pesquisas Arqueologicas, Faculdade de Filosofia, Ciencias e Letras. Santa Cruz do Sul, Rio Grande do Sul, Brazil.

Revista Colombiana de Antropología. Santafé de Bogotá. Bogotá, Colombia.

Revista Española de Antropología Americana. Universidad Complutense. Madrid, Spain.

Revista del Museo de Arqueología y Etnología. São Paulo, Brazil.

Revista del Museo de La Plata. Universidad Nacional de La Plata. La Plata, Argentina.

Revista del Museo Nacional. Lima, Peru.

Revista de Pré-História. Instituto de Pré-História, Universidade de São Paulo. São Paulo, Brazil.

Runa. Universidad de Buenos Aires. Buenos Aires, Argentina.

Shincal. Escuela de Arqueología, Universidad Nacional de Catamarca. Catamarca, Argentina.

Studies in Precolumbian Art and Archaeology. Dumbarton Oaks. Washington, D.C.

Tawantinsuyu: An International Journal of Inka Studies. Gundaroo, New South Wales, Australia.

Temas de Arqueología Brasileira. Instituto Goiano de Pré-história e Antropologia. Goiânia, Brazil.

Textos Antropológicos. Universidad Mayor de San Andrés. La Paz, Bolivia.

University of Pittsburgh Memoirs in Latin American Archaeology. University of Pittsburgh. Pittsburgh, Pa.

Bibliography

CONTENTS

RECENT GENERAL TEXTS

Bonavia, Duccio, Claudia Grimaldo, and Jimi Espinoza. *Bibliografía del Período Precerámico Peruano*. Lima, Peru: Pontificia Universidad Católica del Perú, Fondo Editorial, 2001.

Cardich, Augusto. *Hacia una prehistoria de Sudamérica. Culturas Tempranas de los Andes Centrales y de Patagonia*. La Plata, Argentina: Editorial de la Universidad de La Plata, 2003.

Ledergerber-Crespo, Paulina, ed. *Formativo Sudamericano, Una Revaluación*. Quito, Ecuador: Editorial ABYA YALA, 2000.

Lumbreras, Luis G., ed. *Historia de América Andina, vol. 1: Las sociedades Aborígenes*. Quito, Ecuador: Universidad Andina Simón Bolívar, 1999.

Peregrine, Peter N., and Melvin Ember. *Encyclopedia of Prehistory*. Vol. 7, *South America*. New York: Kluwer Academic/Plenum Press, 2002.

———. *Encyclopedia of Prehistory*. Vol. 5, *Middle America*. New York: Kluwer Academic/Plenum Press, 2002.

Plew, Mark G., ed. *Explorations in American Archaeology: Essays in Honor of Wesley R. Hurt*. Lanham, Md.: University Press of America, 1998.

Salomon, Frank, and Stuart B. Schwartz, eds. *The Cambridge History of the Native Peoples of the Americas*. Vol, 3, *South America*. Part 1. Cambridge, UK: Cambridge University Press, 1996.

GENERAL INFORMATION

Alcina Franch, J. *Bibliografía Básica de Arqueología Americana*. Madrid, Spain: Editorial Cultura Hispánica, 1983.

Blake, Michael, ed. *Pacific Latin America in Prehistory: The Evolution of Archaic and Formative Cultures*. Pullman, Wash.: Washington State University Press, 1999.

Bruhns, Karen O. *Ancient South America*. Cambridge, UK: Cambridge University Press, 1994.

Carneiro da Cunha, M., ed. *Historia dos Indios no Brasil*. São Paulo, Brazil: Companhia Das Letras, 1992.

Caviedes, César, and Gregory Knapp. *South America*. Englewood Cliffs, N.J.: Prentice Hall, 1995.

Comas, Juan. *Cien años de Congresos Internacionales de Americanistas: Ensayo histórico-crítico y bibliográfico*. Mexico City, Mexico: Instituto de Investigaciones Históricas and Instituto de Investigaciones Arqueológicas, 1974.

Fiedel, Stuart. *Prehistory of the Americas*. 2nd ed. Cambridge, UK: Cambridge University Press, 1992.

Hill, Jonathan D., and Fernando Santos-Granero. *Comparative Arawakan Histories: Rethinking Language Family and Culture Area in Amazonia*. Urbana-Champaign, Ill.: University of Illinois Press, 2002.

Meggers, Betty J., ed. *Prehistoria Sudamericana: Nuevas Perspectivas*. Washington, D.C.: Taraxacum, 1992.

Olson, James S. *The Indians of Central and South America: An Ethnohistorical Dictionary*. New York: Greenwood Press, 1991.

Ortiz Troncoso, O. R., and T. van der Hammen, eds. *Archaeology and Environment in Latin America*. Amsterdam: Universiteit van Amsterdam, 1992.

Oyuela-Caycedo, Augusto, ed. *History of Latin American Archaeology*. Worldwide Archaeology Series 15. Aldershot, UK: Avebury Press, 1994.

Oyuela-Caycedo, Augusto, and J. Scott Raymond, eds. *Recent Advances in the Archaeology of the Northern Andes*. Monograph 39, Institute of Archaeology. Los Angeles, Calif.: University of California, Los Angeles, 1998.

Parodi, Lorenzo R. *La agricultura aborigen Argentina*. 2nd ed. Buenos Aires: Editorial Universitaria de Buenos Aires, 1998.

Politis, Gustavo G., and Benjamin Alberti, eds. *Archaeology in Latin America*. London, New York: Routledge, 1999.

Schobinger, Juan. *The Ancient Americans: A Reference Guide to the Art, Culture and History of Pre-Columbian North and South America*. 2 vols. Armonk, N.Y.: M. E. Sharpe, 2000.

———. *Prehistoria de Sudamérica: Culturas precerámicas*. Madrid, Spain: Alianza Editorial, 1988.

———. *Prehistoria de Suramérica*. 2nd ed. Barcelona, Spain: Editorial Labor, 1973.

Stanish, Charles. "The Origins of the State in South America." *Annual Reviews in Anthropology* 30 (2001): 41–64.

Teruggi, Mario E. *Museo de La Plata: 1888–1988 Una centuria de honra*. La Plata, Argentina and Boston, Mass.: Fundación Museo de La Plata and Fundación Banco de Boston, 1988.

Willey, Gordon R. *An Introduction to American Archaeology*. Vol. 2. *South America*. Englewood Cliffs, N.J.: Prentice Hall, 1971.

Wilson, David. *Indigenous South Americans of the Past and the Present: An Ecological Perspective*. Boulder, Colo.: Westview Press, 1999.

Early Settlers

Borrero, Luis Alberto. "The Prehistoric Exploration and Colonization of Fuego-Patagonia." *Journal of World Prehistory* 13, no. 3 (September 1999): 321–55.

Bryan, Alan L., ed. *New Evidence for the Pleistocene Peopling of the Americas*. Orono, Maine: Center for the Study of the First Americans, 1984.

Dillehay, Thomas D. *The Settlement of the Americas: A New Prehistory*. New York: Basic Books, 2000.

Dillehay, Thomas D., G. A. Calderón, G. Politis, and M. C. Beltrao. "Earliest Hunters and Gatherers of South America." *Journal of World Prehistory* 6 (1992), no. 2: 145–203.

Gruhn, Ruth. "Current Archaeological Evidence of Late Pleistocene Settlement of South America." In *New Perspectives on the First Americans*, edited by Bradley T. Lepper and Robson Bonnichsen, 27–34. Orono, Maine: Center for the Study of the First Americans, 2004.

Lavallee, Daniele. *The First South Americans: The Peopling of a Continent from the Earliest Evidence to High Culture*. Salt Lake City, Utah: University of Utah Press, 2000. Originally published in French in 1995 by Hachette.

Miotti, Laura. "Quandary: The Clovis Phenomenon, the First Americans, and the View from Patagonia." In *New Perspectives on the First Americans*, edited by Bradley T. Lepper and Robson Bonnichsen, 35–40. Orono, Maine: Center for the Study of the First Americans, 2004.

Miotti, Laura, M. Salemme, and N. Flegenheimer, eds. *Where the South Winds Blow: Ancient Evidence of Paleo South Americans*. College Station, Tex.: Center for the Study of First Americans, Texas A&M University, 2003.

Núñez, Lautaro, and B. Meggers, eds. *Investigaciones Paleoindias al Sur de la Línea Ecuatorial*. Estudios Atacameños 8, special number. San Pedro de Atacama, Chile, 1987.

Specific Topics

Ad Hoc Panel of the Advisory Committee on Technology Innovation, Board on Science and Technology for International Development, National Research Council. *Lost Crops of the Incas: Little-Known Plants of the Andes with Promise for Worldwide Cultivation*. Washington, D.C.: National Academy Press, 1989.

Allison, M., E. Gerszten, J. Munizaga, C. Santoro, and G. Focacci. "La práctica de la deformación creaneana entre los pueblos andinos precolombinos." *Chungará* 7 (1981).

Arriaza, Bernardo T. *Beyond Death: The Chinchorro Mummies of Ancient Chile*. Washington, D.C.: Smithsonian Institution, 1995.

———. *Cultura Chinchorro: Las momias más antiguas del mundo*. Santiago, Chile: Editorial Universitaria, 2003.

Aschero, C. A., M. A. Korstanje, and P. M. Vuoto, eds. *En los tres reinos: Prácticas de recolección en el Cono Sur de América*. San Miguel de Tucumán, Argentina: Instituto de Arqueología y Museo—Ediciones Magna Publicaciones, 1999.

Bauer, Brian S., and David S. P. Dearborn. *Astronomy and Empire in the Ancient Andes: The Cultural Origins of Inca Sky Watching*. Austin, Tex.: University of Texas Press, 1995.

Benson, Elizabeth P., ed. *Pre-Columbian Metallurgy of South America*. Washington, D.C.: Dumbarton Oaks, 1979.

Blower, David. "The Many Facets of *Mullu*: More than Just a *Spondylus* Shell." *Andean Past* 6 (2000): 209–228.

Boomert, Arie. "Gifts of the Amazons:'Green Stone' Pendants and Beads as Items of Ceremonial Exchange in Amazonia and the Caribbean." *Antropologica* 67 (1987): 33–54.

Bouchard, J. F., and M. Guinea, eds. *Relaciones interculturales en el area ecuatorial del Pacífico durante la época precolombina*. BAR International Series 503. Oxford: Oxford University Press, 1989.

Burger, Richard, F. Asaro, H. Stross, and E. Salazar. "An Initial Consideraction of Obsidian Procurement and Exchange in Prehispanic Ecuador." *Latin American Antiquity* 5 (1994): 228–56.

Burger, Richard L., Karen L. Mohr Chávez, and Sergio J. Chávez. "Through the Glass Darkly: Prehispanic Obsidian Procurement and Exchange in Southern Peru and Northern Bolivia." *Journal of World Prehistory* 14, no. 3 (September 2000): 267–362.

Cardale de Schrimpff, Marianne. "Prehistoric Salt Production in Colombia, South America." In *Salt: The Study of an Ancient Industry*, edited by K. W. De Brisay and K. A. Evans, 5–11. Colchester, UK: Colchester Archaeological Group, 1975.

Cardenas-Arroyo, Fernando, Tamara Bray, and Carl K. Langebaek, eds. *Intercambio y comercio en los Andes: La interacción tierras altas-tierras bajas desde una perspectiva arqueológica y etnohistórica*. 49 Congreso Internacional de Americanistas, Bogotá, Colombia. Simposio ARQ-13, 1988.

Cartmell, Larry W., A. C. Aufderheide, and C. Weems. "The Frequency and Antiquity of Prehistoric Coca Leaf Chewing Practices in Northern Chile: Radioinmunoassay of a Cocaine Metabolite in Mummy Hair." *Latin American Antiquity* 2 (1991), no. 3: 260–68.

Ceruti, María Constanza. *Arqueología de alta montaña*. Salta, Argentina: Editorial Milor, 1997.

Denevan, William M. *Cultivated Landscapes of Native Amazonia and the Andes*. Oxford, UK: Oxford University Press, 2001.

Di Capua, Constanza. "Las 'Cabezas Trofeo': Un Rasgo Cultural en la Cerámica de la Tolita y de 'Jama-Coaque' y Breve Análisis del Mismo Rasgo en las Demás Culturas del Ecuador Pre-Colombino." *Antropología Ecuatoriana* 1 (1978): 72–164.

Dillehay, Thomas D. *Tombs for the Living: Andean Mortuary Practices*. Washington D.C.: Dumbarton Oaks, 1995.

Dillehay, Thomas, and Patricia Netherly, eds. "La frontera del estado Inca." In *Proceedings of the 45th International Congress of Americanists, Bogota, Colombia, 1985*. British Archaeological Reports, International Series 142. Oxford, UK: British Archaeological Reports, 1987.

Dransart, Penelope Z. *Earth, Water, Fleece and Fabric: An Ethnography and Archaeology of Andean Camelid Herding*. London: Routledge, 2002.

Drennan, Robert D., and Mora C. Santiago. *Archaeological Research and Heritage Preservation in the Americas*. Washington D.C.: Society for American Archaeology, 2001.

Dubelaar, C. N. *Bibliography of South American and Antillean Petroglyphs*. Publication of the Foundation for Scientific Research in the Caribbean Region 129. Amsterdam: Foundation for Scientific Research in the Caribbean Region, 1991.

Falchetti, Ana María. "El poder simbólico de los metales: la *tumbaga* y las transformaciones metalúrgicas." *Boletín de Arqueología* 14 (1999), no. 2: 53–82.

Gil, Adolfo. "Cultígenos prehispánicos en el sur de Mendoza. Discusión en torno al límite meridional de la agricultura andina." *Relaciones de la Sociedad Argentina de Antropología* 22–23 (1997–1998): 295–318.

Gonzalez, Alberto Rex. *Las placas metálicas de los Andes del Sur: Contribución al estudio de las religions precolombinas*. Materialen zur Allgemeinen und Vergleichenden Archaeologie, Band 46. Mainz, Germany: Verlag Philipp von Zabern, 1992.

Gonzalez, Luis R. "Bronce bajo el sol. Metalurgia prehispanica en el Noroeste argentino." In *Masked Histories: A Re-Examination of the Rodolfo Schreiter Collection from North Western Argentina*, 97–131. Etnologiska Studier 43. Goteborg, Germany: Etnografiska Museet, 1999.

Hardoy, Jorge. *Ciudades precolombinas*. Buenos Aires: EUDEBA, 1964. Translated to English as *Urban Planning in Pre-Columbian America* and published by Braziller in New York in 1968.

Hocquenghem, Anne. "Rutas de entrada del *Mullu* en el extremo norte del Perú." *Boletín del Instituto Francés de Estudios Andinos* 22 (1993), no. 3: 701–9.

Hyslop, John. *The Inka Road System*. Orlando, Fla.: Academic Press, 1984.

Langebaek, C. H., and F. Cárdenas Arroyo, eds. *Caciques, intercambio y poder: interacción regional en el área intermedia de las Américas*. Bogotá, Colombia: Universidad de los Andes, 1996.

Loza, Carmen Beatriz. "Quipus and quipolas at the Museum fur Volkerkunde, Berlin. Genesis of a reference collection (1872–1999)." *Baessler Archiv* 47 (1999), no. 1: 39–75.

Mora, Santiago, ed. *Ingenierías Prehispánicas*. Bogotá, Colombia: Instituto Colombiano de Antropología and Fondo Eléctrico Nacional (FEN), 1990.

Muelle R., Jorge C. "Espejos precolombinos del Perú." *Revista del Museo Nacional* 9 (1940), no. 1: 5–12.

Museo Arqueológico Rafael Larco Herrera. *Spondylus: Ofrenda sagrada y símbolo de paz*. Lima, Peru: Fundación Telefónica, 1999.

Oliveira Freitas, Fabio, G. Bendel, R. G. Alaby, and T. A. Brown. "DNA from Primitive Maize Landraces and Archaeological Remains: Implications for the Domestication of Maize and its Expansion into South America." *Journal of Archaeological Science* 30, no. 7 (July 2003): 901–8.

Olsen, Dale A. *Music of El Dorado: The Ethnomusicology of Ancient South American Cultures*. Gainesville, Fla.: University Press of Florida, 2002.

Oyuela Caicedo, A. "Rock versus Clay." In *The Emergence of Pottery*, edited by W. K. Barnett and J. W. Hoopes, 133–44. Washington, D.C.: Smithsonian Institution Press, 1995.

Perera, Miguel Angel. *Arqueología y arqueometría de las placas líticas aladas del occidente de Venezuela*. Caracas, Venezuela: Universidad Central de Venezuela, 1979.

Perez Gollán, José Antonio, and Inés Gordillo. "Vilca/Uturuncu. Hacia una arqueología del uso de alucinógenos en las sociedades prehispánicas de los Andes del Sur." *Cuicuilco: Revista de la Escuela Nacional de Antropología e Historia*, nueva época, 1 (1994), no. 1: 99–140.

———. "Iconografía religiosa andina en el NOA." *Boletín del Instituto Francés de Estudios Andinos* 15 (1986), nos. 3–4): 61–72.

———. "Los suplicantes: una cartografía social." In *Arte Prehispánico: Creación, desarrollo y persistencia*, edited by Romualdo Brughetti and Ruth Corchera, 21–36. Buenos Aires, Argentina: Academia Nacional de Bellas Artes, 2000.

Rostworowski, María. "Peregrinaciones y procesiones rituales en los Andes." *Journal de la Société des Américanistes* 89 (2003), no. 2: 97–123.

Ruppert, Hans. "Zur Verbreitung und Herkunft von Turkis und Sodalith in Praekolumbischen Kulturen der Kordilleren." *Baessler Archiv, Beitrage zur Volkerkunde* 30 (1982): 69–124.

———. "Geochemische Untersuchungen an Turkis und Sodalith aus Lagerstatten und praekolumbischen Kulturen der Kordilleren." *Berliner Beitrage zur Archaeometrie* 8 (1983): 101–210.

Sanoja O., Mario. *Los hombres del maíz y de la yuca: ensayos sobre los sistemas agrarios precolombinos del Nuevo Mundo*. Caracas, Venezuela: Editores Monte Avila, 1982.

Schobinger, Juan. *Arte prehistórico de América*. Mexico City, Mexico: Consejo Nacional para la Cultura y las Artes, 1997.

Shimada, Izumi, ed. *Andean Ceramics: Technology, Organization, and Approaches*. Philadelphia, Pa.: Museum Applied Science Center for Archaeology, University of Pennsylvania Museum of Archaeology and Anthropology, 1998.

Torres, M. C., and A. Llagostera, eds. "Archaeology of Hallucinogens in the Andean Region." *Eleusis* 5. Journal of Psychoactive Plants and Compounds. Telesterion, Dozza, 2001.

Vargas-Arenas, I., M. Toledo, L. Molina, and C. Montcourt. *Los artifices de la concha*. Caracas, Venezuela: FACES, Universidad Central de Venezuela,

Alcaldía del Municipio Jiménez, Lara, Funda Cultura, Museo Arqueológico de Quíbor, 1997.

Wassen, Henry. "Algunos datos sobre el comercio precolombino." *Revista Colombiana de Antropología* 4 (1955): 87–110.

Wheeler, Jane. "Patrones prehistóricos de la utilización de los camélidos sudamericanos." *Boletín de Arqueología*, Pontificia Universidad Católica del Perú, 3 (2000): 297–305.

Yacobaccio, H. D., P. S. Escola, F. X. Pereyra, M. Lazzari, and M. D. Glascock. "Quest for Ancient Routes: Obsidian Sourcing Research in Northwestern Argentina." *Journal of Archaeological Science* 31 (2004): 193–204.

Zucchi, Alberta, and William M. Denevan. *Campos Elevados e Historia Cultural Prehispánica en los Llanos Occidentales de Venezuela*. Caracas, Venezuela: Universidad Católica Andrés Bello, 1979.

COUNTRIES

Argentina

Berberián, Eduardo E., and Axel E. Nielsen, eds. *Historia Argentina Prehispánica*. 2 vols. Cordoba, Argentina: Editorial Brujas, 2001.

Berón, Mónica, and Gustavo Politis, eds. *Arqueología Pampeana en la década de los '90*. Mendoza, Argentina: Museo de Historia Natural de San Rafael, Mendoza/INCUAPA, UNICEN, 1997.

Briones, Claudia, and José Luis Lanata, eds. *Archeological and Anthropological Perspectives on the Native Peoples of Pampa, Patagonia, and Tierra del Fuego to the Nineteenth Century*. Westport, Conn.: Bergin and Garvey, 2002.

Cardich, Augusto, and R. Paunero. "Mid-Holocene Herding in Central Patagonia." *Research and Exploration* 10 (1994), no. 3: 368–69.

Durán, Víctor. *Poblaciones Indígenas de Malargüe: Su Arqueología e Historia*. Facultad de Filosofía y Letras. CEIDER. Seire Libros No. 1. Mendoza: Universidad Nacional de Cuyo, 2000.

Fernández Distel, Alicia. "Las cuevas de Huachichocana, su posición dentro del precerámico con agricultura incipiente del Noroeste Argentino." *Beitrage zur Allgemeinen und Vergleichenden Archaeologie* 8 (1986): 353–430.

Flegenheimer, Nora, and M. Zarate. "Considerations on Radiocarbon and Calibrated Dates from Cerro La China and Cerro El Sombrero, Argentina." *Current Research in the Pleistocene* 14 (1997): 27–28.

Gambier, Mariano. *Prehistoria de San Juan*. 2nd ed. San Juan, Argentina: Ansilta Editora, 2000.

Garcia, Alejandro, M. Zarate, and M. M. Paez. "The Pleistocene/Holocene Transition and Human Occupation in the Central Andes of Argentina: Agua de la Cueva Locality." *Quaternary International* 53/54 (1999): 433–52.

———. *Los Primeros Pobladores de Los Andes Centrales Argentinos*. Mendoza, Argentina: Zeta Editores, 2004.

Gil, Adolfo F., and Gustavo A. Neme, eds. *Entre montañas y desiertos: arqueología del sur de Mendoza*. Buenos Aires: Publicaciones de la Sociedad Argentina de Antropología, 2002.

Gonzalez, Alberto R. "Cincuenta años de Arqueología del Noroeste Argentino (1930–1980): Apuntes de un casi testigo y algo de protagonista." *American Antiquity* 50 (1985), no. 3.

Gradin, Carlos J., and Fernando Oliva, eds. *La región pampeana su pasado arqueológicó*. Selección de trabajos presentados al 1er Congreso de Arqueología de la Región Pampeana Argentina, Venado Tuerto, Santa Fe, República Argentina. Laborde, Argentina: 2004.

Laguens, Andrés G. *Arqueología del contacto hispano indígena: un estudio de cambios y continuidades en las Sierras Centrales de Argentina*. British Archaeological Report International Series 801. Oxford, UK: British Archaeological Report, 1999.

Mazzanti, Diana L., Monica A. Beron, and Fernando W. Oliva, eds. *Del mar a los salitrales: diez mil años de historia pampeana en el umbral del tercer milenio*. Buenos Aires: Sociedad Argentina de Antropología, 2002.

Ortiz, Gabriela, and Beatriz Ventura, eds. *La mitad verde del mundo andino: investigaciones arqueológicas en la vertiente oriental de los Andes y las Tierras Bajas de Bolivia y Argentina*. San Salvador de Jujuy, Argentina: Universidad Nacional de Jujuy, 2003.

Politis, Gustavo, and María Gutierrez. "Gliptodontes y cazadores-recolectores de la Región Pampeana Argentina." *Latin American Antiquity* 9 (1998), no. 2: 111–34.

Politis, Gustavo, Gustavo Martinez, and Mariano Bonomo. "Alfarería temprana en sitios de cazadores-recolectores de la Región Pampeana (Argentina)." *Latin American Antiquity* 12 (2001), no. 2: 167–80.

Raffino, Rodolfo A. *Poblaciones indígenas en Argentina: Urbanismo y proceso social precolombino*. Buenos Aires: Tipográfica Editora Argentina, 1988.

Schobinger, Juan. "Sacrifices of the High Andes." *Natural History* 100 (1991), no. 4: 62–68.

Schobinger, Juan, ed. "*La 'Momia' del Cerro El Toro. Investigaciones arqueológicas en la Cordillera de la Provincia de San Juan*." Supplement to Volume 21 of *Anales de Arqueología y Etnologia*. Mendoza, 1966.

Schobinger, Juan, comp. *El santuario incaico del Cerro Aconcagua*. Cuyo, Argentina: Universidad Nacional de Cuyo, 2001.

Tarragó, Myriam N. *Los pueblos originarios y la conquista*. Nueva Historia Argentina, vol. 1. Buenos Aires: Editorial Sudamericana, 1999.

Bolivia

Arellano, Jorge. *Mollo: Investigaciones arqueológicas*. La Paz, Bolivia: Imprenta Nacional, 1985.

Bennett, Wendell C. "Excavations at Tiahuanaco." *American Museum of Natural History, Anthropological Papers* 34 (1934), no. 3: 359–494.

——. "Excavations in Bolivia." *American Museum of Natural History, Anthropological Papers* 35 (1936), no. 4: 329–50.

Berenguer, José. *Tiwanaku: Señores del lago sagrado*. Santiago, Chile: Museo Chileno de Arte Precolombino, 2000.

Bermann, Mark P. *Lukurmata: Household Archaeology in Prehispanic Bolivia*. Princeton, N.J.: Princeton University Press, Princeton, 1994.

——. "Domestic Life and Vertical Integration in the Tiwanaku Heartland." *Latin American Antiquity* 8 (1997), no. 2: 93–112.

Dearborn, David S. P., Brian Bauer, and Matthew Seddon. "The Sanctuary of Titicaca: Where the Sun Returns to Earth." *Latin American Antiquity* 9 (1998), no. 3: 240–58.

Escalante Moscoso, Javier F. *Arquitectura prehispánica en los Andes bolivianos*. La Paz, Bolivia: CIMA Producciones, 1993.

Giesso, Martin. "Stone Tool Production in the Tiwanaku State: The Impact of State Emergence and Expansion on Local Households." 2 vols. PhD diss., University of Chicago, 2000.

Hastorf, Christine Anne. "Community with the Ancestors: Ceremonies and Social Memory in the Middle Formative at Chiripa, Bolivia." *Journal of Anthropological Archaeology* 22 (2004), no. 4: 305–32.

Hastorf, Christine Anne, ed. *Early Settlement at Chiripa, Bolivia: Research of the Taraco Archaeological Project*. Contributions of the University of California Archaeological Research Facility, no. 57. Berkeley, Calif.: University of California, Berkeley, 1999.

Higueras-Hare, Alvaro. *Prehispanic Settlement and Land Use in Cochabamba, Bolivia*. PhD diss., University of Pittsburgh, 1996.

Janusek, John Wayne. "Tiwanaku and Its Precursors: Recent Research and Emerging Perspectives." *Journal of Archaeological Research* 12 (2004), no. 2: 121–83.

——. *Identity and Power in the Ancient Andes: Tiwanaku Cities Through Time*. New York: Routledge, 2004.

Kolata, Alan L. *The Tiwanaku: Portrait of an Andean Civilization*. Cambridge, Mass.: Blackwell Publishers, 1993.

Kolata, Alan L., ed. *Tiwanaku and Its Hinterland: Archaeological and Paleoecological Investigations in the Lake Titicaca Basin of Bolivia*. Smithsonian Series in Archaeological Inquiry 2. Washington, D.C.: Smithsonian, 2003.

Manzanilla, Linda. *Akapana: Una pirámide en el centro del mundo*. Mexico City, Mexico: Instituto de Investigaciones Antropológicas, UNAM, 1992.

Ponce Sanginés, Carlos. *Las culturas Wankarani y Chiripa, y su relación con Tiwanaku*. Academia Nacional de Ciencias de Bolivia 25. 2nd ed. La Paz, Bolivia: Academia Nacional de Ciencias, 1970.

———. *Tiwanaku: Espacio, Tiempo y Cultura: Ensayo de síntesis arqueológica*. La Paz, Bolivia: Editorial Los Amigos del Libro, 1972.

———. *Tiwanaku: 200 años de investigaciones arqueológicas*. La Paz, Bolivia: Producciones Cima, 1995.

Ponce Sanginés, Carlos, and G. Mogrovejo T. *Acerca de la Procedencia del Material Lítico de los Monumentos de Tiwanaku: Examen Arqueológico*. Vol. 2. Academia Nacional de Ciencias de Bolivia 21. La Paz, Bolivia: Academia Nacional de Ciencias, 1970.

Ponce Sanginés, Carlos, Johan Reinhard, Max Portugal, Eduardo Pareja, and Leocadio Ticlla. *Exploraciones arqueológicas subacuáticas en el lago Titikaka: Informe científico*. La Paz, Bolivia: Editorial La Palabra Producciones, 1992.

Ryden, Stig. *Archaeological Researches in the Highlands of Bolivia*. Goteborg, Sweden: Elanders Boktryckeri Aktiebolog, 1947.

———. *Andean Excavations I: The Tiahuanaco Era East of Lake Titicaca*. The Ethnographical Museum of Sweden Monograph Series 4. Stockholm: The Ethnographical Museum of Sweden, 1957.

———. *Andean Excavations II: Tupuraya and Cayhuasi: Two Tiahuanaco Sites*. The Ethnographical Museum of Sweden Monograph Series 6. Stockholm: The Ethnographical Museum of Sweden, 1959.

Stanish, Charles, and Brian S. Bauer, eds. *Archaeological Research on the Islands of the Sun and Moon, Lake Titicaca, Bolivia: Final Results from the Proyecto Tiksi Kjarka*. Cotsen Institute of Archaeology at UCLA Monograph 52. Los Angeles, Calif.: Cotsen Institute of Archaeology at UCLA, 2004.

Brazil

Brasil: 50 mil anos; Uma Viagem ao Passado Pré-Colonial. São Paulo, Brazil: Editora da Universidade de São Paulo, 2001. Published in conjunction with the exhibition "Brasil: 50 mil anos" held at Superior Tribunal de Justiça in Brasília.

DeBoer, W. R., K. Kintigh, and A. G. Rostoker. "Ceramic Seriation and Site Reoccupation in Lowland South America." *Latin American Antiquity* 7 (1996): 263–78.

Brochado, José Proenza. *An Ecological Model of the Spread of Pottery and Agriculture into Eastern South America*. Ann Arbor, Mich.: University Microfilms, 1984.

Dias Jr., Ondemar F. "Considerações a respeito dos modelos de difusão da ceramica tupi-guarani no Brasil." *Revista de Arqueología* 2 (1994–1995), no. 8: 113–32.

Gonzalez, E.M.R. "Os grupos ceramistas pré-coloniais do centro-oeste brasileiro." *Revista do Museu de Arqueología e Etnologia* 6 (1996): 83–121.

Guidon, Niede. "On Stratigraphy and Chronology at Pedra Furada." *Current Anthropology* 30 (1989), no. 5: 641–42.

Heckenberger, Michael J., J. B. Petersen, and E. G. Neves. "Village Size and Permanence in Amazonia: Two Archaeological Examples from Brazil." *Latin American Antiquity* 10, no. 4 (December 1999): 353–76.

Kashimoto, Emília Mariko, and Gilson Rodolfo Martins. "Archaeology of the Holocene in the Upper Paraná River, Mato Grosso do Sul State, Brazil." *Quaternary International* 114 (2004), no. 1: 67–86.

Kern, Arno Alvarez. *Le précéramique du plateu sud-brésilien*. Universidade Federale do Rio Grande do Sul, Publicações Avulsas 1. Porto Alegre, Brazil: Universidade Federale do Rio Grande do Sul, 1982.

———. *Arqueologia pré-histórica do Rio Grande do Sul*. Porto Alegre, Brazil: Editorial Mercado Aberto Porto Alegre, 1991.

Martin, Gabriela. *Pré-Historia do Nordeste do Brasil*. 3rd ed. Recife, Brazil: Editora Universitaria Universidade Federal de Pernambuco, 1999.

Meggers, Betty. "Desenvolvimento cultural pré-histórico nas terras baixas tropicais da América do Sul: Amazonas e Orinoco." *Fronteiras: Revista de História* 2 (1998), no. 4: 9–38.

Oliveira, Jorge Eremites de. "A Arqueología Brasileira da década de 1980 ao início do século XXI: uma avaliação histórica e historiográfica." *Estudos Ibero-americanos* 28 (2003), no. 2: 25–52.

Oliveira, Jorge Eeremites de, and S. A. Viana. "O Centro-Oeste antes de Cabral." *Revista USP* 44 (2000), no. 1: 142–89.

Prous, André. "L'Archéologie au Brésil: 300 siècles d'occupation humaine." *L'Anthropologie* 90 (1986), no. 2: 257–306.

———. *Arqueología Brasileira*. Brasilía: Editoral Universidade de Brasilia, 1992.

Prous, André, and W. Piazza. *Documents pour la préhistoire du Brésil meridional. 2. L'état de Santa Catarina*. Cahiers d'Archeologie d'Amérique du Sud 4. Paris: École des Hautes Études en Sciences Sociales, 1997.

Riberiro, Pedro Augusto Mentz. "A Tradiçao Umbu no Sul do Brasil." *Revista do CEPA* 17 (1990), no. 20: 129–52.

Roosevelt, Anna C. *Moundbuilders of the Amazon: Geophysical Archaeology on Marajó Island, Brazil*. Orlando, Fla.: Academic Press, 1991.

Roosevelt, Anna C., R. Housley, M. Imazio da Silveira, S. Maranca, and R. Johnson. "Eighth Millenium Pottery from a Prehistoric Shell Midden in the Brazilian Amazon." *Science* 254 (1991): 1621–24.

Roosevelt, Anna C., M. Lima da Costa, C. Lopes Machado, et al. "Paleoindian Cave Dwellers in the Amazon: The Peopling of the Americas." *Science* 272 (1996): 373–84.

Schmitz, Pedro I. "Prehistoric Hunters and Gatherers of Brazil." *Journal of World Prehistory* 1 (1987): 53–126.

———. *Sitios Arqueológicos no Pantanal de Matto Grosso do Sul. Pesquisas, Antropologia* 54. São Leopoldo, Brazil: Instituto Anchietano de Pesquisas/ UNISINOS, 1998.

Schmitz, Pedro I., ed. *Casas subterrâneas nas terras altas do sul do Brasil. Pesquisas, Antropologia* 58. São Leopoldo, Brazil: Instituto Anchietano de Pesquisas, UNISINOS, 2002.

Schmitz, Pedro I., M. B. Ribeiro, A. F. Miranda, de, et al. *Arqueologia nos cerrados do Brasil Central, sudoeste da Bahia e leste de Goiás: O Projeto Serra Geral. Pesquisas, Série Antropologia* 52. São Leopoldo, Brazil: Insituto Anchietano de Pesquisas, UNISINOS, 1996.

Simões, Mario F. *Indice das fases arqueológicas brasileiras. Publicaçoes Avulsas do Museu Paraense Emilio Goeldi* 18. Belem, Brazil: Museu Paraense Emílio Goeldi, 1972.

Souza, A. M. de. *História da Arqueología Brasileira. Pesquisas, Antropologia* 46. São Leopoldo, Brazil: Instituto Anchietano de Pesquisas, UNISINOS, 1991.

Tenório, Maria Cristina, org. *Pré-História da Terra Brasilis*. Rio de Janeiro: Editora Universidade Federal do Rio de Janeiro, 2000.

Wüst, Irmhild, and C. Barreto. "The Ring Villages of Central Brazil: A Challenge for Amazonian Archaeology." *Latin American Antiquity* 10, no. 1 (March 1999): 3–23.

Chile

Cornejo, Luis, and Javier Simonetti. "De rocas y caminos: espacio y cultura en los Andes de Chile Central." *Revista Chilena de Antropología* 14 (1997–1998): 127–43.

Dillehay, Tom D. "Mapuche Ceremonial Landscapes, Social Recruitment and Resource Rights." *World Archaeology* 22 (1990), no. 2: 223–41.

——. *The Archaeological Context and Interpretation*. Vol. 2, *Monte Verde: A Late Pleistocene Settlement in Chile*. Washington, D.C.: Smithsonian Institution Press, 1997.

Hidalgo, Jorge, Virgilio Schiappacasse, Hans Niemeyer, Carlos Aldunate, and Ivan Solimano, eds. *Culturas de Chile desde sus orígenes hasta los albores de la Conquista*. 4th ed. Santiago, Chile: Editorial Andrés Bello, 2000.

Le Paige, Gustavo. "El Precerámico en la cordillera atacameña y los cementerios de la época agroalfarera de San Pedro de Atacama." *Anales de la Universidad del Norte* 3 (1964): 5–267.

Mostny, Grete. *Prehistoria de Chile*. Santiago, Chile: Editorial Universitaria, 1974.

Nuñez, Lautaro, J. Varela, R. Casamiquela, V. Schiappacasse, H. Niemeyer, and C. Villagrán. "Cuenca de Taguatagua en Chile: el ambiente del Pleistoceno superior y ocupaciones humanas." *Revista Chilena de Historia Natural* 67 (1994): 503–19.

Niemeyer, Hans W., Miguel Cervellino, and Gastón Castillo. *Culturas prehistóricas de Copiapó*. Copiapó, Chile: Museo Regional de Atacama, 1998.

Orellana Rodriguez, Mario. "Relaciones culturales entre Tiwanaku y San Pedro de Atacama." *Dialogo Andino* 4 (1986): 247–57.

——. *Historia de la Arqueología en Chile*. Santiago, Chile: Bravo y Allende Editores, 1996.

Sanhueza, Lorena, and Fernanda Falabella. "Las comunidades alfareras iniciales en Chile Central." *Revista Chilena de Antropología* 15 (1999–2000): 29–47.

Stehberg, L. Rubén. *Instalaciones incaicas en el norte y centro semiárido de Chile*. Colección de antropología 2. Santiago, Chile: Dirección de Bibliotecas, Archivos y Museos, Centro de Investigaciones Barros Arana, 1995.

Colombia

Angulo, V. C. *La Tradición Malambo*. Bogotá, Colombia: Fundación de Investigaciones Nacionales. Banco de la República, 1981.

Botiva Contreras, A., G. Cadavid, L. Herrera, A. M. Groot, and S. Mora. *Colombia Prehispánica*. Bogotá, Colombia: Instituto Colombiano de Antropología, 1989.

Cardale, Marianne, W. Bray, T. Gahwiler, and L. Herrera, eds. *Calima: Diez mil años de historia en el Suroccidente de Colombia*. Bogotá, Colombia: Fundación Pro Calima, 1992.

Cavelier, I., and S. Mora, eds. *Ambito y ocupaciones tempranas de la América tropical*. Bogotá, Colombia: Fundación Erigaie, ICAN, 1995.

Correal, G. "Evidencias culturales durante el Pleistoceno y Holoceno de Colombia." *Revista de Arqueología Americana* 1 (1990): 69–90.

Drennan, Robert D. *Las sociedades prehispánicas del Alto Magdalena*. Bogotá, Colombia: Instituto Colombiano de Antropología e Historia, 1999.

Eden, J. M., W. Bray, L. Herrera, and C. McEwan. "Terra Preta Soils and Their Archaeological Context in the Caquetá Basin of Southeast Colombia." *American Antiquity* 49 (1984): 125–40.

Enslow, Sam. *The Art of Prehispanic Colombia: An Illustrated Cultural and Historical Survey*. Jefferson, N.C.: McFarland & Company, Inc., 1990.

Gnecco, Cristobal, ed. *Perspectivas regionales en la arqueología del Suroccidente de Colombia y norte de Ecuador*. Popayán, Colombia: Universidad del Cauca, 1995.

Gnecco, Cristobal, and Santiago Mora. "Tropical Forest Occupations at San Isidro and Peña Roja, Colombia." *Antiquity* 71, no. 273 (September 1997): 683–90.

Herreman, Frank, and Mireille Holsbeke, with a contribution by Jean-François Bouchard. *Power of the Sun: The Gold of Colombia*. Antwerp, Belgium: Ethnographic Museum, 1993.

Labbé, Armand J. *Shamans, Gods, and Mythic Beasts: Colombian Gold and Ceramics in Antiquity*. Seattle, Wash.: The American Federation of Arts and the University of Washington Press, 1998.

Lange, Frederick. *Wealth and Hierarchy in the Intermediate Area*. Washington, D.C.: Dumbarton Oaks, 1992.

Langebaek, Carl, A. Cuéllar, and A. Deber. *Medio Ambiente y Poblamiento en la Guajira: Investigaciones Arqueológicas en el Rancherío Medio*. Estudios Antropológicos 1. Bogotá, Colombia: Departamento de Antropología, Universidad de los Andes, 1998.

Langabaek, Carl, and Alejandro Deber. *Arqueología en el bajo Magdalena: un estudio de los primeros agricultores del Caribe colombiano*. Informes arqueológicos del Instituto Colombiano de Antropología e Historia, no. 1. Bogotá, Colombia: Instituto Colombiano de Antropología e Historia, 2000.

Oyuela-Caycedo, Augusto, and Scott Raymond. *Recent Advances in the Archaeology of the Northern Andes: In Memory of Gerardo Reichel-Dolmatoff*. The Institute of Archaeology Monograph 39. Los Angeles: University of California, Los Angeles, 1998.

Reichel-Dolmatoff, Gerardo. *Arqueología de Colombia: un texto introductorio*. Bogotá, Colombia: Fundación Segunda Expedición Botánica, 1986.

———. *Colombia Indígena*. Medellin, Colombia: Editorial Colina, 1998.

Rojas de Perdomo, Lucía. *Manual de Arqueología Colombiana*. Bogotá, Colombia: Carlos Valencia Editores, 1985.

———. *Arqueología Colombiana: Visión Panorámica*. Santafé de Bogotá, Colombia: Intermedio Editores, Círculo de Lectores, S.A., 1995.

Ecuador

Almeida Reyes, Eduardo. *Estudios arqueológicos en el Pucara de Rumicucho*. Quito, Ecuador: Banco Central de Ecuador, 2000.

Alvarez, A., S. Alvarez, C. Fauria, and J. G. Marcos, eds. *Primer encuentro de investigadores de la costa Ecuatoriana en Europa: Arqueología, Etnohistoria, Antropología Sociocultural*. Quito, Ecuador: Abya-Yala, 1995.

Burger, Richard L., F. Asaro, H. V. Michel, F. H. Stross, and E. Salazar. "An Initial Consideration of Obsidian Procurement and Exchange in Prehispanic Ecuador." *Latin American Antiquity* 5 (1994), no. 3: 228–55.

Currie, E. "Archaeology, Ethnohistory and Exchange Along the Coast of Ecuador." *Antiquity* 69 (1995): 511–26.

Damp, J. *La primera ocupación Valdivia de Real Alto: Patrones económicos, arquitectónicos e ideológicos*. Quito, Ecuador: Corporación Editora Nacional, 1988.

Guffroy, J., ed. *Loja Préhispanique: Recherches archéologiques dans les Andes méridionales de l' Equateur*. Éditions Recherche sur les Civilizations 32. Paris: Institut Français d'Études Andines, 1987.

Guinea, Mercedes, Jorge Marcos, and Jean-François Bouchard, coordinators. *El Area Septentrional Andina: Arqueología y etnohistoria*. Biblioteca ABYA-YALA 59. Quito, Ecuador, 1998.

Idrovo Urigüen, Jaime. *Tomebamba: Arqueología e Historia de una Ciudad Imperial*. Quito, Ecuador: Banco Central del Ecuador, 2000.

Marcos, Jorge. *Real Alto: La historia de un centro ceremonial Valdivia*. 2 vols. Biblioteca Ecuatoriana de Arqueología 1. Guayaquil, Ecuador: Escuela Politécnica del Litoral, 1988.

Marcos, Jorge, ed. *Arqueología de la costa ecuatoriana. Nuevos enfoques*. Biblioteca Ecuatoriana de Arqueología 1. Guayaquil, Ecuador: Escuela Politécnica del Litoral, 1986.

Porras, Pedro I. *Arqueología del Ecuador*. Otavalo, Ecuador: Editorial Gallocapitán, 1980.

Raymond, J. Scott, and Richard L. Burger, eds. *Archaeology of Formative Ecuador: A Symposium at Dumbarton Oaks, 7 and 8 October 1995*. Washington, D.C.: Dumbarton Oaks, 2003.

Salazar, Ernesto. "El intercambio de obsidiana en el Ecuador precolombino: perspectivas teórico-metodológicas." In *Arqueología en America Latina Hoy*, edited by G. Politis, 116–31. Bogotá, Colombia: Biblioteca Banco Popular, Fondo de Promoción de la Cultura, 1992.

———. *Entre mitos y fábulas: El Ecuador Aborigen*. Quito, Ecuador: Biblioteca General de Cultura, 1998.

Staller, John Edward. "Reassessing the Developmental and Chronological Relationships of the Formative of Coastal Ecuador." *Journal of World Prehistory* 15, no. 2 (June 2001): 193–256.

Stothert, K. E. "The Preceramic Las Vegas of Coastal Ecuador." *American Antiquity* 50 (1985), no. 3: 613–37.

Valdez, Francisco, and Diego Veintimilla. *Amerindian Signs: 500 Years of Precolumbian Art in Ecuador*. Quito, Ecuador: Dinediciones, 1992.

Villalba, Marcelo. *Cotocollao: Una aldea formativa del valle de Quito*. Miscelánea Antropológica Ecuatoriana, Serie Monográfica 2. Quito, Ecuador: Museos del Banco Central de Ecuador, 1988.

Zeidler, J. A., and Deborah M. Pearsall, eds. *Regional Archaeology in Northern Ecuador*. Vol. 1, *Environment, Cultural Chronology and Prehistoric Subsistence in the Jama River Valley*. Memoirs in Latin American Archaeology 8. Pittsburgh: University of Pittsburgh, 1994.

Guyana/Suriname/Guyane

Boomert, Arie. "Agricultural Societies in the Continental Caribbean." In *UNESCO General History of the Caribbean*. Vol. 1, *The Autochthonous Societies*, edited by Jalil Sued Badillo, 134–94. New York: UNESCO, 1991.

———. "The Saladoid Occupation of Wonotobo Falls, Western Surinam." In *Proceedings of the Ninth International Congress of the Study of the Pre-Columbian Cultures of the Lesser Antilles*, edited by Suzanne M. Lewenstein, 97–120. Montreal: Université de Montréal, 1983.

———. "The Sipaliwini Archaeological Complex of Suriname." *Nieuwe West-Indische Gids* 54 (1980), no. 2: 94–108.

———. *Trinidad, Tobago and the Lower Orinoco Interaction Sphere: An Archaeological/Ethnohistorical Study*. Alkmaar, The Netherlands: Cairi Publications, 2000.

Delpuech, André, Jean-Pierre Giraud, and Albert Hesse. *Archéologie précolombienne et coloniale des Caraibes: Éditions du Comité des travaux historiques et scientifiques*. Actes des congres nationaux des societies historiques et scientifiques 123. Antilles-Guyane: 1998, 2002.

Evans, Clifford, and B. Meggers. *Archaeological Investigation in British Guiana*. Smithsonian Institution Bureau of American Ethnology Bulletin 177. Washington, D.C.: Smithsonian Institution, 1960.

L'archéologie en Guyane. Cayenne, Guyane: Édition APPAAG (Association pour la Protection du Patrimoine Archéologique et Architectural de la Guyane), 1997.

Mazière, G. "L'archéologie amérindienne en Guyane. Etat actuel de la recherche." *Bulletin de la Société Préhistorique Française* 91 (1994), no. 4–5: 333–42.

Rostain, Stéphen. "Archeologie du littoral de Guyane, une region charniere entre les influences culturelles de l'Orenoque et de l'Amazone." *Journal de la Société des Américanistes* 80 (1994): 9–46.

Rostain, Stéphen, and Aad H. Versteeg. "Recherche sur l'archéologie de la côte occidentale de Guyane." *Journal de la Société des Américanistes* 89 (2003), no. 1: 161–75.

Vacher, Stephane, Sylvie Jérémie, and Jérôme Briand, eds. *Amérindiens du Sinnamary (Guyane): Archéologie en forêt équatoriale*. Documents d' Archéologie Française 70. Paris: Éditions de la Maison des Sciences de l'Homme, 1998.

Versteeg, A. H. "C-14 Datings from Archaeological Sites in Suriname." *Mededelingen Surinaams Museum* 32 (1980): 38–57.

——. "The Prehistory of the Young Coastal Plain of West Suriname." *Ber. Rijksd. Oudheidk. Bodemonderzoek* 35 (1985): 653–750.

Versteeg, A. H., and F. C. Bubberman. *Suriname before Columbus*. Paramaribo: Stichting Surinaams Museum, 1992.

——. "Inhabitation and Environment in the Guianas between 10.000 and 1.000 BP." Paper presented at the Seminaire Atelier Peuplements anciens et actuels des Forêts tropicales at Laboratoire Ermes/Orstom, Orléans, France, October 16, 1998.

Williams, Dennis. *Ancient Guyana*. Georgetown, Guyana: Department of Culture, 1985.

——. *Prehistoric Guyana*. Kingston, Jamaica: Ian Randle Publishers, 2003.

Paraguay

De Morais, Jose Luiz, and José Antonio Perasso. *Tecno-tipología de estructuras de lascamiento del sitio Marcelina-Kué (Itapúa – Paraguay)*. Ensayos de Arqueología Paraguaya I. Asunción, Paraguay: Arte Nuevo Editores, 1984.

Pallestrini, Luciana, J. Gomez Perasso, and Ana M. Castillo. *El hombre prehistórico del Py-Pucú: Esbozo arqueo-etnológico*. Asunción, Paraguay: RP Ediciones, 1989.

Peru

Aldenderfer, Mark. *Montane Foragers: Asana and the South-Central Andean Archaic*. Iowa City: University of Iowa Press, 1998.

Alva, Walter, and Christopher Donnan. *Tumbas Reales de Sipan*. Los Angeles: Fowler Museum of Cultural History, University of California, 1993.

Bauer, Brian. *The Development of the Inca State*. Austin: University of Texas Press, 1992.

Bawden, Garth. *The Moche*. Cambridge, Mass.: Blackwell Publishers, 1996.

Benson, Betty, and Anita G. Cook, eds. *Ritual Sacrifice in Ancient Peru: New Discoveries and Interpretations*. Austin: University of Texas Press, 2001.

Bonnier, Elisabeth, and H. Bischof. *Arquitectura y Civilización en los Andes Prehispánicos. Prehispanic Architecture and Civilization in the Andes*. Archaeologica Peruana 2. Mannheim, Germany: Sociedad Arqueológica Peruano-Alemana, Reiss-Museum, 1997.

Brooks, Sarah, Michael Glascock, and Martin Giesso. "Source of Volcanic Glass for Ancient Andean Tools." *Nature* 386 (1997): 449–50.

Burger, Richard L. *Chavin and the Origins of Andean Civilization*. London: Thames and Hudson, 1992.

Burger, Richard L., and Frank Asaro. *Trace Element Analysis of Obsidian Artifacts from the Andes: New Perspectives on Pre-Hispanic Economic Interaction In Peru And Bolivia*. Lawrence Berkeley Laboratory Report 6343. Berkeley, Calif.: University of California, Berkeley, 1977.

Burger, Richard L., and Frank Asaro. "Obsidian Distribution and Provenience in the Central Highlands and Coast of Peru." *Contributions of the University of California Archaeological Research Facility* 36 (1978): 61–83.

Burger, Richard L., Frank Asaro, Paul Trawick, and Fred Stross. "Alca Obsidian Source: The Origin of Raw Material for Cusco Type Obsidian Artifacts." *Andean Past* 5 (1997): 185–202.

Burger, Richard L., and Lucy Salazar-Burger. "Ritual and Religion at Huaricoto." *Archaeology* 33 (1980): 26–32.

Burger, Richard L., and Lucy Salazar, eds. *Machu Picchu: Unveiling the Mystery of the Incas*. New Haven, Conn.: Yale University Press, 2004.

Burger, Richard L., Katharina J. Schreiber, Michael Glascock, and José Ccencho. "Jampatilla Obsidian Source: Identifying the Geological Source of Pampas Type Obsidian Artifacts from Southern Peru." *Andean Past* 5 (1997): 225–239.

Canzianai Amico, José. *Asentamientos Humanos y Formaciones Sociales en la Costa Norte del Antiguo Perú (del Paleolítico a Moche V)*. Lima, Peru: Ediciones INDEA, 1989.

Castillo, J. C. *Personajes Míticos, Escenas y Narraciones en la Iconografía Mochica*. Lima, Peru: Pontificia Universidad Católica del Perú, Fondo Editorial, 1989.

Cook, Anita G. "The Stone Ancestors: Idioms of Imperial Attire and Rank Among Huari Figurines." *Latin American Antiquity* 3 (1992), no. 4: 341–64.

——. *Wari y Tiwanaku: entre el estilo y la imagen*. Lima, Peru: Pontificia Universidad Católica del Perú. Fondo Editorial, 1994.

D'Altroy, Terence N. "Recent Research on the Central Andes." *Journal of Archaeological Research* 5 (1997): 3–73.

D'Altroy, Terence N., and Christine A. Hastorf, eds. *Empire and Domestic Economy*. New York: Kluwer Academic/Plenum Publishers, 2001.

Dillehay, Tom D., J. Rossen, and P. Netherly. "The Nanchoc Tradition: The Beginnings of Andean Civilization." *American Scientist* 85 (1997): 46–55.

Donnan, Christopher B., ed. *Early Ceremonial Architecture in the Andes*. Washington, D.C.: Dumbarton Oaks, 1985

——. *Moche Portraits from Ancient Peru*. Austin: University of Texas, 2004.

Frye, Kirk L., Mark Aldenderfer, and Michael Glascock. "The Aconcahua Obsidian Source and Its Relation to South Central Andean Exchange Systems." Paper presented at the 38th Annual Andean Meeting, Berkeley, Calif., 1998.

Glowacki, Mary, and Michael Malpass. "Water, Huacas, and Ancestor Worship: Traces of a Sacred Wari Landscape." *Latin American Antiquity* 14 (2003), no. 4: 431–48.

Goldstein, Paul. "Tiwanaku Temples and State Expansion: A Tiwanaku Sunken-Court Temple in Moquegua, Peru." *Latin American Antiquity* 4 (1993), no. 1: 22–47.

Gonzalez Carré, Enrique, E. Bragayrac Dávila, C. Vivanco Pomacanchari, V. Tiesler Blos, and M. Lopez Quispe, eds. *El Templo Mayor en la ciudad de Wari*. Ayacucho, Peru: Laboratorio de Arqueología, Facultad de Ciencias Sociales, Universidad Nacional de San Cristobal de Huamanga, 1996.

Grieder, Terence, Alberto Bueno, C. Earle Smith Jr., and Robert Malina. *La Galgada, Peru: A Preceramic Culture in Transition*. Austin: University of Texas Press, 1988.

Haas, Jonathan, Sheila Pozorski, and T. Pozorski. *The Origins and Development of the Andean State*. New Directions in Archaeology. Cambridge, UK: Cambridge University Press, 1987.

Hastorf, Christine Anne, T. K. Earle, H. E. Wright, L. LeCount, G. Russell, and E. Sandefur. "Settlement Archaeology in the Jauja Region of Peru: Evidence from the Early Intermediate Period through the Late Intermediate Period: A Report on the 1986 Field Season." *Andean Past* 2 (1989): 81–129.

Heyerdahl, Thor, Daniel H. Sandweiss, and Alfredo Narváez. *Pyramids of Túcume: The Quest for Peru's Forgotten City*. New York: Thames and Hudson, 1995.

Hocquenghem, Anne Marie. "Les combats mochicas: essai d'interpretation d'un materiel archaeologique à l'aide de l'iconologie, de l'ethno-histoire et de l'ethnologie." *Baessler-Archiv, Neue Folge* 26 (1978): 127–57.

Hyslop, John. "An Archaeological Investigation of Lupaca Kingdom and its Origins." PhD diss., Columbia University, 1976.

———. *Inka Settlement Planning*. Austin: University of Texas Press, 1990.

Isbell, William H. *Mummies and Mortuary Monuments: A Postprocessual Prehistory of Central Andean Social Organization*. Austin: University of Texas Press, 1997.

Isbell, William H., and Gordon F. McEwan, eds. *Huari Administrative Structure: Prehistoric Monumental Architecture and State Government*. Washington, D.C.: Dumbarton Oaks, 1991.

Isbell, William H., and H. Silverman, eds. *Andean Archaeology III*. New York: Springer, 2006.

Kaulicke, Pert, and William H. Isbell. *Huari y Tiwanaku: Modelos vs evidencias, Primera parte*. Boletín de Arqueología Pontificia Universidad Católica del Perú 4. Lima, Peru: Universidad Católica del Perú, 2000.

Keatinge, Richard, ed. *Peruvian Prehistory*. Cambridge, UK: Cambridge University Press, 1988.

Larco, Rafael. *Los Mochicas*. 2 vols. Lima, Peru: Museo Arqueológico Rafael Larco Herrera, 2001.

Lavallée, Danielle. "L'occupation préhistorique des hautes terres andines." *L'Anthropologie* 89 (1985): 409–30.

———. *Telarmachay: Chasseurs et Pasteurs Préhispaniques des Andes*. Vol. 1. Lima, Peru: Institut Français d'Études Andines, 1985.

Lecoq, Patrice, and Erwan Duffait. "Choqe K'iraw au Perou: Un Nouveau Machu Picchu?" *Archeologie* 411 (May 2004): 50–63.

Lumbreras, Luis G. *Chavín de Huantar en el nacimiento de la Civilización andina*. Lima, Peru: INDEA, 1989.

MacNeish, Richard S., R. K. Vierra, A. Nelken-Terren, and C. J. Phagan. *Prehistory of the Ayacucho Basin, Peru*. 3 vols. Ann Arbor, Mich.: Robert S. Peabody Foundation for Archaeology, University of Michigan Press, 1980–1983.

Makowski, K., C. B. Donnan, I. Amaro Bullon, L. J. Castillo, M. Diez Canseco, O. Eléspuru Revoredo, and J. A. Murro Mena. *Vicús*. Lima, Peru: Banco de Crédito del Perú, 1995.

Masuda, Shozo, Izumi Shimada, and Craig Morris, eds. *Andean Ecology and Civilization*. Tokyo: University of Tokyo Press, 1985.

Moore, Jerry. *Architecture and Power in the Prehispanic Andes*. Cambridge, UK: Cambridge University Press, 1996.

Morris, Craig. *Huanuco Pampa—An Inca City and Its Hinterland*. London: Thames and Hudson, 1985.

Morris, Craig, and A. von Hagen. *The Inka Empire and Its Andean Origins*. New York: Abbeville Press, 1993.

Moseley, Michael. *The Incas and Their Ancestors: The Archaeology of Peru*. 2nd ed. London: Thames and Hudson, 2001.

Moseley, Michael, and K. C. Day, eds. *Chan Chan: Andean Desert City*. Albuquerque: University of New Mexico Press, 1982.

Orefici, Giuseppe. *Nasca: Archeologia per una ricostruzione storica*. Milan, Italy: Jaca Books, 1992.

Paul, Anne. *Paracas Ritual Attire: Symbols of Authority in Ancient Peru*. Norman: University of Oklahoma Press, 1990.

Paul, Anne, ed. *Paracas Art and Architecture: Object and Context in South Coastal Peru*. Iowa City: University of Iowa Press, 1991.

Quilter, Jeffrey. "Moche Politics, Religion, and Warfare." *Journal of World Prehistory* 16, no. 2 (June 2002): 145–95.

Ravines, Rogger. *Panorama de la Arqueología Andina*. Fuentes e investigaciones para la historia del Perú 6. Lima, Peru: Instituto de Estudios Peruanos, 1982.

Rick, John W. *Prehistoric Hunters of the High Andes*. New York: Academic Press, 1980.

Schreiber, Katharina. *Wari Imperialism in Middle Horizon Peru*. Museum of Anthropology, University of Michigan, Anthropological Papers 87. Ann Arbor: University of Michigan, 1992.

Shady, Ruth. *La ciudad sagrada de Caral, Supe en los Albores de la civilización en el Perú*. Lima, Peru: Universidad Nacional Mayor de San Marcos, 1998.

Shady Solis, Ruth, J. Haas, and W. Creamer. "Dating Caral, a Preceramic Site in the Supe Valley on the Central Coast of Peru." *Science* 292 (April 2001): 723–27.

Shimada, Izumi. *Pampa Grande and the Mochica Culture*. Austin: University of Texas Press, 1994.

Silverman, Helaine, and William H. Isbell. *Andean Archaeology*. 2 vols. New York: Kluwer Academic/Plenum Publishers, 2002–2004.

Stanish, Charles. *Ancient Titicaca: The Evolution of Complex Society in Southern Peru and Northern Bolivia*. Berkeley: University of California, 2003.

Uceda, Santiago, and E. Mujica. *Moche: Propuestas y Perspectivas*. Lima, Peru: Travaux de l'Institut Français d'Études Andines, 1994.

Uceda, Santiago, E. Mujica, and R. Morales. *Investigaciones en la Huaca de la Luna 1995*. Trujillo, Peru: Facultad de Ciencias Sociales, Universidad Nacional de la Libertad–Trujillo, 1997.

Ziolkowski, Mariusz, M. F. Padur, A. Krzanowski, and A. Michczynski. *Andes Radiocarbon Data Base for Bolivia, Ecuador and Peru*. Warsaw and Gliwice: Andean Archaeological Mission of the Institute of Archaeology, Warsaw University and Gliwice Radiocarbon Laboratory of the Institute of Physics, Silesian Technical University, 1994.

Uruguay

Consens, Mario. *El pasado extraviado: Prehistoria y arqueología del Uruguay*. Montevideo, Uruguay: Librería Linardi y Risso, 2003.

Consens, Mario, José M. López Mazz, and M. del Carmen Curbelo, eds. *Arqueología en el Uruguay: 120 años después*. Trabajos presentados en el VIII Congreso Nacional de Arqueología Uruguaya. Montevideo, Uruguay: Imprenta Surcos, 1995.

Durán, Artigas, and Roberto Bracco, eds. *Simposio internacional de arqueología de las tierras bajas*. Montevideo, Uruguay: Ministerio de Educación y Cultura, 2000.

Hilbert, Klaus. *Aspectos de la Arqueología en el Uruguay*. Materialen zur allgemeinen und vergleichenden Archäologie 44. Mainz, Germany: Verlag P. von Zabern, 1991.

López Mazz, José M. "Las estructuras tumulares (cerritos) del litoral atlántico uruguayo." *Latin American Antiquity* 12, no. 3 (September 2001): 231–55.

López Mazz, José M. and Mónica Sans, eds. *Arqueología y bioantropología de las tierras bajas*. Montevideo, Uruguay: Facultad de Humanidades y Ciencias de la Educación, Universidad de la República, 1999.

Ministerio de Educación y Cultura. *Misión de Rescate Arqueológico Salto Grande: República Oriental del Uruguay*. 2 vols. Montevideo, Uruguay: 1989.

Nami, Hugo. "Consideraciones tecnológicas preliminares sobre los artefactos líticos de Cerro de los Burros (Maldonado, Uruguay)." In *Comunicaciones Antropológicas, Museos Nacionales de Historia Natural y Antropologia* 21, vol. 3., 1–23. Montevideo, Uruguay: 2001.

Suarez, R. and J. López. "Archaeology of the Pleistocene-Holocene Transition in Uruguay: An Overview." *Quaternary International* 109-110 (2003): 65–79.

Venezuela

Arte prehispánico de Venezuela. Caracas, Venezuela: Galería de Arte Nacional, 2000.

Barse, W. P. "Preceramic Occupations in the Orinoco River Valley." *Science* 250 (1989): 1388–90.

Fernandez, Francisco, and Rafael Gasson, comps. *Contribuciones a la arqueología regional de Venezuela*. Caracas, Venezuela: Fondo Editorial Acta Científica Venezolana, 1993.

Gassón, Rafael A. "Prehispanic Intensive Agriculture, Settlement Patterns and Political Economy in The Western Venezuelan Llanos." PhD diss., University of Pittsburgh, 1998.

———. "Quirípas and Mostacillas: The Evolution of Shell Beads as a Medium of Exchange in Northern South America." *Ethnohistory* 47 (2000), nos. 3–4: 581–609.

———. "Orinoquia: The Archaeology of the Orinoco River Basin." *Journal of World Prehistory* 16, no. 3 (September 2002): 237–311.

Jaimes, A. "Visión Crítica sobre la Arqueología de cazadores-recolectores en el Occidente de Venezuela. Bases para una reinterpretación." *Boletín del Museo Arqueológico de Quibor* 5 (1996): 37–62, Edición Especial 30 Aniversario.

Oliver, José R. "The Archaeological, Linguistic, and Ethnohistorical Evidence for the Expansion of Arawakan into Northwestern Venezuela, and Northeastern Colombia." PhD diss., University of Illinois at Urbana-Champaign, 1989.

Redmond, Elsa M., and C. S. Spencer. "Savanna Chiefdoms of Venezuela." *National Geographic Research and Exploration* 10 (1994): 422–39.

Salazar, L. A. and A. J. Vargas. *Prehistoria de Venezuela*. Caracas, Venezuela: Fondo Editorial Tropykos, 1992.

Sanoja, Mario, and Iraida Vargas-Arenas. *Orígenes de Venezuela: Regiones Geohistóricas Aborígenes hasta 1500 D.C.* Caracas, Venezuela: Comisión Presidencial del Vto Centenario de Venezuela, 1999.

Scaramelli, Franz, and Kay Tarble. "Contenido arqueológico y etnográfico de los sitios de interés espeleohistórico del Orinoco medio, Bolivar, Venezuela." *Boletín de la Sociedad Venezolana de Espelología* 30 (1996): 20–32.

Wagner, Erika. *Relaciones prehispánicas de Venezuela*. Caracas, Venezuela: Asociación Venezolana de Arqueología, Asociación Venezolana para el Avance de la Ciencia, 1984.

HISTORICAL SOURCES

Note: This section covers 180 years of South American archaeology (1825–2005) from the opening of the first museums.

Derby, O. "The Artificial Mounds of Marajo." *American Naturalist* 13 (1879): 224–29.

Ferreira Penna, D. S. "Breve noticia sobre os sambaquis do Pará." *Arquivos do Museu Nacional do Rio de Janeiro* 1 (1876): 85–99.

Figueira, José. "Los primitivos habitantes del Uruguay." In *Uruguay en la exposición histórico americana de Madrid*, 121–221. Montevideo, Uruguay: Memoria, 1892.

Hartt, C. F. "The Ancient Indian Pottery of Marajó." *American Naturalist* 5 (1871): 259–271.

———. "Brazilian Rock Inscriptions." *American Natualist* 5 (1871), no. 3: 139–147.

Im Thurn, Everard. "Notes on the Indians of Guiana: No 2. Indian Antiquities." In *Demerara papers, Being papers on different subjects concerning British Guiana, contributed to the Royal Gazette of that colony*. Georgetown, British Guiana: Royal Gazette, 1879.

Wiener, C. "Estudo sobre os sambaquis do sul do Brasil." *Arquivos do Museu Nacional do Rio de Janeiro* 1 (1876): 388–405.

Winter, Alexander. *Indian Pictured Rocks in British Guiana*. London: Judd, 1981.

About the Author

Martin Giesso (Licenciado, Universidad Nacional de La Plata, 1981; MA, University of Chicago, 1990; PhD, University of Chicago, 2000) is lecturer at the Department of Anthropology at Northeastern Illinois University in Chicago. He was also lecturer at the Department of Latin American and Latino Studies of the University of Illinois at Chicago. After graduating from La Plata, he was director of the Museo Municipal in Eldorado (Misiones, Argentina), an archaeological and historical museum in the region between Argentina, Paraguay, and Brazil. From there he explored pre-Columbian Guaraní sites and colonial Jesuitic missions. For his doctoral dissertation, he studied the ancient city of Tiwanaku in Bolivia. His research specialties and interests include Andean complex societies, craft specialization, lithic analysis, and archeometry.

Dr. Giesso is a member of the Society of American Archaeology, the International Association of Obsidian Studies, and AAPRA (Asociación de Arqueólogos Profesionales de la República Argentina). He was also assistant editor for current research on the Southern Cone of the journal *American Antiquity*.

Dr. Giesso has undertaken archaeological investigations in Argentina and Bolivia and has lived and traveled in Bolivia, Argentina, Peru, Paraguay, Brazil, and Uruguay. He is currently active in research on long-distance circulation of goods in central Argentina, central Chile, and in the highlands of Bolivia.

Dr. Giesso has written articles in English, Spanish, and Portuguese, which have been published in the United States, Great Britain, Brazil, Argentina, Chile, and Bolivia.